Social Work in Adult Services in the European Union

Selected Issues and Experiences

Social Work in Adult Services in the European Union

Selected Issues and Experiences

Edited by

Józefa Brągiel,

Iwona Dąbrowska-Jabłońska

and

Malcolm Payne

ISBN 978-1-84890-027-1

College Publications
Scientific Director: Dov Gabbay
Managing Director: Jane Spurr
Department of Computer Science
King's College London, Strand, London WC2R 2LS, UK

http://www.collegepublications.co.uk

Photographs:
Cover. Sculpture: Adam and Eve (2001), Faculty of Pedagogical Sciences, University of Opole:.
Sculptors: Damian Jureczko and Grzegorz Wiercigrosz, superviser: Professor Marian Molenda. Photograph: Malcolm Payne

Cover designed and created by Laraine Welch
Printed by Lightning Source, Milton Keynes, UK

Contents

Introduction

PART I   Contemporary issues in social work with adults in EU countries

PART 2   Dimensions of practice in social work with adults

List of Figures and Tables

Acknowledgements

The authors and editors wish to thank the translators of their individual chapters, and in particular Jacek Jędrzejowski, who was the interpreter for the conference where these papers originated and translated the majority of papers prepared at Opole University.

Introduction

Józefa Brągiel, Iwona Dąbrowska-Jabłońska and Malcolm Payne
Opole University

Social work, exclusion and adult services in Europe

Social work, as a form of assistance to citizens experiencing difficult situations, has evolved in different countries in varying economic, social, socio-political and cultural environments. Also, its contemporary form, range and dynamics are dependent on these social factors. The experience from different European countries discussed in these papers, demonstrates, first, how social work implements a social policy commitment to a European social model that sees it as a state responsibility to respond to important personal issues in people's lives. Second, they emphasise in different ways how social work enables social policy and social services to respond to the social difficulties that lead to the exclusion of adults from fulfilling lives and social experiences. With a strong central European perspective, these papers speak from states that, twenty years on, are well-advanced in the social transition that has gone alongside the economic transition from socialist planned economies. These papers amply demonstrate the emergence of a central European social model. Contributing to the broader European social model, these central European perspectives focus strongly on the role of the state in responding not only to difficult social situations, but to the emotional and personal needs that flow for adults dealing with such issues. In this way they offer strong statements in favour of a role for social work within policy responses to social issues. Moreover, they demonstrate a broad interpretation of social work, incorporating perspectives from social pedagogy which will be unfamiliar to Western European readers..

This book, then, bears witness to the great number of responses to social issues and the struggle to achieve a particular central European model of response. But this can only be achieved through testing out ideas in a broad forum. The European Union offers opportunities for exchanging knowledge and practical experience, making use of good, effective solutions that have been successfully introduced in other member states, and considering how that may be implemented skilfully on the ground in other countries. Among the issues dominating debate at present in social work, it is possible to distinguish some common themes arousing interest and concern to the member-states of the EU, as follows:

- The role of social work as an element of social policy response of individual states in achieving their interpretation of the doctrine of the *welfare state*;
- Social work as a response to social exclusion;
- Social work as a professional activity to promote social changes, solving problems in human relationships, as well as empowering people in attaining a state of wellbeing;
- Social work as a form of interference in interactions between individuals and their social environments;
- Social work with people of different age groups;
- Social work in new areas of social concern;
- Human rights and the principle of social justice as a foundation of social work;
- The support through personal help of individual action;
- Help aimed at activating the self-help potential in individuals as a model of social work;
- Social work education and competences (cf. *A new definition of social work*, http://ptps.ops.pl/kacik.htm, data of 24 February, 2009).

Many of these issues were raised and discussed during a conference organised by the Social Pedagogy Unit of Opole University, which was held on 14-15 May 2008. The conference was entitled *Praca socjalna z dorosłymi w krajach Unii Europejskiej* (Social Work with adults in the EU). The present volume contains some of the papers, presented during the conference. The publication itself is a result of a three-way cooperative venture, led by Opole University. It brings together perspectives from Opole University, its partner universities in central Europe and a variety of social work provider agencies within the *Leonardo da Vinci* programme coordinated by Przemysław Kaniok, a research worker of the Institute of Pedagogical Sciences of Opole University. The programme operated from 2006-2008, including seven agencies: St Christopher's Hospice (London), Princess Alice Hospice (Esher), British Association of Social Workers (London), Garth Care Home (Kington), Trinity Hospice (London),

The Blue Cross Centre (Wuppertal) and the Kofoeds School (Copenhagen).

As part of the programme of cooperation, thirteen students of Opole University took part in practice placements within the *Leonardo da Vinci* programme. Through this, they had a unique opportunity to become acquainted with the particular nature of work carried out in centres abroad and then compare it with the experience and practices of the counterparts at home. Apart from that, the international exchange of knowledge and experience of people practically engaged in this sphere of public activity and researchers created an unusual opportunity for sharing reflections on the systems of social services and the contents and methods of social work in different countries of the EU. It also provided a chance to consider social workers' preparation and professional development. This is crucial to achieving the capacity to respond effectively, imaginatively and quickly to the requirements for practice in rapidly changing societies and social realities.

Managers of the social service provision where the practice placements were held wrote papers offering information about and reflection on the social care systems in their setting and country. Researchers from universities with which Opole University has had cooperation agreements over many years, also contributed to the knowledge and understanding about social care as it is developing particularly in mid-Europe in this publication. Our colleagues of the Catholic University of Ružomberok and the Matej Bel University in Banská Bystrica (Slovak Republic), the University of Hradec Králové (Czech Republic) contributed additional perspectives on a variety of social service systems for adults. And finally, some of the papers were written in collaboration with employees of the Opole Municipal Family Aid Centre through their research cooperation with Opole University.

The structure of the book

The papers included in the volume are grouped in two parts.

Part I contains articles dealing with contemporary issues in social work and social policy in the member states of the European Union, setting a policy context for practice changes explored in part 2. Smutek and Smutkova review a range of current policy thinking that underlies social care policy developments. Payne identifies the principles of personalisation and dignity; new implementations of the concept of individualizing services that are beginning to have an impact on in social care services in the UK. Prior presents a thoughtful analysis of many of the same trends from a private sector perspective; her analysis of the pressures on and need for quality care in private sector settings offers an unusual and thought-provoking perspective demonstrating the importance of a business analysis where private sector services are part of the mixed economy of care.

In the first of two papers exploring social work education, Novotná and Žilová explore the importance of social skills as a component of social work practice and education. Then, Surrey draws directly on her experience of Polish placement students in the UK and new perspectives in the literature on loss and bereavement to argue for these concepts to be central to preparation for social work internationally.

Two papers on aspects of social policy for particular service user groups follow. First, Žilová and Novotná discuss different approaches to meeting the needs of older people in the EU, from a central European perspective, and drawing on research from the Slovak republic. Finally in Part 1, Weissbrot-Koziarska offers a critical review of services for unemployed people in Poland, drawing particularly on examples of local experience demonstrating how their social situation leads to both practical and emotional social exclusion and arguing for a role for social work in tackling these issues.

Part 2 focuses on a social work role in services for particular groups of adult service users. It starts from services responding to issues for adults in communities and families, moving on to discussion of generic services for a wide range of adult service users excluded in various ways from a normalised social life, and then to communities of service users who are disabled, older people in the population and who are carers. Sikora and Wójcik describe programmes of social work aiming to help Roma communities in Poland, designed to prevent social marginalization of this ethnic group, which is a significant population in central Europe. Two papers from a research programme at Opole University into family care for children and young people focus on the shift from institutional to family-based care for children in Poland, which reflects international trends, over many years. Kurcz, in presenting new approaches in social work with foster families, draws attention to the importance of working with the impact on adult foster carers of their role with deprived children, particularly where professional or emergency foster care presents them with serious challenges. Brągiel and Kozak examine how social workers deal with the transition from care into adulthood, exploring the issues that arise in enabling care leavers to achieve adult self-reliance. Niklova explores preventive social work with families coping with family members whose behaviour such as drug abuse and youth offending that presents social problems for the social environment in which they live.

Two papers follow which explore in detail the complex practice issues that arise for social workers in interpersonal practice. Špániková and Janigová explore the psychological concept of social facilitation as a model of practice for helping people deal with discriminatory and behaviour in groups. Sikorski focuses on the therapeutic micro skills that are crucial in developing effective interpersonal social work practice, enabling practitioners to explore and work on the quality of clients' psychological lives.

The following three papers focus on services for particular social groups who are excluded from ordinary social life. Meldgaard describes the work of Kofoeds School, an agency in Copenhagen working with homeless people, and Ligus presents the work of the Blue Cross Centre in Wuppertal, working with chronically addicted alcoholics. Janigová and Špániková discuss the development of alternative community punishment in the Slovak Republic, drawing on European models of practice.

Two papers on disabled people in Poland discuss social work and inclusion in higher education. Górnicka describes the Polish implementation of UK personalisation policy outlined by Payne, extending the analysis by examining the advantages and practical issues in providing personal assistants for disabled people. Dąbrowska-Jabłońska argues that disabled people are often marginalised and excluded by major institutions, drawing on disabled people's accounts of applying for and adjusting to higher education for the social and education professions.

Finally, two papers explore work with older people and carers of dying people. Jasiński, a leading figure in the University of the Third Age in Poland, examines the value of community education through the university in the lives of older people. Reith describes and evaluates a group for carers of dying people in a UK hospice.

The organizers of the conference and the editors of this volume appreciate the authors' efforts to prepare the materials that provide much valuable information and analysis. This volume offers the inspiration of exploring different approaches within Europe to developing social work and the professional skills of social work practitioners to combat social exclusion and respond to social issues with commitment and concern. These collected materials in their variety facilitate the exchange of experiences in working towards action to resolve the many social issues that affect the member states of the EU and their achievement of a social policy model that incorporates a social work practice that is both personalised and socially committed.

Opole, Poland 2009

PART I

Contemporary issues in social work with adults in EU countries

1   Contemporary modernization processes and shifts in power relationships in social work

Martin Smutek, Lucie Smutková[1]
Department of Social Work and Social Policy, Faculty of Education, Hradec Králové University, CZ

Introduction

Contemporary European welfare states are faced with significant social changes linked to nature of post-industrial societies, which are sometimes described as information or knowledge societies. Such societies develop changes in labour markets, in education and in social care systems. Examples of these changes are pressure on labour forces to be flexible, education to be lifelong and clients or social service users to be empowered.

According to Chytil (2007), social work is connected with the development of modernity; this is the type of society where social work originated and it is time to debate the consequences of modernization for social work. Modernity is in its second wave today, the first having had its impact just after the second world war. The second wave of modernity creates societies in which services have the most important place, rather than manufacturing. Recently this development is leading to a loss of confidence, since the future development of a service-based society has raised a number of uncertainties.

Metamorphoses in the social role of social work exemplify the shifts in power in society. Currently, there are concerns about the power of such social institutions as social work over its clients, for example, disabled people or families. In the context of this paper, power is taken as overall social power of the social institution 'social work',

A number of reform processes are simultaneously affecting welfare states today. General trends are the reduction of welfare benefits, tightening of eligibility for services and the reform of big social programmes such as pension systems to reduce their financial burden on the state. The institutional environment of social work is also changing, for example with changes in activation regimes for unemployed people, that is, policies that require unemployed people to make efforts to find work as a condition of receiving benefits. All these policy actions, which may generally be

---

[1] E-mail: martin.smutek.2@uhk.cz; lucie.smutkova@uhk.cz.

described as 'welfare reforms', are examples of efforts to reduce the costs of welfare provision. See Esping-Andersen 1996, Pierson 2001, Taylor-Gooby 2004, Fenger and Henman 2006 for firther discussion.

These changes also bring various kinds of new risks, often called 'the new social risks' of post-industrial societies. According to the Taylor-Gooby (2004) 'new social risks' are defined as risks that people face during their lifecycle as the result of the socio-economic changes taking place in contemporary European societies. Four main processes are described:
1. There is continual growth of female employment, while the economic activity of men is declining.
2. There is continual growth in the population of older people.
3. Labour markets are characterised by rapid change.
4. There is significant expansion of the private sector, as a result of restrictions in the social role of modern welfare states.

'New social risks' are also linked to shifts in gender roles of men and women, and with the consequences of lack of qualification, so that poorly qualified workers are unable to be sure of finding work. 'New social risks' are also part of the process of reducing welfare costs in contemporary welfare states in Europe. The result is the growth of private sector provision with the state commissioning social programmes from external providers, rather than providing services directly. Some authors (for example Keller, 2005, 2007) speak about contemporary modernization as 'regression', because most modernization processes are characterised by efforts to reduce cost, and tighten eligibililty for benefits.

The result of these social changes should be flexible employees, prepared for rapid change and able to adapt rapidly to new circumstances. The negative side of this process is growth of economic pressure on the average employee's shoulders. The burden of uncertainties in the market are shifting from employer to employee.

Types of welfare reforms and reactions of welfare states
Many contemporary welfare reforms are inspired by the 'new public management', which emerged in public administration during the late 1980s (see, for example, Osborne and Gaebler 1992). More recently, the concept of governance in public administration has been preferred. Taylor-Gooby (2004) identifies the range of circumstances that probably initiates the need of welfare reform. He splits this set into four groups of circumstances:
1. demographic changes
2. globalisation
3. labour market changes
4. political and social changes.

He goes on to identify three main types of welfare reforms:
1. re-commodification
2. cost-containment
3. recalibration.

According to Fenger and Henman (2006:6) an additional type of strategy would be:
4. administration reform.

De-commodification is the situation where people have a social right to services, as a consequence of which they can maintain their standard of living even when they are not employed. De-commodification leads to the welfare state's adbility to control the social situation of people (see Esping-Andersen 1990). Re-commodification is the effort to turn back this process, to reduce alternatives to participation in the labour market and to reduce social benefits as an incentive to take up those alternative (see Pierson 2001). This emphasis on work, in such policies as workfare programmes adopted from the USA, and the British policy of conditionality, points up the significance of re-commodification in today's Europe.

Cost containment is the second reform strategy. Although successful re-commodification is reduces costs, cost containment strategies are a different way to control costs. Cost containment includes a wide range of substrategies such as tightening eligibility criteria and reducing benefits (Pierson 2001).

Recallibration means efforts to adapt contemporary welfare states to be consistent with shared social goals and people's views of the role of social security in society (Pierson 2001). According to Pierson, there are two different types of recallibration: rationalization and updating. Rationalization means reforming social programmes to achieve their goals more effectively. Updating means efforts to adapt programmes to changing demands of the society and changing unwritten social norms.

Administrative reform is proposed by some authors as a futher reform strategy. It means reforms in implementation and in management structures of social programmes, without necessarily changing the goal of the programme. This concept covers shifts such as decentralization, privatization or restructuring administrative responsibility (Fenger and Henman 2006:7).

Pierson suggests that the reform strategy or strategies selected by governments depend on the model of the welfare state held by important actors within any particular society. Esping-Andersen's (1990) well-known study points to different types of regime in welfare states, which differ in important respects from each other and produce different dynamics in the restructuring of welfare (Pierson 2001):

- In liberal regimes, re-commodification and cost containment strategies are dominant; there is a vision of workfare state.
- In social democratic regimes, there are cost containment and rationalization strategies are the main focus.
- In conservative regimes, cost containment and updating strategies are preferred.

Pierson (2001) does not discuss administrative reform as alternative strategy, and this welfare reform strategy is therefore not included in this analysis (Fenger and Henman 2006:7).

Governance

Modernization of welfare states may also be achieved by recent trends to substitute 'governance' for government. Debate on the meaning and implications of the shift to 'governance' is linked to changing face of welfare, and with the changing role of the state in the 'welfare triangle' of social institutions concerned with welfare, the market, state and civil society. Debate about governance developed mainly in the early 1990s among different authors with a range of points of view (see Osborne and Gaebler 1992; Rhodes, 1996).

Governance usually refers to socio-economic development processes concerned with changes:

1. between state and other major actors in society
2. changes in configuration of civil society and its relationships with the state
3. changes in inner mechanisms of the state.

Thus, a focus on governance suggests that there is no one mode of government and the state is not always the dominant actor.

There are many definitions of governance (each stressing different points of view) (see Kooiman 2005). Some of main characteristics (according to Fitzpatrick 2005:159; see also Newman 2001, Clarke and Newman 1997 or Ling 1998):

- Governance enables a shift from Weberian bureaucratic hierarchy to more horizontal models (for example, market competition, networks of agencies).
- Governance refers to the vaporisation of administrative boundaries.

- Governance means that the state is integrating itself into broad partnerships among many agencies; state governing bodies no longer manipulate society.
- The state becomes steerer than rower (Osborne and Gaebler 1992), more facilitator than controllor.

Such changes are the essence of the shift 'from government to governance', impling a shift from an instrumental to a process point of view.

Table 1.1 *Differences between 'old' government and 'new' governance*

	'old' government	*'new' governance*
Source of power	state	state with civil society
Main actors	public sector and administrative bodies	public, private and third sector
Dependency	on elites (who have power)	participation of all elites
Activities oriented towards	organisations	processes
Emphasize on	organizational structure	inputs, outputs and policies
Philosophy of policies	direct care (paternalism)	choices, serving, steering
Role of government	care, control	steering, helping, cooperation, negotiation
Form of government performance	hierarchy (top down) and authority	partnership and nets

Source: Leach and Percy-Smith, 2000:5; Peters, 2003:5-8; (quoted by Vymětal, 2005).

Consequences of modernization for social work
The processes of globalization and individualization are two dimensions going hand in hand. The first implies that there is no longer space for state to dominate all actors and the second implies that people became rather active 'consumers' than passive 'soldiers'. The Keynesian welfare state is shifting somewhat towards a Schumpeterian workfare state, where control over clients is an important factor.

Such trends of rising control over clients (with a practice focus on assessing their claims rigorously) may give an impression of rising power of social institutions (state or nonstate) over clients. On the other hand, the opposite consequence also arises. Power is reduced because the total number of clients is reduced, although there may be a problem that the population is undeserving. The state is losing part of its influence over parts of population who were controlled in the past. But another consequence of shifts in the overall power relationship means that reducing costs of financial benefits will not reduce the overall number of clients of the welfare state. Clients are likely to be shifted from one area of the welfare state to another area, for example from primarily receiving financial benefit to receiving or being required to receive counselling, as part of a process of being required to make efforts to find work.

Chytil (2007) suggests that the development of theories and methods of social work is closely linked to the development of modernity. 'All theoretical concepts are in the main context of industrial modernity and are not going beyond this. They are not reflecting the challenges of postindustrial modernity, they are still thinking traditionally, seeing social problems as stemming from society and individuality within it. They don't know how to respond to the common situation that arises when risks are produced by society, but need to cope with them as rigorously individualised. …They do not reflect that social work is losing legitimacy and, because of economic rationalisation, is loosing financial stability' (Chytil 2007: 66). One of the characteristic aspects of modernization is extensive rationalisation to achieve cost and efficiency savings and colonization of the public sector by private mechanisms.

Another issue is that education for social work does not reflect common shifts in modernity. Instead of giving students broad spectra of norms, values and ideas, in modernity, it is reduced to only one function - to raise economic functioning of human capital. An orientation towards competencies available to meet service demands, rather than education in ideas and values and social science understanding that underpins technical skills. The consequence is that social workers are not able to react in flexible ways to social trends and are unable to reflect critically on tendencies towards modernization (Chytil 2007:66).

Individual social work, groupwork and community work
The individualisation of the society is stronger and stronger and it reduces the flexibility of formal as well as informal systems of help. Case management techniques seek to modernize social work, to adapt it to general trends where economic racionality is the main objective. But an excessive focus on technical-rational techniques may lead to reduction or elimination of public sector financing of social work. Some authors (see Chytil, 2007; Keller, 2007) are sceptical that there is a future for social work. Some others

(e.g. Janebová 2005) present this like 'apocalyptic' vision of the future of social work.

While this doubt arises mainly for individual social work, it also raises similar questions about the future of groupwork. Scepticism about the ability of groupwork to survive in modernizing services focuses on some of its main goals, such as education and development. These are often primarily in the interest of the individual, and might not be supported in post-industrial societies.

Community social work - as the youngest method – responds to modernization in a relatively active and strategic way, but its theoretical concepts also have not yet produced a critique of modernization (Chytil 2007).

Conclusions: the need for further discussion
In general, discussion of the effects of modernization on social work is marginal to much of the policy debate. In the Czech Republic, there is little systemnatic public debate about the changing social role of social workers and their ability to survive rapid modernization. Issues such as social responsibility of social workers should be debated as well as the supply of social workers for society.

Historical and institutional characteristics of welfare states still play an important role in national policies. Neverthless these characteristics are more and more influenced by decisions at the international level. This is particularly so in regional groupings of nations such as the European Union, where states are incorporated into slow and longterm processes of developing social policy jointly. Authors such Pierson (1998), Ferrera et al. (2000) or Geyer (2000) argue that the probability of such an extensive impact for European social policy in social services is likely to be limited. Instead of trying to influence such emerging policy we argue that policy to examine differencies that characterise Eeuropean areas. Any concept of social policy is universal for all member countries must start from important differences between states (Šimková, 2007). So the key analytical question for the near future is how EU social policy interacts with different national social policy regimes.

The way street-level bureaucrats (see Lipsky, 1980) are influenced by welfare reforms is also an important analytical question for the future. According to Henman and Fenger (2006, see Table 2) we can distinguish three ways in which welfare reforms are implemented by street-level workers. First, the traditional bureaucratic model tries to reduce the discretion, or free decision-making on organisational matters among street-level workers. This model tries to increase effectiveness by centralising power and control. Second, the new public management (NPM) model, is oriented towards outcomes and high performance and uses quasi-market mechanisms. Finally, the implementation model, the governance model, sees street-level bureaucrats as developers of relationships with variety of actors, including clients and employers...

Table 2 *Three models of welfare administration*

	Participants	*Practice*	*Processes*
Bureaucratic	state agencies	street-level workers apply rules and norms	national state is the main actor
New Public Management	private agencies and NGOs like partners	street-level workers are attempting to increase productivity	coordination and control role for the national state
Governance	net of governments, private actors, NGOs etc.	street-level workers works with different interests	international, national and local levels simultaneously

Source: Henman and Fenger 2006: 262-263

Welfare reform has replaced the traditional bureaucracy '...with either neo-liberal managerial forms of administration or with consensual governance forms. Both types have in common that they are now much more sensitivene to the context in which they operate than the traditional bureaucracy was. Introduction of (such) welfare reforms requires a reinforcement of the role of local-level organisations in welfare administration'.(Henman and Fenger 2006:261).

Although possible forms of implementation of welfare reforms were discussed above, key questions are still to be resolved:
- How do welfare reforms interact with national regimes of welfare?
- How are the capacities of subsystems of welfare systems, such as labour market policy, social security policy, changing?
- Are the capacities of these subsystems to solve social problems increasing or declining?
- What are the consequences for the role of social work, in its various forms?

Bibliography

Bache, I. and Flinders, M. (2005) *Multi-level Governance*. Oxford: Oxford University Press.

Clarke, J. and Newman, J. (eds.) (1997). *The Managerial State*. London: Sage Publications.

Colebatch, H. K. (2005) *Úvod do policy*. Brno: Barrister and Principal.

Esping-Andersen, G. (1990) *The Three Worlds of Welfare Capitalism*. Princeton: Princeton University Press.

Fenger, M. and Henman, P. (2006) Introduction: Administering Welfare Reform. In Henman, P. and Fenger, M. (eds) *Administering Welfare Reform*. Bristol: The Policy Press: 1-17.

Fitzpatrick, T. (2005) *New Theories of Welfare*. Basingstoke: Palgrave Macmillan.

Henman, P. and Fenger, M. (2006) Reforming Welfare Governance: Reflections. In Henman, P. and Fenger, M. (eds) *Administering Welfare Reform*. Bristol: The Policy Press: 257-278.

Chytil, O. (2007) *Důsledky modernizace pro sociální práci*. Sociální práce/Sociálna práca, 4/2007: 64-71.

Janebová, R. (2005) K čemu je sociálním pracovníkům teorie aneb postmoderní feministická perspektiva o „krizi poznání". In Smutek, M. (ed.) *Možnosti sociální práce na počátku 21. století*. Hradec Králové: KSPSP UHK: 69-78.

Keller, J. (2005) *Soumrak sociálního státu*. Praha: Sociologické nakladatelství.

Keller, J. (2007) *Teorie modernizace*. Praha: Sociologické nakladatelství.

Kooiman, J. (2005) Social-Political Governance: Overview, reflections and design. In Hodges, R. (ed.) *Governance and the Public Sector*. Cheltenham: Edward Elgar: 61-83.

Lipsky, M. (1980) *Street-Level Bureaucracy – Dilemmas of the Individual in Public Services*. New York: Russell Sage Foundation.

Pierson, C. (1991) *Beyond The Welfare State*. Pennsylvania: Pennsylvania State University Press.

Smutek, M. (2008) Modernizace sociálního státu a analýza moci (celospolečenské hledisko a hledisko klient-pracovník). In Janebová, R., Kappl, M. and

Smutek, M. (eds) *Sociální práce mezi pomocí a kontrolou*. Hradec Králové: Gaudeamus: 254-266.

Smutek, M. (2007) Sociální politika, sociální stát a modernizace. In: Smutek, M. and Sveřepa, M. (eds) *Sociální práce a sociální služby*. Hradec Králové: Gaudeamus: 14-23.

Smutková, L. and Smutek, M. (2008) Uplatňování moci řadových probačních úředníků při realizaci institutů probace a mediace. In: Janebová, R., Kappl, M. and Smutek, M. (eds) *Sociální práce mezi pomocí a kontrolou*. Hradec Králové: Gaudeamus: 214-228.

Smutková, L. and Smutek, M. (2006) Problematika moci v pomáhajících profesích a balancování vztahu s klientem. In: Smutek, M. and Kappl, M. (eds) *Proměny klienta služeb sociální práce – Social Work Client Metamorphoses*. Hradec Králové: Gaudeamus: 466-476.

Šimková, E. (2007) Úloha sociálních služeb a kvalita života na venkově. *Sociální práce/Sociálna práca*, 3/2007: 97-101.

Taylor-Gooby, P. (2004) *Welfare State Reform and New Social Risks*. Kent: University of Kent.

Valadas, C. (2006) The Fight Against Unemployment as a main Concern of European Social Policy: The Implications of a new, local-level approach. In Henman, P. and Fenger, M. (eds) *Administering Welfare Reform*. Bristol: Policy Press: 213-231.

Vymětal, P. (2006) Proměny teoretických koncepcí governance. In Němec, J. and Šůstková, M. (eds.) *III. Kongres českých politologů*. Praha: Olomouc: Česká společnost pro politické vědy: 534-547.

Winkler, J. (2007) *Vývoj institucionální kapacity politiky zaměstnanosti*. Paper given at the conference: Monitoring trhu práce a politiky zaměstnanosti. Brno: 14th November 2007.

2   Adult social services in the UK: recent developments

Malcolm Payne
Policy and Development Adviser, St Christopher's Hospice London,
Visiting Professor, Opole University

Introduction: UK adult social care

Social care services for adults in the UK is provided mainly by the adult
social services departments of local municipalities, known as local councils
or local authorities (LAs). Adult social care is separated from children's
social care, which is administered by LA education departments.

Four main groups of people receive adult social care in the UK:

- Older people, people of pensionable age, which is being equalised
  over a period to 65 years; many older people receive social care
  because of disabilities that arise as they age.
- Younger people, that is under pensionable age, with disabilities
- People with learning disabilities
- Mentally ill people.

Most of these groups' care needs derive from illness, disability or the
increasing frailty of old age, and therefore most adult social care is closely
related to healthcare services. However, there are administrative, legal and
financial differences between social and health care (Glasby and Littlechild,
2004). In particular, there are significant issues around the relationship
between local and central government. Healthcare is provided free of charge,
financed from national taxation and managed as a national service. There are
charges for social care, which is financed from local taxation, although with
a substantial national subvention. It is administered according to local
political priorities by LAs, following national legislation and policy
guidance from central government. The difference in charging policies for
the services is largely historic and reflects the political priority given to
healthcare. Among the reasons for charging for social care is to demonstrate
its value and cost to service users, to ration provision and to reduce costs.
Charging also reflects a distinction between social needs that are part of
everyday life, such as bathing, dressing and eating for which people seen as
responsible and health needs, which are defined in the NHS Act 2006 as

requiring medical treatment or nursing care. Healthcare aims to return people to state in which they can manage their own health and care.

Adulthood as an issue in service provision

Four aspects of adulthood raise issues for the way in which social care is provided:

- Autonomy: adults are expected to be self-managing in their care and to make their own decisions about lifestyle, medical and social care and treatment. They have to give their consent for involvement by professionals. This has two consequences for social care. First, people cannot be compelled to accept care or treatment, even where professionals and family members think this would be desirable. Second, people who have lost the capacity to exercise their autonomy, for example through brain damage, learning disabilities or dementia in old age, need someone else to exercise their autonomy. The recent Mental Capacity Act 2005 makes provision for various relatives or professionals to make decisions for people who are unable to do so themselves (DCA, 2007). Where care decisions are being made, an independent mental capacity advocate (IMCA) is contracted by the LA to represent their interests; IMCAs are often social workers.
- The expectation that in most respects an adult is a fully developed person. Full-time, compulsory education ends at 16 years. Thus, although young people take part in further of higher education, they are regarded as fully developed. Issues arise for social care services where this is not so. For example, people with learning disabilities may need further social education and personal development opportunities, people with disabilities may be delayed in their education or require re-education and training after an accident or disabling illness, and older people may lose physical and mental capacities and have to relearn skills, or develop alternative interests to achieve a fulfilling lifestyle. Such developmental provision may seem a luxury compared with meeting basic social or health care needs, but is integral to helping people achieve a satisfying life. Social care services may therefore have to justify resources allocated to personal development and education for adults.
- Adults are financially responsible for their own existence. This is reflected in the charging policies discussed above and also in stigma if people are financially dependent.
- Adults are expected to be competent to meet their own needs in all domains of living. Where they are not able to do so, they may be

stigmatised as inadequate, dependent or demanding, and services provided for them regarded as a low priority.

The domains of life within which adults expected to be responsible for meeting their own needs are:

- Health, including mental health
- Education
- Housing, and therefore avoiding homelessness maintaining their own house in a reasonable state
- Employment, and therefore avoiding unemployment and preparing fro their own retirement
- Justice, obeying the law, both civil and criminal.
- Income, including making appropriate transfers to provide for pensions and insurance, avoiding dependence on social security if possible and taking responsibility for mitigating their poverty (Kamerman, 2002).

Social care services
Social care services, therefore, may help people meet their needs in each of these areas. In the UK, it is conceived as a service that is:

- Multisectoral, that is providers of social care operate in the public, private and voluntary, not-for-profit or third sectors of the economy
- It is also closely integrated with the informal sector, with the contributions of users' own self-care and their carers (the British term) or informal caregivers (the internationally recognised term)
- It involves 'provision' or care rather than therapeutic social work
- It provides services rather than trying to achieve social and behaviour change
- It maintains the social lives of people with long-term disabling conditions, rather than being concerned with short-term problem-solving
- It covers all groups of service users, including children, but children are usually provided for separately from adults (Payne, 2009).

Social care is a long-term service. It provides for people who are very physically, psychologically or emotionally dependent on other people and who need care:

- For long periods of the day

- Over a long timescale, and
- Covering many aspects of their lives (Parker, 1981).

This requires services that are able to provide continuity. However, since these are personal services, they require a high ratio of staff to service users, and staff have to be employed on shifts. Users receiving services at home often experience 'serial carers', a succession of different carers who perform particular tasks, leaving to move to the next care task in someone else's home. Where care is provided in residential care homes, staff work shifts, and it may be hard to achieve consistency and good relationships between paid carers and service users.

In addition to its association with healthcare, social care is also connected with accommodation, since many people's care requires specialised accommodation. Most services are domiciliary and are provided in people's own homes alongside informal care by relatives and others in the service users' social network. Some users are helped by living in sheltered housing, which may be specially adapted for disabled people. 'Very sheltered' or 'extra care' housing allows extensive personal care is provided within the user's own accommodation. Occasionally there are adult placement schemes where users live within and receive care from another person's family, similar to foster care for children. A small number of people are helped in care homes where there is shared communal accommodation, and this may be supplemented by nursing care in care homes with nursing (CHNs), commonly called by the traditional name, 'nursing homes'.

Social work in social care
Since most services are provided in people's homes, social care requires an intrusion in the autonomy and privacy of services users, who may have to have specialised equipment around their home and strangers visiting to provide intimate services, such as bathing.

The main social work practice in adult social care is care management, which developed during the 1980s from American case management (Payne, 1995). It was introduced by the NHS and Community Care Act 1990 as a way of managing a newly-established quasi-market system of provision. This gave LAs the role of planning services in their area from all the sectors of the economy. A plan setting out the services available was established, the care manager assessed service users' needs and commissioned the services from the various providers. LAs themselves provided some services, including social work, usually provided directly by the care manager.

The care management process is a traditional social work circle, in which the assessments lead to a care plan, increasingly provided in a document, which defies the needs, the services to be provided, the charges and a date when the plan will be reviewed, usually annually. The services are organised and the care manager monitors how the services fit together, making adjustments as required, and evaluates whether they are meeting the user's needs at the annual review (Payne, 1995).

Two recent developments have adapted this cycle of practice. Since the 1980s, a growing movement representing the needs of informal carers has grown up. Successive legislation has tried to incorporate within care management practice the growing public concern for the support of carers (CSCI, 2006). As a result, carers are entitled to a separate assessment of their needs, for example for respite, pursuing education or employment, and a plan for meeting their needs must be incorporated into care plan.

Another development is direct payments or independent budgeting. These are part of an international trend, and of a 'public choice' policy agenda characteristic of many Western governments. The 'ordinary living' movement of physically disabled people sought to improve housing and public facilities so that service users could have lifestyles similar to those enjoyed by non-disabled people. After a negotiated assessment of needs, elements of a care plan are agreed, and the budgets to provide these are paid to the service user, helpers or families. Many people employ their own care assistants and this maintains continuity and user control of the arrangements in their own home. In some areas, a user-controlled organisation offers an alternative way of managing services, without the practical difficulties for families of employing carers directly. Although this is a more flexible system of care, which is supported by service users because of the freedom of choice it offers, there are concerns that not every person receiving social care wants to be entrepreneurial and manage their own provision or has family members willing to help them. They may also choose carers to meet their own preferences, without considering the training and general suitability of the employee for a career in social care in the future.

Recent policy trends
Four important policy developments have been designed to respond to many of these issues:

- Partnership developments

Partnership between users, carers and professionals is an essential part of achieving the continuity required by caring and public choice policy agenda.

However, partnership policy is not limited user-carer-practitioner cooperation, but wider issues of public service management. Partnership policy aims to achieve coordination of policy between central; and local government, organisations in the private, public and not-for-profit sectors of the economy, between community and public organisations, between planners and commissioners of services and the providers of them, and between service users, providers and educators and researchers. In particular, partnership policy is an attempt to overcome professional and organisational divisions between health and social care. Because these are a direct result of the differences in financing and organisation discussed above, however, there are always going to be divisions between different professional, disciplinary and organisational interests in social care. I would argue that it is more appropriate to encourage professional discretion among good quality staff in the lower reaches of organisations, rather than develop a rhetoric of organisational coordination.

- Participation policies

Participation polices are an attempt to generate user and carer involvement not only in the organisation of personal services but also in planning and management of services. It is almost becoming an orthodoxy in public services. One of the reasons is to create a sense of inclusion to combat the intrusion of social care services and practitioners in private arenas, which is the concomitant of the development of community care in people's homes. Another is to demonstrate public involvement and support for the rationing decisions required to provide care to the growing numbers of older people and others who are unable to live independent lives. Other sources of the pressure to generate participation are a longstanding approach to managing the impact of professional discretion and producer or provider interests on services and the perception that the care management process has become a bureaucratised process of rationing services, rather than responding flexibly to users' and carers' needs..

- Personalisation policy

Personalisation policy is a recent development seeking to develop user and carer participation through increasing their involvement in planning and managing their own services (Leadbetter and Lownsborough, 2005). The main practice implication of this is to generalise the experiments on direct payments and independent budgeting, making them more widely available. The government hopes that the social work role will shift towards advocacy and support for service users and carers managing their own services.

- Dignity

Dignity policy is an attempt by policy-makers to influence the quality of service provided by influencing public demand and practice guidance (Lewis, 2006). This is particularly important because social care offers largely practical services delivered by lot-paid and poorly-trained staff. It is not clear that politicians and policy-makers can influence quality in this way.

Conclusion

I have argued in this paper that social care services for adults have to respond to four major characteristics of adulthood: adults' assumed autonomy, full psychosocial development, their competence to manage their lives in all domains of living and their financial independence. Because they provide personal care, social care services involve intrusion upon the privacy of adults who are assumed to be competent and independent in managing their affairs. The existing system of community care for adults in the UK relied upon a practice of care management by social workers devising a package of services for people in need drawing on providers from different sectors of the economy. However, this has become increasingly seen as over-bureaucratised and concerned with rationing services. Therefore, recent policy developments have focused on social inclusion of service users and their carers through a public choice agenda of partnership, participation and personalisation policies, which also aims to limit professional discretion and the impact of producer interests on service quality. Dignity policy is an example of an attempt to influence professional and organisational practices, necessary because social care mainly employs poorly qualified and paid staff, requiring guidance to maintain personalisation policies.

References

Charnley, H. (2001) Promoting independence: a partnership approach to supporting older people in the community. In Balloch, S. and Taylor, S. (eds) *Partnership Working: Policy and Practice*. Bristol: Policy Press: 143-64.

CSCI (2006) *The State of Social Care*. London: Commission for Social Care Inspection.

DCA (2007) *Mental Capacity Act 2005: Code of Practice*. London: TSO.

Glasby, J. and Litttlechild, R. (2004) *The Health and Social Care Divide: The Experiences of Older People*. (2nd edn) Bristol: Policy Press.

Kamerman, S. B. (2002) Fields of practice. In Mattaini, M. A., Lowery, C. T. and Meyer, C. H. (eds) *Foundations of Social Work Practice: A Graduate Text*, Washington DC: NASW Press: 319-39.

Leadbetter, C. and Lownsborough, H. (2005) *Personalisation and Participation: The Future of Social Care in Scotland: Final Report*. London: Demos.

Lewis, I. (2006) *Dignity in Care*. (Gateway ref: 7388) London: Department of Health.

Parker, R. (1981) Tending and social policy. In Goldberg, E. M. and Hatch, S. (eds) *A New Look at the Personal Social Services*. London: Policy Studies Institute: 17-32.

Payne, M. (1995) *Social Work and Community Care*. Basingstoke: Macmillan.

Payne, M. (200() *Social Care Practice in the Community*. Basingstoke: Palgrave Macmillan.

3   Developing services, knowledge and skills - the 21st century challenge

Patricia Prior
Garth Care Services, Herefordshire, UK

Introduction

This paper considers the challenge of developing services, knowledge and skills during the twenty-first century within a private sector care organisation in the UK, providing a case study of innovation and development in a comparatively new context for care services. The debate about the level and structuring of financing for services for adults; is a complex area of discussion beyond the scope of this paper. Chapter 1 indicates the policy developments that have influenced recent developments. Traditionally, service development has been seen as a role of the state, in which agencies that provide services participate. However, to participate effectively, a provider needs its own policies based on its role within the mixed economy of care (Means et al, 2008: 67-74).

The context of this case study is Garth Care Homes, a care home business established in June 1988 with a range of services that has developed over the period of the last twenty years. It is a family business structured legally as a partnership with leadership from a husband, wife and son team. It currently provides a care home (for social care) and a care home with nursing (in the official terminology, usually called a nursing home). These are residential homes in which people are provided with accommodation and care together; in the case of nursing homes a registered nurse is available to undertake nursing interventions where these are required. Another aspect of the provision is homecare or domiciliary services providing care in people's own homes, and a number of independent living apartments, where people can maintain their own residence near the care and nursing homes, but supported by homecare and meals provision. This is a fairly comprehensive range of provision within one organisation, and a similar range of provision is available in most European countries (Le Bihan and Martin, 2006).

The organisation also has an education and training centre, which is accredited to provide EDEXCEL and BTEC awards in health and social care; these organisations accredit training provided by both colleges and by employers to the same standard. The centre offers a range of qualification to staff as part of their employment, to enable their personal and career development, but also to improve the quality of the service.

The challenge of quality
Providing good-quality care services for people with nursing and social care needs in the UK is always a challenge, as it is elsewhere. A private sector organisation must start from the need to maintain a functioning business, because this is the instrument through which the existence of secure services for the service users is maintained, and the quality of the provision may be enhanced. The key to achieving that is to manage the company with the main aim of providing services of the highest possible quality.

Public demonstration of the quality achievement may be measured by the regulator for care services, currently the Commission for Social Care Inspection (CSCI), which is due to be merged with other regulators in the field into the Care Quality Commission during 2009. CSCI inspects all care service providers regularly and this gives a comparative measure of quality: Garth Care Homes are currently awarded three stars (***), the highest, 'excellent' rating. Standards in the education and training department are measured by EDEXCEL twice a year through an external verification process, involving visits by one of their external verifiers; the standard achieved is also the highest, A+.

Maintaining such standards requires keeping abreast of and responding to social change in a practical way. This is because as social expectations change, so also do the requirements of services. Therefore, it is important for companies not to assume that present good provision will always be appropriate, but to build an understanding of social trends as a basis for strategic development of services.

Social trends affecting care services
The company is therefore currently looking at the next generation of UK elders, those born towards the end and after the second world war. The birth rate boomed and service people returned home from war and resumed their normal lives, almost immediately increasing the birthrate as they started families in the security of the post-war economy and the creation of a welfare state, including a comprehensive health service. The oldest resultant age group of children are now about aged around 60 have been called the 'baby boomers'. They – we - were the first generation of young people to be called 'teenagers' in the late 1950s and '60s. They - we - had their own type of music that adults disliked; because they disliked it, we liked it even more. This was a questioning generation, able to be critical because of the security of the welfare state.

This generation experienced Elvis Presley, rock and roll, the Beatles, hippies, flower power, perhaps 'free love' and a 'psychedelic' time; some experimented with drugs. Some British celebrities of that era such as the musician and Band Aid founder Sir Bob Geldorf, and the feminist Germaine Greer, have written about their personal expectations of future care in older age. These are people that have grown up with ambitions and high expectations, living in a period of sustained growth and a society that was rebuilding and reimagining itself in the post-war period.

My personal life echoes this generational experience. I was born and brought up in a small coal mining community, where both my parents worked to provide opportunity and education for their daughters. In my family, education was seen as the way out of poverty, and following a career pathway was encouraged. My mother always said in defence of educating her daughters: 'Educated mothers will nurture more educated children'. This was also the time when the contraceptive pill was developed, so the 'baby boom' children, my generation, also had choices in this aspect of their lives and chose not to have as many children. So, the birth rate dropped, and now UK is left with fewer people to pay for and to care for greater number of people marching towards older age.

Current and future consequences

This brief account of recent social trends affecting the quality of care provision raises a number of issues for consideration. It is clear that:

- Increased personal services will be needed but there will be fewer people to provide them
- There will be greater and higher expectations of a wider range of types of care. For example, some large-scale providers have already developed villages for people over fifty-five years of age, with leisure facilities such as golf, theatres, leisure pools but with a nursing home on site for possible more intensive or end-of-life care.
- This generation has an increased awareness of the rights and choices available to them, and government policy supports the wish for greater choice
- A number of pieces of legislation set requirements for high standards, again particularly in the realm of individual choice. The Care Standards Act 2000 makes provision for independent regulation of care providers and professionals, the Carers (Equal Opportunities) Act 2004 reinforces existing legislation giving rights to assessment of needs and services for carers, the Mental Capacity Act 2005 makes provision for advance care planning

and the protection and support of people who are no longer able to make decisions for themselves; and many others are being brought forward.
- Legislation is also under consideration for the protection of vulnerable adults; this has already been legislated for in Scotland.

Much of this change is geared towards the rights of individuals to make their own life decisions, provided they have the capacity to do so, and the promotion of the quality of care. The England government's 'dignity in care' programme is one example of the policy shift towards concern for the quality of life among people receiving care services. A rapid pace of change is being set, encouraged by primary and secondary legislation and policy initiatives. These are significant drivers in setting the way that services will be commissioned and provided.

Cooperation is the only way forward
Although government has set the policy and legislative drivers, the mixed economy of care assumes an involvement from all sectors of the economy working together, to provide each with its own distinctive contribution. Thus, more may be achieved by cooperation between health and local authorities, private and voluntary sector organisations rather than by competition among them or dominance of decision-making by any one provider. The challenge for younger people and for services is to care for a generation that has had more opportunities than previous generations. People of this generation are generally more affluent than previous generations, with their own homes and private pensions which they want to use to buy or contribute to their own care, which in turn enables them to enforce their own preferences as customers, rather than be provided for by paternalistic services. This customer relationship is a service relationship that private sector providers operating a business model are particularly well-fitted to offer.

I count myself as being fortunate to have a foot in both camps. I am of the boom generation and still in a position to be able to help influence change in my community. Throughout my career, I have been forever optimistic about changing systems and structures to make life better for people, families in my particular locality. Thus, it is important for a business not only to respond to individual wishes, but also to meet its interpretation of the needs of local communities. Paternalism by public authorities or by charitable organisations in the voluntary sector can limit the impact of the decision-making freedom that the coming generation of elders will require. Local authorities and representative bodies have roles in acting as bridges and interpreters between national policies and local providers responding to their own conception of personal needs. The relationship required between public, private and voluntary sector providers and planners thus needs a continuing dialogue about needs, demands, wishes and financing.

A private sector organisation therefore needs to contribute to the mix both imagination and careful analysis of business risks and opportunities, which can guide what can and should be provided. The key is to listen to the views and aspirations of people who are likely to use the services. The quality of peoples' everyday lives will be supported by translating their aspirations and needs into timely and relevant services. These can often be a minimal provision, perhaps fifteen minutes of input a couple of times a day. But such interventions can reduce a the potential for care needs to escalate into a crisis management situation, which should always be avoided.

What people say they want

A recent priority listing taken from the Commission of Social Care Inspection (CSCI) providing feedback from service users states that:

- Services for people should be provided by people and organisations that genuinely understand the people that use them
- They want proper and accurate assessment of their individual needs
- Care should be led by their needs, not just fitting in with the services available
- Care should not be governed by cost and targets
- People want to be treated as individual persons and not just as numbers
- People require continuity of services, which should only change as their needs change
- Services should allow for spontaneity
- Services should empower people to exercise choice and be in control of their lives
- Services should allow people to be cared for in their own homes
- Wherever possible, people they wish to lead their lives as independently as possible.

Future opportunities to development person-centred care

The picture of needs that we gain from understanding the social trends, responding to service users' feedback suggests changing business needs. This is because people who would previously been admitted into care homes should now be supported at home, This will, logically, decrease the need for social care home places, but probably not for nursing home places, where people may have less choice in meeting their needs appropriately. Therefore as a business, we will need to look at increasing our home care availability and maintaining or increasing nursing home capacity. In this way, we can take up the opportunity to meet a wide range of needs in the community as part of a future development of services.

To replace long term places we should as a business seek to develop 'respite care' and set up active day care support services, available seven days a week. Perhaps we should also be setting aside specific days for different specialisms, for both example elderly mentally infirm people and younger physically disabled people might benefit from care focused on their specific needs. Similarly, setting up carers' support groups to help people cope with caring for a relative at home offers a means of meeting others who are also caring for loved ones, together with some education and training in areas they are finding difficult to manage.

Extending current home cooked meals provision to cover a larger area, meet more dietary and social needs might also be of benefit. Increasing the stock of supported living apartments might also increase flexibility of care. For people approaching the end of life, or where there are palliative care needs, where people wish to be nursed at home, the service could develop a rapid response team. Health care assistants with specific skills in end-of-life care could also usefully support community nursing and palliative care specialist nurses in their roles.

Provision of this kind can contribute to a flexible person-centred care, which would respond to the wishes pf everyone, whatever their impairment, to be facilitated in making choices about their care, with support if needed.

Just thinking about new services is not the whole story, because a competent and skilled workforce is needed to provide them. Caring for people is labour-intensive, and requires a skilled work force to provide these services in a sound and effective way that enables choice and flexibility.

Therefore, business planning in this field requires consideration of workforce development alongside service development. Being proactive in developing appropriate education and training is essential, both toe offer the quality of care and life that service users want and also to enable the business to function. Being able to offer the opportunity of qualification and staff development is the core of any business in a person-centred industry. It enables the service to maintain a clear vision and support that vision with achievement. Similarly, supporting nurse education, by providing placements for student nurses, enables skills transfer to a new generation of nurses and builds interest among professionals in this important and developing area of employment and service. Providing adaptation training to enable overseas nurses to take up employment in the uk also addresses staff shortages. In-house provision of accredited national vocational qualifications through accredited training can attract staff who have opportunity to achieve qualifications at work, whilst earning a living, and opportunity for advancement.

Garth Care homes has also been involved in providing training for students at Opole University as part of the European da Vinci programme; a wonderful group of dedicated young Polish people were inspirational. Residents and patients also gained much from the students' contribution to their daily living. It also enabled students to take home with them both positive and negative issues upon which to reflect and add to their life experience.

Conclusion

This paper has argued that service development and planning requires cooperation between the sectors involved in a mixed economy of care, each bringing its distinctive role and experience. A private sector organisation, focusing on business planning, brings a particular perspective focusing on customer needs, responding to social change among the coming generation of elders and its rising expectations. A much broader and more flexible service can be envisaged. Workforce development, education and training is a crucial aspect of enhancing services, without which service development cannot be achieved.

References

Le Bihan, B. and Martin, C. (2006) A comparative case study of care systems for frail and elderly people: Germany, France, Spain, Italy, United Kingdom and Sweden. *Social Policy and Administration.* 40(1): 26-46.

Means, R., Richards, S. and Smith, R. (2008) *Community Care: Policy and Practice.* (4th ed.) Basingstoke: Palgrave Macmillan.

4 Social skills as a component of education and personal development for helping professionals

Alena Novotna and Anna Žilová[2]
The Catholic University in Ružomberok, Slovak Republic

Introduction
This paper discusses the importance of empathy and assertiveness in facilitating helping professionals and their clients to work together; these social skills are also beneficial for professionals in their personal lives.

Relationships and the helping professions
Helping people in everyday life means that people, as part of their everyday social relations and without necessarily being asked to help, influence positively the way others solve their personal problems by helping them achieve greater self-realisation. It is a common response to human needs in our society.

Professional assistance is not the same as everyday help. When help as part of everyday life fails, professional aid may be used instead of it. Úlehla (1999: 9) comments: 'professional help is used when the other methods by which people solve their problems fail, or these methods cannot be accessed for personal or social reasons'. It is a professional requirement that professionals 'know what to do'. This means that they have evidence that supports their behaviour based on practical experience and understanding derived from theoretical knowledge.

Each helping profession has its own frame of action, unique relations with clients, its own boundaries of responsibility and professional identity.

The quality of human relations between helping professionals and individuals that they are helping is of crucial importance. Personal relationships with clients demands more than fairness, esteem or etiquette but acceptance, empathy, non-judgemental attitudes and clients´ positive feelings that professionals want to help them. However, achieving any activities within helping processes merely meets the requirements of law or

---

[2] novotna.a@gmail.com; zilova@fedu.ku. sk

the agency unless these characteristics of relationships between professionals and clients are achieved.

The professions of social work and social educator or pedagogue are part of the helping professions, and their work therefore requires a focus on relationships in all aspects of human beings.

The social skills of helping practitioners
Capacities and skills are developed through experiences within all social relationships, permitting clear, smooth, acceptable and meaningful communication. These capacities may be described as social skills.

Social skills used by helping professions are divided into groups:

- Skills used with clients who are dependent on help from others; these are focused on:

    - protecting clients (e.g. acceptance),

    - forming a close and interactive relationship between professional and client (e.g. empathy).

- Skills used to achieve self-realisation for clients and the social and psychological confidence of the practitioner (e.g. assertiveness, mental health, ability to prevent burn-out, self-understanding),
- Skills necessary to intervene through communication between professional and client – verbal, non-verbal communication,
- Skills used as part of the process of helping - concrete thinking processes, using knowledge, skills in social communication, self-understanding (e.g. teaching skills)(Buda, 1998: 50)

Empathy in practice and in the personal life of helping professions
Empathy as a psychological skill
Empathy is seen as a tool for creating personal relationships between practitioners in helping professions and clients. 'Generally, empathy is a personal skill, which enables people to put themselves into the psychological state of another person as part of the communication between them. Using this skill, professionals can feel and understand others' emotions, motives and burdens in ways that cannot come from interpersonal interactions. The main tool of this understanding is that within their own personality, others' feelings and passions are experienced through empathy. It may be

understood as personalities putting themselves in another's place or people being reflected within others' psychological experiences' (Buda, 1994: 50).

Everyone possesses the capacity to put themselves in another's place, feel the psychological balance of the other, and the other's emotions. This capacity assists in building relationships with those we help.

Empathy as an empathic response
The word 'empathy' refers to empathic responses – it means to demonstrate the capacity to be empathic to others. Empathy may be expressed both verbally and non-verbally.

The verbal empathic response has three basic interlocking steps:

- put oneself in the client's situation,
- consciously processing what the client feels,
- the empathic response – expressing the client's situation in words, so that the client may in turn expresses understanding that the practitioner experiences something about his/her feelings and way of life.

The non-verbal empathic response can be expressed by: touch, gaze, stance, and eventually by offering a chair, embrace, handshake or other non-verbal and para-language. This empathic response, in the same way as verbal empathic responses, has three basic interlocking steps that end in:

- action by which we express our empathy to the client's situation and by which we demonstrate our perception of his/her situation, that we respect and accept him/her. The client often conveys thought verbal or non-verbal communication awareness of what we express through the empathy.

Empathy may be understood:

- from the social point of view as the humanisation of interpersonal relationships,

- from the individual point of view – as making social education, and achieving individual mental and social health[3], facilitating communication and increasing sensitivity to the others' needs.

We can see the outcomes of empathy in both formal and informal interpersonal relations; the next section focuses on formal relations.

The consequence of empathy in formal relations

'Empathy is a basic requirement for understanding and acceptance others as human beings. It expresses the willingness to accept the other unconditionally. It means to accept him with esteem and respect' (Praško and Prašková, 1996: 40).

In relationships with clients, we want to focus on an outcome of empathy among individuals who are dependent on help from others because they can not manage difficult situations in their lives. Expressing empathy helps clients in various ways:

- It enables clients the opportunity to experience how they feel,
- It decreases clients' feelings of helplessness in not being able to understand and describe their situation and despite this enables the helping practitioner to understand it,
- It enables the practitioner to concisely interpret the situation in ways that help clients,
- It strengthens clients in managing their situation,
- It develops clients' capacity to make sense of their situation,
- It gives clients confidence, especially where the problem is stigmatised.

Acceptance of other people's behaviour and feelings does not mean acting submissively. Roche-Olivar (1992: 98) describes authentic acceptance as 'something very active', because it assumes the capacity to try to understand the other person in his life circumstances and accepting the other; this enriches 'ego and self-confidence'.

---

[3] People with good mental health can express their social identity and can develop it as part of their social environrment without disrupting relationships between them and their social environment to the extent that social intervention is necessary to eliminate or reduce unbalanced or disturbed relationships. An inidividual's social health is closely connected to the social health of groups, communities and societies in which they participate.

The empathy of helping professions helps clients recognise and accept themselves with positives and negatives in the same way that the practitioner accepts them.

Communicating assertive behaviour and its outcomes

Assertive behaviour is behaviour by which we empower ourselves in relations with others, without aggression, and without subordinating our interests. In other words, assertive behaviour is open and direct behaviour. According to Herdová (1997:3) 'assertive behaviour is a collection of tactics that help implement valid demands or say no to impossible claims so as not to harm others' rights'.

We differentiate between:

- assertive communication,
- assertive behaviour.

Assertive communication is a conversation between two or more persons, characterised by the need to insist on our own identity and rights, ask for answers, even to ask too much, while respecting both ourselves and others.

Assertive people's behaviour communicates their assertiveness, respecting both their own and others' rights. In assertive people as they communicate, we may observe what we might describe as 'me-language'. This means communication in the first person singular. Sentence construction is clear and lucid, avoiding long and complex phrases and sticking to the topic. Assertive behaviour focuses on problem-solving. Solutions are suggested and offered; compromises found. Assertive people remain calm, self-possessed and self-confident. Assertive people are good partners, knowing when to talk or to be silent. They do not let themselves be manipulated or pressed to accept unacceptable things. They know how to make their points and achieve respect for their rights.

Assertive behaviour is behaviour like this, which involves open, direct, adequate and honest expression of one's ideas, feelings, opinions and internal psychological state whether these may be seen as positive or negative. Assertive people are aware of their own behaviour and accept responsibility for it, knowing how this behaviour is appropriate t achieving successful outcomes in communication. They listen to others, present themselves as relaxed, responsible and intelligible. In this behaviour, we can clearly see interest in teamwork, not in victory.

The impact and outcomes of assertive behaviour in helping processes
The impact of assertive behaviour on assertive helping practitioners
Assertive behaviour in practitioners helps clients by modelling the behaviour of an individual who expects and receives help, but is at the same time also participating in a process of providing help.

The impact of assertive behaviour on helping actions may be seen in the following:

- assertive helping practitioners have greater self-esteem, self-confidence enabling them to be less dependent on agreement or others' goodwill. Professionals who are open about their needs are more likely to feel satisfaction with their own interventions in clients' situations,
- assertive behaviour creates self-confidence in practitioners, allowing more assertiveness, openness and straightforwardness in expressing emotions, requests and ideas.
- increased self-confidence and equilibrium within helping practitioners allows them to accept others' forcefulness without feeling threatened by it.

Assertive helping practitioners:

- have strong feeling of self-control and control of their enviroments, and is able to accept responsibility,
- manage difficult situations without anxiety, without feeling threatened by things that go wrong,
- learn from mistakes, resolving difficulties without blaming others.
- are flexible in using a range of options, expanding them as they gain experience
- save time and energy by being less pre-occupied by the self-control needed to agree with others, less worried about things going wrong and have to defend themselves against potential criticism
- feel good when they have to negotiate with others

The impacts of assertiveness of helping practitioners on clients
Helping practitioners communicate with clients in order to gain clients' confidence and participation in a mutual endeavour and eventually to help resolve clients' difficulties. Assertive behaviour enables a process to take place of enabling clients to see and use the practitioner's help positively, in the following ways:

- clients feel good when working with an assertive practitioner,
- clients see the practitioner's openness and transparency, and this increases confidence and reduces doubts about the practitioner,
- clients gain self-esteem and respect the practitioner more, and this leads to greater willingness and confidence in their joint work,
- clients also tend to behave more assertively, modelling their behaviour on the practitioner.

The final and central aim of a practitioner's role is to resolve clients' difficult situations. Hence, the outcomes of practitioners' assertive behaviour, discussed above, support problem-solving. Practitioners' assertive behaviour contributes to:

- increased confidence in negotiations and suggestions from both participants, contributing equally,
- meeting common aims – assertive people achieve others' confidence that they will be able to cooperate together,
- encouraging creativity from all participants,
- effectively using practitioners' and clients' contributions positively rather than leading to conflict,
- creating mutual respect generating increased commitment and motivation on both sides,
- reducing participants' doubts when dealing with difficult situations or decisions.

Situations in which assertive behaviour is useful

Assertiveness and assertive behaviour are not a direct means of problem-solving. However, by facilitating open and trouble-free communication among people, they set the conditions within which problem-solving may take place. Dealing with specific issues may not require practitioners to behave assertively all the time. However, it is useful to identify situations in which assertive behaviour may be appropriately applied. These are when practitioners want to:

- achieve compliance on specific issues, by asserting the right to say 'no, I don't want to do that', or 'I cannot' without needing to justify their response.
- openly express feelings, opinions, attitudes,
- confront dishonest comments in a way that does not conflict with either their own feelings or values, or those of others,
- appropriately criticise and respond to criticism
- appropriately praise and accept approval from others,

- manage difficult or negative situations conveniently,
- talk reasonably and effectively at meetings or conferences
- improve atmosphere and communication with others,
- negotiate effectively and do not withdrawing from important issues
- debate vigorously when it is necessary and appropriate.

It is possible to acquire and develop the capacity to be assertive. Self-education, self-training and learning from social experience may all be helpful, but specific assertiveness training may be helpful in social education. The main aims of such training is to acquire the feeling of self-esteem, better self-evaluation and self-confidence, to release people from doubt and uncertainty in social situations, to know how to sustain the important personal goals, to gain a spontaneity and openness in interpersonal relations and develop the other skills discussed above (Praško and Prašková, 1996: 66)

Bibliography

Buda, B. (1994) *Empatia – psychológia vcítenia a vžitia sa do druhého* (Empathy: The psychology of putting oneself in another's place). (2nd edition). Nové Zámky: Psychoprof.

Buda, B. (1998) *Čo vieme o empatii? (What we know about the empathy?)* Bratislava: Pravda.

Herdová, Z. (1997) *Asertívne správanie (Assertive behaviour)*. Bratislava: IVS.

Praško, J. and Prašková, H. (1996) *Asertivitou proti stresu (With the assertiveness against the stress)*. Havlíkuv Brod.

Roche-Olivar, R. (1992) *Etická výchova (Ethical education)*. Bratislava: Orbis Pictus, Istropolitana.

Úlehla, I. (1999) *Umění pomáhat (The Art of Helping)*. Praha: Slon.

Žilová, A. (2003) *Kapitoly z teórie sociálnej práce* (náuka o sociálnej práci) *(Readings on the theory of social work* (the science of social work). (2nd edition) Badín: Mentor.

5   Loss, death and dying: issues for social work education in the EU

Margaret Surrey
Formerly of Trinity Hospice, London

Introduction

This paper explores issues about death, dying and bereavement facing students gaining practice experience in a broad spectrum of social work with adults in EU countries, drawing on knowledge and experience in the field of palliative care in the UK, and the experience of supervising students from Opole University in Trinity hospice, a UK palliative care service operating in an inner-London area. Many students from Opole University were placed during 2007 in nursing homes and hospices in the UK, becoming involved in social work with individuals and families involving death, dying, loss and grief. Their practice experience involved either social work support for patients and families experiencing physical death, or social work with adults experiencing the loss of their home, or loss because of changed circumstances, changes in their family and cultural issues.

A recent book, *Negotiating Death in Contemporary Health and Social Care* by Margaret Holloway, Professor of Social Work at Hull University, England considers the history of the care of dying people and specifically looks at demography and culture in the context of death, dying, loss and grief work. It considers, among many things, causes of death and place of death within a multi-cultural context, and the role of the social worker, using case studies in considering these issues.

Within health and social care, culturally appropriate services and practice are crucial, both in the context of pre-death, post death, dying and wider experiences of loss. To achieve this, practitioners must have a critical understanding of loss and grief work within different cultures, societies and countries. Nyatanga (2002) says the principles of hospice and palliative care (and I would add in nursing home care, and care of adults generally) may be presented globally, but variously interpreted in different countries. The flourishing of bereavement theories in the United States, the UK and Northern Europe suggests that grief counselling, both within and without social work, is going on at sufficient levels to stimulate theoretical development; but how is this perceived within a social work base and across EU countries?   Does social work training focus on and cover issues of palliative care, death and dying, loss, grief work and mourning within these countries? Certainly, within social work training in the UK within the universities where I am tutoring, reference may be made to the concept of these issues within the human growth and development module, but with minimal emphasis – perhaps an hour and a half - focussed specifically on death, loss and grief.

Erikson's (1950) theory of life stages of development has had a strong influence on social work education, and often, the emphasis has been on childhood and adolescence. Reconsidering the theory again for this paper, I was reminded of the latter three stages of Erikson's theory, which focus on adulthood. Each stage arises during a period of life where the individual faces certain important psychological issues:

- Young Adulthood, ages 19-40 - Intimacy versus Isolation
- Middle Adulthood, ages 40-65 – Generativity versus Stagnation
- Late Adulthood, ages 65 upwards - Integrity versus Despair

Focusing on those words 'isolation', 'stagnation' and 'despair', we are immediately drawn to think of loneliness, loss and grief in its widest sense. For adults whose life has no meaning, or where social change has meant a change in lifestyle, often this is accompanied by a sense of loss and mourning.

An important focus of this conference is expressed in its objectives as: directions of development of social work with adults as a reaction to social change. My experience suggests that social workers must be better equipped to ensure that individuals and groups are supported appropriately when they are experiencing significant events and transitions in their lives arising from social change. Transition is the movement from one stage or phase to the next, and is often closely linked with crisis or loss. Thompson (1991: p 4) calls these events 'turning points,…situations which push our usual coping mechanisms beyond their usual limits of effectiveness'. Loss is closely linked to this, and it could be argued that all crises involve a degree of loss because they involve a change in some way. Loss is often associated with death; however we should recognise that loss is a much broader concept – home, country, functional ability, status, illness, admission to care are examples. Loss can produce a significant psychological reaction known as grief, but this must also be seen in its social context of mourning. It is into life stage events of this kind that social workers must become involved and be able to function in a professional manner.

Holloway (2007) book is a welcome addition to the literature, addressing death, loss and mourning in the new context if the social change occurring at the beginning of the twenty-first century. These subjects are still hidden, not widely discussed, in the UK. Is this also true of other EU countries? Do these countries follow the same trend, or is it a more widely acceptable subject for discussion? To achieve the best social work, practitioners in each country need to explore the contemporary social and cultural responses to death, dying and loss in the public debate and private experience of people in their country. However, the last fifteen months of the monthly periodical *Social Work Education* contains frequent discussion of social work with children, women, gender and sexuality. These are all mentioned but the equally important personal and social experiences of death, loss or mourning and not referred to, and there is little coverage of older adults. When looking at random articles from the European Commission Research into Social Sciences and Humanities website covering, amongst many things, family structure and lifestyle, culture, education and medical services, it is difficult to find references to the impact of death and loss amongst adults in EU countries. Does culture play a part? Are there death rituals, or is death and loss a private part of life? Should social workers be involved in these issues, and if so, how should social work training reflect this?

Often social workers in palliative care and nursing and residential care homes have had little or no formal training in death and loss, grief and mourning, yet they are expected to come alongside service users and families during these times of life changing events. As social norms change and people are living longer, should our social workers have more training in mid life to old age, death, dying, loss and mourning? Coleman and O'Hanlon (2004: p 24) in their book *Ageing and Development*, say of Erikson's eight-stage model of human development: 'One of the lasting achievements (of his Eight stages model) is to have brought to the forefront of gerontological concerns questions to do with the psychological and social conditions necessary for later life to flourish'.

Holloway (2007) is also not afraid to consider such subjects as grief amongst cultures; complicated grief; dying, bereavement and grief in old age; dying in the 21st Century including assisted dying, euthanasia and suicide. Health and social care professionals may not be comfortable with such subjects, yet they clearly have a profound impact on those with whom we work, and therefore our training needs to pay attention to them. My teaching experience with social work students suggests that they must manage complex ethical issues, dilemmas and conflicts. We will all have our own views on these delicate subjects, but as professionals we must consider our own value base in order to be able to assist our clients for whom these issues are literally matters of life or death.

Conclusion

Should social work with adults in EU countries place more emphasis in its education on learning about the effects of loss in whatever form that might affect a person? Should there be standardised training across all EU countries to influence the incorporation of appropriate curricula needed to ensure that all practitioners are competent in these important areas of human experience? One organisation in the UK made up of people in the caring professions have started Prime - Partnerships in Medical Education, visiting other countries (mostly Eastern Europe) to teach and share their experiences with medical students. Is this something for qualified social work practitioners to consider? Should all universities follow the trend of some, and to quote from one UK university website "we are able to arrange placements overseas in the USA and Europe." Obviously Opole has adopted this method – should this be encouraged across all EU countries?

Bibliography

Coleman, P. and O'Hanlon, A. (2004) *Ageing and Development*. London: Arnold .

Erikson, E. (1950) *Childhood and Society*. New York: Norton.

Holloway, M. (2007) *Negotiating Death in Contemporary Heath and Social Care*. Bristol: Policy Press.

Nyatanga. B. (2002) Culture, palliative care and multiculturalism. *International Journal of Palliative Nursing* 8(5): 240-246:

Thompson, N. (1991) *Crisis Intervention Revisited*. Birmingham: Pepar.

Social Work Education Routledge

Various articles www.ec.europa.eu/research/social-sciences/knowledge/projects accessed 19th March 2008

6   Research reflections on meeting the needs of older people in the Slovak Republic

Anna Žilová and Alena Novotná[4]
The Catholic University in Ružomberok, Sloval Republic

Introduction

As societies develop, social change and other 'social turbulence', both in the community at large and in particular localities, modify people's personal preferences, and also change the quality of their circumstances, their extent and nature, and opportunities for meeting personal needs. The following paper deals with such changes in the Slovak Republic. Nationwide and regional research on older people in Slovakia have established a close connection between their needs and their social background.

Demographic change in Slovakia (Hegyi, 2000: 40) from 1989 shows an increase in the average duration of life of men from 66.8 to 68.9 years, and women from 75.4 to 76.7 years. The proportion of the Slovak population at or above retirement age will increase from about 17.5% in 1995 to about 23.7% in 2015. In 2004, there were 1,022m citizens above retirement age, about 18.9% of the total population (Štatistická ročenka SR 2005, 2005: 63).

The ageing process leads to changes over time. The idea of an 'ageing process' is concerned with changes after adolescence; such changes are frequently seen frequently negatively (Hartl and Hartlová, 2000: 561; Strmeň and Raiskup 1998: 269) describe old age as a phase in development characterised by physiological, mental and social changes, involving respectively metabolic changes, increased emotional instability and reduced adaptability in social situations. Older people are called 'seniors' in academic and professional discourse. Čornaničová (1998: 26) states that the term 'senior' began to be used spontaneously as a semantically neutral term in educational practice. It replaced terminology drawn from medical, psychological, sociological and other disciplines to describe older people; being used as administrative terms in relation to retirement. However, the term 'senior' is not accepted in the educational or social sciences.

---

[4] novotna.a@gmail.com; zilova@fedu.ku.sk

Seniors' needs

Among the needs of older people as well as of other age groups are: physiological needs, safety needs, social needs, needs for self-determination and needs for self-fulfilment. The degree and quality to which they may be satisfied depends on individual circumstances (including potential for family support), social exchanges and social resources which the senior has and that can be used depending on events that affect the individual. The following research studies show how a range of seniors´ needs are perceived and evaluated in Slovakia:

1. **Physiological needs** are basic needs; not meeting them can affect the broad health and physical condition of older people. This includes nutrition, excretion, breathing, sleep and rest, exercise and mobility.   A regional study, including surveys with a multiple choice questionnaire (N = 184) and interviews with seniors in the region of Liptovský Mikuláš, shows that significant problems that seniors face are: housekeeping 64.1% of subjects; transport services 59.9%; communication with neighbourhood, medical and business   services, 39.0%; shopping 34.10% (Džubáková and Žilová, 2003: 56).
2. **Safety needs** may affect three areas of life: economic, physical and psychological safety.

For economic needs to be acknowledged as met, human beings have to get to the point of accepting that they have adequate living conditions. Where economic needs are not met, older people feel anxious and have concerns about the future. The subjects in Table 1 subjectively considered their households as in need in all aspects of life (Bednárik, 2004: 12; present authors' calculation of percentages; N = 575).

Table 6.1 *Perception of household needs*

Household of ▶ Year ▼	single men	single women	couples
2004	85.3%	88.7%	80.7%
1999	72.7%	76.0%	66.2%

The respondents' subjective feeling of poverty in 2004 emerged from comparison with friends (63.6% of respondents), with not having enough to buy necessities (63.5%), with having no income for hobbies (56.3%) and with inability to give presents (56.3%).

The physical safety of older people is important because seniors with mobility difficulties often fear falling and injury. Mobility aids, and physical help from family members or a health visitor can strengthen the perception of physical safety. Mental safety means to have feeling of certainty, not to have fears and not to feel alone.

Research in 2004 (Bednárik, 2004: 8; present authors' calculation of percentages) shows that 30.6% of elder respondents in living settings for older people were beoing abused. According to their views, reasons for ill-treating older people are: efforts to gain money, a place to live, other property or a house (21.6% of respondents), the fact that family can not manage the care of older person (15.9%), that people around seniors are self-centred and seniors obstruct their wishes (16.3%). An important feature of this research is that 46.2% of respondents avoided answering the questions.

Comparing the results of this research in 2004 with similar research in 1999, it seems that older people in 2004 felt worse than older people in 1999 and they had more troubles. The most significant decline of living conditions affected single men, 66.4% of respondents in 1999 were quite or mostly satisfied, but in 2004 only 47.1% of single older men chose this answer. However, single women came second in the amount of change. In 1999, when the questions were asked of the single women, 70.3% were quite or mostly satisfied, but only 52.4% of respondents were in the category in 2004. The differences between older people living as couples were less marked: 71.9% in 2004 and 51.8% in 1999.

3. **Social needs.** People, old as well as young, cannot be alone for a long time; they need human contact and communication with others. Among social needs are: the need to be of self-aware, the need to belong to a group, the need to love and be loved, and the need to speak and to be heard.

The factors that seniors consider to be of most and middling importance in the multiple choice survey of the exctent to which they were feeling satisfied with their social environment were: satisfactorily healthy conditions 96.9% of respondents, being self-contained in everyday activities, 84.9%; strong family relationships 85%; contacts with another people 78.4%, be financial self-contained 80.7%, participating in social events 36.2%, carrying on their hobbies 49.4% (Bednárik, 2004: 17; present authors' calculation of percentages). If older people needed help, they would turn first to their close family 81.5%; relatives or friends 73.9%; their family doctor 69.0%; municipal services 46.0%, church agencies 23.9%; private agencies 1.4%; or nobody 14.6% (Džubáková and Žilová, 2003: 54-7; present authors' calculation of percentages). The existence of social support for seniors is a significant factor in the level of their satisfaction (Balogová, 2005: 70-73).

Of social workers, the seniors, evaluating what they wanted from social contact in residential care homes, expected the ability to take a kind and respectful approach (72.5%) and patience (27.1%). According these preferences, there is the question whether the expectation of these abilities of social workers is not reportly accurately because of their absence in the observed social environment. (Karkusová and Žilová, 2003: 61). These results illustrate the significant influence of social background on how people adapt to a care home environment. The respondents' preferred staff behaviour which helps them adapt (multiple choice survey, N = 24) communication with staff (79.2%), smiling (66.7%), willingness to help (50.0%), willingness to listen (41.7%). (Zamborová and Žilová, 2004: 53).

4. **Need for self-determination.** This is the autonomy to be free, to make decisions by oneself. Being appreciated by others and respect from others is a part of this aspect of autonomy. The need to be of value, to do things for others may be included to this category of needs. Taken together, these needs, and meeting them, are significant determinants of the quality of life and of the subjective evaluation of their achievement and contentment. These areas of need have not been explored by research in Slovakia.
5. **Needs for self-fulfilment.** These needs include the need of to be independent, affiliation needs and self-fulfilment in itself (Pichaud and Thareauová, 1998: 37 – 41; Matulayová, 2001: 225 et seq,): The need of independence means not to be dependent on help and services of other people and agencies.

The need for self-fulfilment (feeling of value and being satisfied) which is connected with valuation of the senior's own and occupations. Attitudes to their own life and its achievements depend on the goals that the senior fulfilled in earlier parts of the life course. The most frequently selected satisfactions from a multiple choice list by seniors were the presence in their actual life and its achievements multiple choice of:

feeling safe in a well-functioning family	87.4 % of respondents
well-behaved children	86.0 %
adequate family life assurance	75.2 %

self-realisation in working life	77.1 %
able to save money for children	48.8 %
able to carry out useful tasks for others	75.9 %
being able to own property for their old age	71.4 %

The most frequently unfulfilled aims were: saving for children (19.6% of respondents), saving something for their own old age (14.7%) (Bednárik, 2004: 17).

Affiliation needs (the feeling of belonging to the particular social group). Older people are the part of the social structure of any society. Therefore it is necessary, accepting demographic predictions, to draw and adapt social policy to protect older people against the social risks of old age, ensure that the health service provides protection against the fear of illness and to guarantee to provide for the cost of living for people who are unable to save for the necessities of life for themselves (social security). It will also be necessary to support the expansion of a range of care services with the aim maintaining the quality of life in old age at the best possible level.

Levická (2002: 102) introduces the main aims of social service as the protection and care of social welfare and maintaining the accepted level of the quality of life for citizens established in public policy. Since the state is a guarantor of its citizens' living standards, it is expected to manage and maintain the costs of these services. However, the state is not the only or main provider of social services. There are many opportunities in a society that are raised in the field of social work.

Social policy analysis in social work have developed, during the last hundred years, different views about the role of government in developing social services deriving from its absolute responsibility for development, its operational role and its control function. Matulayová (2001: 235) suggests that the social services may be divided into three groups:

- the public sector, social services that are directed and financed by the national state and autonomous authorities
- the private or business sector, social services provided as alternatives and supplements to state services
- the third sector (or not-for-profit and voluntary sector) is a varied group of organisations, from local associations to major

professional organisations. The scale of the services provided by volunteers. They cover all segments of social work from children to the hospice services. Volunteers undertake both manual jobs and also direct works with clients and they organize and finance these activities. The volunteers act in these ways as a supplement to the state services.

In spite of the fact that care homes are not so popular with seniors, the number of applications for places is expanding. Several factors influence this situation: the rise in the number of senior in a population, changes of social and economic conditions in a society, and the decline of traditional three-generation family for a variety of reasons. For example, relatives may be afraid of losing their jobs if they are responsible for taking care of seniors at home. For these reasons, the role care homes as an element of social services provision is not replaceable in at least some cases. Therefore, it is necessary to consider them as a permanent part of provision, even if they are not a positive choice for many people.

The main role of care homes is to provide accommodation, health and cultural care and opportunities for leisure pursuits. These cultural activities follow the abilities and interests of residents to ensure adequate quality of life.

Older people either decide or are forced by their circumstances to go to the care homes. Bartošovič (2002: 4) proposes factors that can influence the decision to enter a care home: poor health, loss of capacity to care for oneself, poor family relationships, not having children able or willing to provide care, a feeling of separateness, psychological factors, the fact they do not want to case difficulties for their children, poor housing conditions, other social factors, feeling uncertainty because of other people's attitudes towards them. These data are supported by the results of the regional research which confirms that the most significant reason of the decision to go to the retirements homes the health of the resident (65%) (Morongová and Žilová, 2003: 58, N = 100), other important responses were: feeling lonely (25%) and family pressures (5%).

Conclusion
Based on the research reviewed here, on what older people thought about ways of meeting their needs in the Slovak Republic, we can see:

- Basic subsistence needs are the main reason why older people's life situation becomes problematic

- A characteristic feature of older people's behaviour is to save for financial 'worse times'
- Seniors want to retain the capacity to help their children financially,
- Health and being self-caring are the most important factors in a satisfactory social environment, but satisfactory relationships with family and social networks and financial independence are also important.
- Seniors expect that their main need will be help with physically difficult household tasks, but other needs that they want help with are in maintaining social contacts and in transport,
- Older people expect practitioners working with them to display a reasonable degree of professional behaviour, such as maintaining a kind and respectful attitude, and patience.

Bibliography

Balogová, B. (2005) *Seniori*. (Seniors). Prešov: Akcent Print. 2005, 158 str.

Bartošovič, I. (2002) Niektoré identifikačné a sociálne charakteristiky obyvateľov domovov dôchodcov. (The identification and social characteristics of retirement home residents). In: *Práca a sociálna politika. (The situation and social policy)*. Roč. 10(3): 4.

Bednárik, R. (2004) *Sociálno-ekonomická situácia starších ľudí na Slovensku (sociologický výskum)*. (The social and economic situation of older people in Slovakia: sociological research). SŠPR. 42 str. Bratislava: SSPR.

Čornaničová, R. (2004) *Edukácia seniorov*. (The education of seniors). Bratislava. UK. 1998. 156 str.

Džubáková, M. (2003) *Sociálne služby pre seniorov v meste Liptovský Mikuláš*. Diplomová práca. Konzultantka Anna Žilová (Social services for seniors in Liptovský Mikuláš)(Dissertation supervised by Anna Žilová). Banská Bystrica: PF UMB.

Hartl, P. and Hartlová, H. (2000) *Psychologický slovník*. (Dictionary of Psychology), Prague: Portál. 2004. 774 str.

Hegyi, L. (2000) Starostlivosť seniorov z aspektu verejného zdravotníctva: Zborník príspevkov z 8. stredoeurópskeho sympózia o sociálnej gerontológii. (Care of seniors from the point of view of public health service: Proceedings of the 8th Central European Conference on Social Gerontology), 93 str., Bratislava: Charis: 2000.

Karkusová, M, (2003) *Sociálna práca v domove dôchodcov*. Diplomová práca. Konzultantka Anna Žilová (Social services in retirement homes) (Dissertation supervised by Anna Žilová), Banská Bystrica: PF UMB.

Levická, J. (2002) *Metódy sociálnej práce*. (Social Work Methods). 1228 str. Bratislava: Vev, s.r.o.,

Matulayová, T. (2000) In: Hroncová, J. Hudecová, A. and Matulayová, T.: *Sociálna pedagogika a sociálna práca* (Social Pedagogy and Social Work). Banská Bystrica: PF UMB. 2000, 293 str.

Pichaud, C. and Thareauová, I. (1998): *Soužití se staršími lidmi*. (Co-existence with older people). 156 str. Praha (Prague): Portal. 1998.

Morongová, I. (2003) *Sociálna práca v Domove dôchodcov a Domove sociálnych služieb v Klenovci*. Diplomová práca. Konzultantka Anna Žilová, (Social services in Retirement Homes in Klenovec) (Dissertation supervised by Anna Žilová), Banská Bystrica: PF UMB

Strmeň, L. and Raiskup, C. J. (1998) *Výkladový slovník odborných výrazov používaných v psychológii*. (Monolingual dictionary of technical terms in psychlogy)., Bratislava: IRIS.

Štatistická ročenka SR (2005) (Statistics year-book SR 2005)., Bratislava: VEDA.

Zamborová, K.)2004) *Adaptácia seniorov na život v podmienkach Domova dôchodcov a Domova sociálnych služieb*. Diplomová práca. Konzultantka Anna Žilová (The adaptation of seniors to living conditions in retirement home)(Dissertation supervised by Anna Žilová). Banská Bystrica: PF UMB.

7   Social policy on unemployment in Poland

Anna Weissbrot-Koziarska
Opole University, Poland

Introduction
Polish society in recent decades has been one of risk in nearly all domains of life. Difficulties frequently appear in the life of individual citizens, which prevent them from realising their own needs, in political, social and cultural spheres. As a consequence, we must deal more often now with 'families-at risk'. The direct factors that shape this state of things include, among others, separations resulting from living abroad, the growing number of divorces, increasing poverty in society and unemployment. The impossibility of realising many needs has brought about a change in the situation resulting from loss of employment, while increasing poverty often leads to destruction of the individual and the individual's family. The family, as a social group, only functions appropriately when conditions for its integration are satisfied. There is no family where there are no common norms or values, or where there is a lack of mutual influences exerted by family group members on one another (Kawula 1999: 246).

One of many examples of difficulties in everyday life in the contemporary world is the phenomenon of unemployment which appeared at the end of 1990 and started rising very rapidly. At the moment it affects the whole country. That unexpected change in the labour market took everybody by surprise: society lacked experience of resolving problems faced by people without jobs. Additionally, nobody seemed prepared to deal with the crisis on such a massive scale, which resulted in the feeling of helplessness and redundancy. Apathy and helplessness of unemployed people were the main causes of many socioeconomic problems that affected our country, which in turn changed the direction of the Polish social policy.

In this paper, I focus on the phenomenon of unemployment in Poland, with the aim of showing its consequences for the individual and the family. I also discuss the opportunities of gaining support from social workers and help from social agencies designed to eliminate this unfavourable social change in our country.

The phenomenon of unemployment in Poland

Unemployment is defined in many different ways, including economic, social and political aspects. It affects not only the standard of living and dynamics of economic development, but also, to a considerable degree, influences social and economic mood in a country and the popularity of governments as well (Kwiatkowski 2002: 7). Economists treat unemployment as a category of analysis of labour market; sociologists pay attention to its social consequences, that is, they concentrate on the state of job-related inactivity of people available for work and people who are available for employment. Social pedagogues, in turn, do not only analyse causes of unemployment and its effects, but, their main role is to find ways of helping and supporting individuals whose functioning and socio-cultural development are threatened for that reason.

The unemployment rate in the whole European Union in August 2008 (Eurostat[5]) was 7.2%, with the lowest in the Czech Republic (4.5%), Holland (2.7%) and Austria (3.8%). In Poland, the unemployment rate was decreasing steadily between January and November 2008. A slight increase (by 0.4%) occurred in December 2008 and currently it is 9.5%. However, economists leave no room for doubt that Poland will face a growing number of unemployed people each month in the future, which will result from the economic slowdown that is going on in the world's main markets (Chief Statistical Office 2008).

Unemployment leads to families being increasingly in poverty, which, in consequence, makes it impossible for them to perform basic functions, including cultural and socialising activity. The final effect of the phenomenon is the families' and their members' withdrawal from participation in wider social groups. Apart from that, as Sikora observes (2004: 174) families' increasing poverty exerts a considerable influence on development of children, who, having very limited opportunities to realise plans for their future lives, can only dream about their future. Therefore, one of the basic social goals of the state must be to eliminate the phenomenon of unemployment so as to bring the growing scale of poverty to a standstill. This is important, because as Głąbicka writes (2001: 318), families living in poverty limits the life prospects of their children and is the main cause of family conflict. Moreover, unemployment, which leads to lowering of living standards of families, can result in deterioration of individuals' health,

---

[5] Eurostat measures the harmonized unemployment rate as a percentage of the population ranging between 15-74 years of age, who are without employment, but capable of taking up jobs in the course of next two weeks, who have actively been looking for jobs in recent weeks, in comparison with all people available for work in the particular state.

gradual loss of up-to-date professional qualifications, as well as frustration and alienation in contacts with people and social groups within the closest environment. This, as a result, may lead to problem behaviour among unemployed people and their family members. In such a situation, day support (such as local day-care centres) can prove invaluable as their task is, among others, to support parents' efforts towards rearing children and taking care of them (Dąbrowska-Jabłońska 2004: 281-289).

The consequences of unemployment are visible in individuals' social and personal functioning. The most significant social consequences include a deterioration of living standards, a threat to existence, threats of individual psychological stress, disturbance in family life, damage to moral and ethical stability, the appearance of social problem behaviour, and tensions and social conflicts (Auleytner and Głąbicka 2001: 40-41).

On the other hand, for individuals without a job, finding themselves in this situation results in greater poverty and worsening of their standard of living. Connected with this, a slow process of becoming isolated from society occurs, with an increasing inability to manage leisure time, conflicts and tensions within the family, psychological discomfort, and a sense of helplessness; all factors that limit or prevent participation in political, social and cultural life. Moreover, the family's potential as consumers becomes restricted, which, as a result, endangers its existence. This occurs because the progress of economic and social development through rising production and globalisation causes people to want to live at a higher standard, even if they cannot often afford to do so. The amount and availability of information concerning consumption goods, aggressive advertising and the promotion of a materialistic style of living add to frustration and disappointment (Wszeborowski 2003: 447-448). A significant consequence of unemployment is also spiritual impoverishment of the family, which destroys the unemployed person's psychological well-being and frequently results in humiliation of all the family members. Therefore, combating unemployment often becomes a crucial challenge to both economic and social policies in our country, and achieving results means character of complex actions on the part of persons and institutions responsible for proper functioning of citizens and their families. The actions are complemented by activities of the state and other subjects in the social sphere of preventing unemployment, which aim at limiting its extent and effects.

Unemployment has become an active challenge to the social policy of the state, particularly to social work, since the rise in the unemployment rate enlarges poverty and social problem behaviour. It is mainly social workers who provide effective support in preventing these negative results and effects of unemployment in the family, since they coordinate services for unemployment established by the state with the actual experiences of individual families. It is social workers who help to secure means of existence for all members of a family that loses all sources of income. It is hard for families where one of the adult members is outside the labour market, to shape their development and to perform social functions appropriately.

Public social policy in fighting unemployment
In Poland, the problem of unemployment, unemployed people and their families is dealt with by the social assistance agency, an element of public social policy. It is designed to make it possible for unemployed people and their families to overcome difficult periods of life when their own means are not sufficient (Social Aid Act of 12th March, 2004, Chapter 1, Article 1). Consequently, *Ośrodki Pomocy Społecznej* (Social Aid Centres) were established with the aim of achieving these tasks. They are intended to provide support in the form of social work, specialist counselling and financial aid. Social work is a professional activity directed at supporting individuals and families in strengthening or regaining their abilities to function in society, as well as at creating conditions that can enhance this goal (Social Aid Act of 12th March, 2004, Chapter 1, Article 8). According to the Social Aid Act, social work should achieve this by, among other things, making it possible for those in need to carry out relevant social roles (Chapter 1, Article 6). Apart from crisis intervention, providing shelters, specialist counselling, and similar provision, in accordance with Article 36, social work is one of a group of non-financial services within the social aid system. It is targeted at the following clients:
1. Individuals and families, with the aim of developing or strengthening their activity and independence in life;
2. The local community in order to secure cooperation and coordination of actions on the part of agencies that are vital in satisfying needs of its residents is concerned (Social Aid Act of 12th March, 2004, Chapter 1, Article 45 §1).

Practice consists of helping people to develop and in accompanying them during their passage through difficult periods of their lives, when they are unexpectedly confronted by events that restrict their ability to deal with problems on their own.

Experiencing unemployment is connected with a loss of opportunities for exchanging privileges and duties, and also loss of independence from surveillance by external social institutions. Unemployed people do not possess employment, which is regulated by a contract, and thus they have no steady income as a reward for the job done. Despite the fact that it is the state that is responsible for creating suitable number of workplaces for its citizens, in the conditions of market economy it is unemployed people themselves who are responsible for finding employment on their own. However, before they succeed in doing so, unemployed people are obliged to register at a job centre and regularly confirm their readiness to take up employment offered. *Powiatowe Urzędy Pracy* (County Job Centres) monitor offers of vacancies, changes in the employment structure, run a register of unemployed people and people seeking jobs. This is necessary to secure adequate achievement in preventing unemployment and easing its effects, as well as rational management of budgets for benefits offered to eligible citizens.

One of the more important tasks in state social policy in fighting unemployment is support provided to individuals in overcoming difficult situations, teaching people how to solve problems hampering their functioning, and also leading unemployed people and their families towards self-reliance. When a family is affected by unemployment, its income decreases severely, if not completely, after the term of eligibility for unemployment benefit expires (Matejek 2004: 130). Therefore, a social worker needs to start cooperating with the family by assessing its situation, followed planning assistance to enable the family to regain its living standards. Sometimes, being unemployed generates such dramatically serious problems that they need emotional support to help them handle the difficult situation. Sikorski (2002: 74-140) discusses a model of simultaneous family therapy involving both the adult and children.

Someone without a job, facing difficult material conditions, expects some help, including help from the state, since the material quality of the family's lifestyle arising from unemployment affects the fulfilment of its functions, especially participation in the economy as consumers. This problem is one of the more significant ones that clients of the social aid system identify. Support for long-term unemployed people with fixed negative patterns in their attitudes towards the labour market is a particularly tough challenge (Matejek 2004: 131). It is then a duty of the social worker to stimulate an unemployed person to work out a way of getting out of this difficult situation. Unemployed people need help to rid themselves of any acquired helplessness, achieving a change of the underplayed person's attitudes and helping to form positive attitude in someone remaining without a source of income. Social work in this situation needs to emphasise raising qualifications and work skills by unemployed people so that their chances of finding work improves.

The social policy of the state is directed towards making it possible for individuals to get out of unemployment through taking an active approach and developing effective activities to find new work. The social worker is expected to help unemployed people to alter and improve the current state of their lives. Social work should also play an educational role, shaping and broadening knowledge that facilitates understanding of many aspects of life, and, as a result, – providing better ways of coping with the hardships of daily life (Matejek 2004: 133). Thus, social work help, support and cooperation with unemployed people and their families is crucial. Educating unemployed people towards changing their situations raises their sense of self-confidence and strengthens their belief that it will be possible to return to 'normal' life. Both the individual and society benefits from such a change: economic growth can only take place when citizens of any state are actively employed.

Therefore, preventing unemployment should be one of the elements of state social policy. In the Polish system of combating unemployment, several agencies are involved on the following three rungs:

The first rung (central) is made up of the government, the main organiser and coordinator of the state policy. This includes:

1. the Ministry of Finance, with the relevant minister who prepares the budget of the state, determines the size of *Fundusz Pracy* (Labour Fund) according to the state's resources
2. the Ministry of Labour and Social Policy carrying out the employment responsibilities of the state, with the help of *Urząd Pracy* (Labour Office) and regional and district job centres, and social aid responsibilities by means of regional and local social aid centres. It also coordinates the state's responsibilities for retirement and other pensions, carries out state responsibilities in employment and rehabilitation for disabled people, using resources means from *Fundusz Rehabilitacji Osób Niepełnosprawnych* (Rehabilitation of the Disabled Fund) (Bańka 1995L 28).

The Minister of Social Work and Social Policy has a *Naczelna Rada Zatrudnienia* (Chief Employment Board) as an assessment and counselling body. Its duties include the following

1. issuing assessments of projects and legislation on employment and submitting applications to change existing regulations
2. issuing assessments of Labour Fund plans and working reports on the activity of this fund
3. inspiring enterprises aimed at full worthwhile employment.

The *Sejmik Krajowy* (National Little Parliament) is an association of representatives of communes' self-governments. Its members lead consultation talks with the national government to resolve socioeconomic problems.

The second rung (regional) includes the *Voivode* (the President of the Province), *Wojewódzki Urząd Pracy* (Regional Labour Office), *Wojewódzki Zespół Pomocy Społecznej* (Regional Social Aid Group) and *Sejmik Samorządowy Województwa* (The Local Government Little Parliament of the Province).

The *Voivode*, being a representative of the government, coordinates the activity of parts of the state administration, holds, *ex officio*, the post of *Przewodniczący Rady Zatrudnienia* (President of the Regional Board of Employment) and is responsible for issuing assessments of the direction of employment in the province, of the effectiveness of the use of resources from the Labour Fund. In turn, the Regional Labour Office deals with responsibilities within various aspects of the labour market, prevention of unemployment and moderating its impact in the province. Furthermore, it is a court of second instance in administrative proceedings about employment and unemployment, coordinates the activity of local job offices in the province, and is responsible for planning and distributing resources from the Labour Fund, sends people to work abroad, and carries out tasks relating to employment and rehabilitation of the disabled.

The problem of unemployment is also dealt with by the Regional Social Aid Group, which carries out and coordinates provision, on behalf of the state, of social aid in the area of the province, targeting individuals and families in difficult situations and creating opportunities for them to overcome crises that they are cannot cope with on their own, offering opportunities and entitlements. Then, the Local Government Little Parliament of the Province jointly represents communes (*gminy*) of the province and issues reports on matters of concern to the province, including employment and unemployment.

The third rung (local, the lowest level) is a system of agencies in direct contact with unemployed people, providing services to them, and includes *Rejonowe Ośrodki Pracy* (District Job Centres), Boards of Communes, *Gminny Ośrodek Pomocy Społecznej* (Commune Social Aid Centres). District Job Centres run employment agencies that help unemployed people and those seeking employment to find appropriate work, as well as helping companies find suitable employees. If there is a lack of work opportunities, they offer training or retraining to their clients. They also develop additional work opportunities in companies by offering financial aid. The offices initiate and subsidise interventions and public works, give loans and offer assistance in obtaining credits from banks to start business activity; they also grant and pay out unemployment benefits.

Restraining the rise in the unemployment rate is possible due to the active policy of the state in the labour market, which performs five basic functions:

1. Motivating unemployed people;
2. Decreasing structural problems in the labour market;
3. Raising productivity in the workforce;
4. Influencing the size of employment and unemployment;
5. Ensuring the readiness of the unemployed to take up work (Kwiatkowski 2002: 301-302).

These activities operate through inclusion of people inactive in the employment market in the special programmes, public works, jobs created through public interventions in the market and programmes of loans to unemployed people and companies. These help, first, to reduce the impact of loss of qualifications and skills among unemployed people, and helps them to maintain work-related activity, preventing loss of faith in their own potential, avoiding a feeling of being 'useless'. Also, they do not lose their sense of responsibility for the family and its social roles. Moreover, striving to find work helps to maintain the labour supply.

Ending unemployment is a shared responsibility for all citizens. All political factions should unite in one programme to revive the economy and accelerate development that seeks to create new work places, responding to the severity of the losses which result for unemployed people, their families and the whole of society from unemployment. This issue becomes more important as the population born in the years of demographic boom is entering the age when they are available for work (Wszeborowski 2003: 448-449).

The percentage of the unemployed in Poland is very high (7.4% according to the Chief Statistical Office – http:/www.praca.gov.pl – data of 15th November, 2008), which may cause social policy analysts and pedagogues, to be pessimistic, to see it as a hopeless situation with no way out or prospects, particularly for the generation of young people in education, where facilities have developed so profusely in recent years. This gives rise to a sense of various psychological and social reactions, feelings of being unfairly treated, frustration and social problem and criminal behaviours, as well as to suicide, acts of escape or rebellion, or aggression (Kawula 2003: 210-211).

The high unemployment rate in Poland pushes politicians to make changes in the structure of social aid and social work. This means not only developing effective service responses but also improving professional preparation for social workers dealing with unemployed people and their families, who advise individuals on getting out of crisis situations and to refer people to relevant agencies. Nevertheless, the effectiveness of an unemployed person's response to their position and agencies fighting unemployment must be based on integration. Changing the present state of affairs is possible only when individuals are active themselves in a consistent drive towards resolving their position alongside the agency's role.

Achieving social policy aims in fighting unemployment also requires a focus on protecting employees against losing work through, among other things, legal protection against individual or group redundancies.

State social aid agencies play an important role in reducing the negative effects of unemployment, facilitating the availability of social workers to work on changing crisis situations of unemployed people through helping them find jobs. Unemployed people often use consultations offered by qualified social advisors in social aid centres. Legal and psychological counselling is a form of assistance of significant value here. Therefore, well-organised education to teach skills of coping with problem situations is a vital element of the state's social policy. Furthermore, unemployed people are often clients of Social Aid Centres and benefit from different forms of financial support.

However, aid and support offered to an unemployed person should not be excessive or last for too long, to avoid people becoming dependent on the help to the extent that they are not able to cope with difficult situations on their own. This loss of independence, in the long run, affects both the receiver and provider of the support negatively. Public policy that aims to prevent unemployment uses several economic instruments, both macro- and micro-economic policies. Macro-economic policies use fiscal, budgetary and monetary instruments to reduce unemployment (Kawula 2003: 232). It aims to restrict the unemployment arising from unbalanced market conditions. Microeconomic policy covers instruments that aim to improve the functioning of the labour market and reduce unemployment in particular groups of the workforce in regions, cities, communes, areas of structural unemployment and poverty in Poland (Kawula 2003: 232). The instruments include:

- Public employment programmes creating additional workplaces in economic sectors that do not generate private sector involvement;
- Granting non-returnable financial aid to companies that avoid planned reduction of personnel or create new workplaces;
- Loans to unemployed people to help them develop their own business activity as self-employed people;
- Vocational training that make it possible for the unemployed to gain or change their qualifications;
- Seasonal and other job-creation measures to meet the needs of unemployed people.

These instruments are usually addressed to a particular group of the workforce; they are selective and play an essential role in reducing structural and temporary unemployment. Passive public policy includes various forms of financial aid offered to unemployed people, such as unemployment benefits, one-off insurance or redundancy payment given to those made redundant. Thus, the instruments aim mainly to create employment opportunities and improve the chances of unemployed people finding jobs (Kawula 2003: 234).

The significance of various social provision in supporting unemployed people is of great importance. County Labour Offices run a variety of specialist courses for unemployed people. Moreover, they make the people seeking employment familiar with different job opportunities and assist companies in organising additional vacancies. They also grant loans to unemployed people for business start-ups. In many places various associations and centres that offer free services providing counselling and information services about running a business, within the social work and mutual aid services. Municipal Centres of Social Aid (*Miejskie Ośrodki Pomocy Społecznej*) also give support to unemployed people through granting occasional grants for specific purpose to pay off bills, purchasing medicines, feeding children or organising leisure pursuits. Commune Social Aid Centres also grant regular allowances and others designed for specific purposes.

However, because of the relatively high unemployment rate in Poland, the support offered to unemployed people by the state is insufficient. Still, it is promising that more people will be affected by social change activity, creating innovative helping solutions, and are supported by European funds.

Conclusion

Work is a fundamental need of human beings, a paramount condition of their psychological well-being (Ratajczak 2001: 22). It constitutes a vital aspect of individual functioning. People prepare themselves to work for the greater part of their lives. Therefore, work is a significant element of everyone's proper development: it defines people's well-being and the possibility of their accomplishing their aims in life. Work enables people to carry out a planned life, and is a factor in preventing the exclusion of individuals from society. Moreover, the work people do to a great extent influences the economic development of their country. Hence, unemployment is one of the most important problems of contemporary times and combating it is a crucial task for each state's social policy machinery, including social work. For many citizens, finding themselves without the chance of having regular employment is a very difficult, problem-generating, unprecedented situation. Frequently, many do not know how to behave and cope with the hardship that results. And it is here that social workers can help people adapt through a number of changes, including shifting people's personal reactions to the situation of being without work.

Unemployment is a crisis situation and each crisis is an especially tough experience which often exceeds individuals' capacities for self-help. Therefore, public social policy must on fight unemployment through constant targeting its role in promoting unemployed people's own capacity to respond to their situation. The social aid system has changed constantly during the socioeconomic transformation of Poland. It sought to develop programmes to lower the unemployment rate. Initially, in the 1990s, labour market interventions used public funds (Kabaj 2004: 110). Later, the Ministry of Labour and Social Policy prepared several programmes to combat unemployment, aiming to help people stay out of job market. A strategy developed that assumed that preventing job loss, stimulating unemployed people to find jobs and developing economic activity should be undertaken simultaneously. As a result, the Ministry sets out four priority goals to achieve a more fluid labour market, differentiating programmes and types of activity, strengthening of agencies supporting the labour market, promoting new educational help and disseminating knowledge about the labour market (Kabaj 2004: 114). It should also be effective public policy against unemployment to strive for a global decrease in its scale, seeing that an increasing number of individuals without employment degraded both individuals and the economic health of the whole country.

Bibliography

Auleytner J., Głąbicka K. (2001) *Polskie kwestie socjalne na przełomie wieków* (*The Polish Social Questions on the Turn of Centuries*), Warszawa: Wyższa Szkoła Pedagogiczna Towarzystwa Wiedzy Powszechnej Elipsa

Bańka A. (1995) *Zawodoznawstwo: doradztwo zawodowe: pośrednictwo pracy: psychologiczne metody i strategie pomocy bezrobotnym* (*The Study of Professions: Job Counselling: Job Agency: Psychological Methods and Strategies of Aid to the Unemployed*),, Poznań: . Wyd. Print-B

Chief Statistic Office (2008) *http:/www.praca.gov.pl* (accessed: 15 September, 2008).

Dąbrowska-Jabłońska I. (2004) Świetlica środowiskowa jako forma pracy socjalno-wychowawczej Ośrodka Pomocy Społecznej/ (The local day-centre as a form of social development work of Social Centres). In: J. Brągiel, and P. Sikora (eds), *Praca socjalna - wielość perspektyw. Rodzina-Multikulturowość-Edukacja* (*Social Work – Multiplicity of Perspectives. Family-Multiculture-Education*), Opole: 281-289.

Głąbicka K. (2001) *Polityka społeczna w Unii Europejskie: aspekty aksjologiczne I empiryczne* (*The Social Policy in the EU: Axiological and Empirical Aspects*), Warszawa. Wyższa Szkoła Pedagogiczna Towarzystwa Wiedzy Powszechnej Elipsa.

http:/www.praca.gov.pl – strona internetowa serwisu informacyjnego urzędów pracy (webpage of information service of job offices).

Kabaj M. (2004) *Strategie i programy przeciwdziałania bezrobociu* (*Strategies and Programmes of Prevention of Unemployment*), Warszawa: 'Scholar'.

Kawula S. (1999) Rodziny ryzyka (Families at risk). In: Lalak D., and Pilch T. (eds), *Elementarne pojęcia pedagogiki społecznej i pracy socjalnej* (*The Fundamental Notions of Social Pedagogy and Social Work*), Warszawa: 'Żak: s.244-247.

Kawula S. (2003) Społeczno-pedagogiczne inicjatywy na rzecz walki z bezrobociem w Polsce. (The socio-pedagogical initiatives for fighting the unemployment in Poland). In: Marzec-Holka K. (ed.), *Pomoc społeczna. Praca socjalna. Teoria i praktyka* (*Social Aid. Social Work. Theory and Practice*), vol. I, Bydgoszcz. Wydaw: Akademii Bydgoskiej im. Kazimierza Wielkiego: s. 209-248.

Kwiatkowski E. (2002) *Bezrobocie: podstawy teoretyczne* (*Unemployment: Theoretical Foundations*). Warszawa: PWN.

Matejek J. (2004) Problemy współczesnej rodziny jako wyzwanie dla pracy socjalnej (.Problems of the contemporary family as a challenge to social work). In: Brągiel J. and Sikora P., (eds), *Praca socjalna - wielość perspektyw. Rodzina-Multikulturowość-Edukacja* (*Social Work – Multiplicity of Perspectives. Family-Multiculture-Education*), Opole: 129-134.

Ratajczak Z. (2001) *Bezrobocie. Między bezradnością a nadzieją* (*Unemployment. Between Helplesness and Hope*), Katowice. Wyd. Uniwersytetu Śląskiego.

Sikora P. (2004) Międzygeneracyjna transmisja wartości podkultury biedy w rodzinach dotkniętych ubóstwem (The inter-generation transmission of the value of subculture of poverty in families affected with poverty). In: J. Brągiel and P. Sikora (eds), *Praca socjalna - wielość perspektyw. Rodzina-Multikulturowość-Edukacja* (*Social Work – Multiplicity of Perspectives. Family-Multiculture-Education*), Opole: 169-178.

Sikorski W. (2002) *Psychoterapia grupowa różnych pokoleń* (*Group Psychotherapy of Different Generations*), Warszawa: „Żak".

Szylko-Skoczny M. (red.) (1992) *Społeczne skutki bezrobocia w wymiarze lokalnym* (*The Social Effects of Unemployment in a Local Dimension*), Warszawa. Fundacja im. Friedricha Eberta w Polsce.

Ustawa o pomocy społecznej z dnia 12 marca 2004 r (Social Aid Act of 12th March, 2004).

Wszeborowski K. (2003) Społeczne skutki bezrobocia (The social effects of unemployment). In: Marzec-Holka K.(ed.), *Pomoc społeczna, praca socjalna: teoria i praktyka* (*Social Aid. Social Work. Theory and Practice*), vol. II, Bydgoszcz. Wydaw. Akademii Bydgoskiej im. Kazimierza Wielkiego: 441-449.

PART 2

Dimensions of practice in social work with adults

8   Social work and the phenomenon of social marginalization of the 'alien': experiences of working with the Roma community

Piotr Sikora
Opole University, Poland
Justyna Wójcik
Municipal Family Aid Centre, Opole, Poland

Introduction

The 'alien' plays an important role in the functioning of social systems, in a way facilitating the process of social stratification and internal identification. Merton indicated a number of situations typical of multicultural societies. This included attributing to representatives of groups of 'alien' people a lack of accomplishments (without analysing the entire context of the social system within which the alien group lived) by representatives of the dominant groups, creating untrue images of the 'worse' groups, excessive condemnation of the 'alien' paying no attention to what they do (Merton, 1982: 464-473). Znaniecki (1990: 292) wrote that an 'alien' is not only someone with whom we are not connected by means of any social 'meeting points', and who does not belong to our group. It is also someone who, in a visible manner, differs from us. The decisive factor is that the 'alien', to a given individual or community, are people who are experienced as 'alien' by that individual or community. The reaction towards the 'alien' and the extent to which myself and other members of my community see what is alien in an 'alien' person become dominant in this respect. Exclusion brought about by ethnic factors is a particular type of this social phenomenon in which there is not only a low income level and sometimes severe poverty, but this also overlaps with this specific social reaction, characteristic of relations with the 'alien'. This dimension of the problem reaches beyond a single state, since ethnicity in Europe is treated as one of the more important problems creating divisions that run across out continent (Lister 2007: 114).

The present paper analyses the institutional and cultural reasons for the social marginalization of the Roma people in Poland and also makes references to practice in working with the Roma community in search for effective models and forms of social work in this area. This category of people perfectly fits the sociological concept of the 'alien', since, in Poland, it is the Roma people who have traditionally been one of the most negatively perceived ethnic groups for centuries.

The Roma are the largest ethnic minority in Europe, the number of which is estimated at 10-12 million people (Nowicka 2007: 124). In Poland, according to the data of the Ministry of Interior and Administration, there live about 50 thousand Roma people. There are about 1,000 families of Roma origin living in the Opole Province. Data obtained from centres of social aid indicates that 90% of them are unemployed. Because of that, social assistance has become the basic instrument of attempts to achieve social inclusion of this category of people, and social workers are the professional group who are in the frontline, bearing responsibility for this process.

Institutional barriers to social inclusion of Roma people in Poland
A great number of barriers hamper full participation of Roma people in social life. Social workers, working directly with people experiencing exclusion due to racial, religious, cultural differences, are also required to influence the local policy and role of agencies, but contrary to this mission contribute themselves to these barriers to full social participation.

School
About 70% of the children of Polish Roma people are registered for school attendance. However, in certain communities, the most children do not attend schools. The absence rate among the Roma children is relatively high, since they often leave homes for periods, accompanying their parents in trading activities, or prolong weekends and holidays. The level of education of the majority of Polish Roma people must be rated as very low, illiteracy being a common phenomenon among the older generation. Another cause of the social exclusion of this ethnic group in Poland, connected with how the educational system works, may be seen in the lack of knowledge of the Polish language. Many members of the group do not complete even primary school within the period of compulsory school attendance (Gerlich: 1997). Placing Roma children in special schools, designed for people with intellectual handicap, because of insufficient knowledge of the Polish language is an unacceptable practice. So is that of organising classes exclusively for Roma children as learning in such classes does not levelling up their educational standard and in many cases results in marginalisation of the Roma pupils or even puts them at risk of being discriminated against. Therefore, it seems reasonable to use integrated classes, which offer a chance of levelling up educational handicaps to all pupils who have difficulty in learning. Teaching in such classes creates a suitable atmosphere of cooperation and co-acting. At the same time, schoolchildren must experience the unconditional acceptance of another person, and what respect for others and understanding other people stand for (Weisbrot-Koziarska 2007: 111). Therefore, teaching Roma people at Polish schools requires a

relevant approach within the whole educational system. The above problem affects also other countries of Central and Eastern Europe, stigmatising Roma people with intellectual handicap sometimes for their whole life. In the Czech Republic, 70% and in Slovakia over 50% of children attending special schools are of the Roma origin (Kwadrans 2007: 235).

Roma schoolchildren, according to inquiries which the co-author of this paper carried out in the parents' communities, are a 'laughing stock' at school and are teased by their peers, sometimes including the teachers themselves because of poor school performance. As one of the social workers at the Municipal Family Aid Centre recollects: 'When the social aid centre social worker proposed that the Centre would pay for the children's lunches at the school canteen, he met with instant refusal. Whereas behaviours degrading and discriminating against Roma pupils are impossible during lessons, under the teacher's eye, the canteen is a place where such reactions occur'. Another reason why the Roma people pay so little attention to the education of their children is connected with their customs. For example, getting married exempts them from the duty of learning and marriages of teenagers are a fairly common occurrence among this group. Thus, completing early education at the primary school level is considered to be a success.

Labour market
Statistically, Roma people are most frequently unemployed, registered at the Local Job Office, without the right to receive unemployment benefit, obtaining financial support from the social aid system. Such a situation, obviously, denotes permanent exclusion into the space outside the labour market, since Roma people available for work do not possess any assets to raise their attractiveness in the market, do not hold formal education, knowledge or skills, cannot use the Polish language well enough and are not open to forms of education offered to long-term unemployed people. Nowadays, the most common activity of Roma people available for work is trading. Roma elites mostly invest in fixed assets, such as shops, restaurants, property and filling stations. The occupational situation and social advancement of Roma people are additionally complicated by the fact that their tradition does not permit them to take up employment in a number of trades, for example agriculture, the police forces or the healthcare profession.

Local community
The process of assimilating people from different ethnic origin into a dominant culture operates at two levels: individual and group processes (Mucha 2006: 182). In local communities there is virtually no process of

group exchange between Polish and Roma peoples. Roma people do not play any significant roles in local communities, do not have representation, are not identified as members of the community and have not absorbed local traditions. The Roma community is also marginalized spatially within local communities: in many parts of the region, Roma people reside in particular areas of the town. In Opole, it is worth underlining that the social standing of the area inhabited by the Roma community is regarded as fairly high. This is a result of the flooding which devastated part of the city in 1997, when inhabitants of flooded areas were transferred to other living areas. Roma families living in buildings in poor repair were moved to a housing estate constructed for victims of the flood. That to a large extent improved their living conditions. In other parts of the region, Roma communities remain concentrated in areas of low living standards, with poor infrastructure.

Social aid

The operation of the system of social aid in Poland is regulated by the Social Aid Act of 12th March, 2004. Its aim is prevention of difficult living situations through activities aimed at making individuals and their families independent, as well as working towards their integration with the community. People with Polish citizenship who remain living on the territory of the Republic of Poland have the right to receive benefits from the social aid system. This help is also available to foreigners living there, who hold a permit to settle, rights of residence or asylum granted in the Republic of Poland. The right extends to citizens of the European Union member-states and those of the European Economic Area who are living in on the Republic of Poland and who have obtained a residence permit.

The Act defines the basic situations in which assistance can be granted. They are: poverty, bereavement, homelessness, unemployment, disability, chronic or serious illness, violence in the family, support and protection of mothers and multi-children family, poor child care, poor upbringing and poor household management, especially single-parent families or families with many children, poor adjustment among young people leaving care, difficulty in integrating refugees, difficulties after release from prison, alcohol or drug addiction, accidents or crisis situations, natural disasters. The social aid system does not clearly delineate a role in social integration and re-integration of people marginalized due to their origin, race, or nationality clearly delineated in. Therefore, material aid has become the basic dimension of social intervention with Roma families.

Individuals and families whose incomes are lower than the income threshold are eligible for allowances. Since 1 October, 2006, for single people, the level is fixed at an amount not exceeding PLN 477.00 (about €110), whereas for an individual in a family it is PLN 351.00 (about €85). Exceeding this markedly low income level makes people ineligible for material benefits, and this keeps Roma families stuck in poverty.

Cultural barriers

Roma people are brought up to respect for tradition and customs, to respect older members of the community and high levels of acceptance of decisions taken by elders, even about the most intimate and private matters. This set of principles is *romanipen*, 'the Roma character'. The most important and ultimate reference group is the family, communicating in the Roma language, the family itself consisting of several generations: great-grandparents, grandparents, parents and children. A young Roma man must maintain his family from the age of 15-16 years, while a young housewife must manage household and wifely duties. The sealed nature of this community, reinforced by poor knowledge of the Polish language, poses an effective barrier to a full social integration and participation. It is, at the same time, a dam preventing social workers from intervening. The worker cannot establish even the basic facts about the life of the family, with the exception of those that are essential to granting material benefits. The Roma attach extraordinary significance to cleanliness understood as freedom from defilement. Violation of *romanipen* leads to a person being thought impure. Mutual assistance and integration through work and modesty hold a particular place in this set of principles. Modesty, for a girl or a woman, involves respect towards the body and is such a tightly guarded value that girls bathe dressed in clothes.

Forms of social work as a response to social marginalisation of Roma families – selected examples of practice

A direct reference to social work seeing itself as a profession actively engaged in building democratic societies founded on full participation of all members can be found in the Global Standards of Education for Social Work. In the section establishing the paradigm of the profession, the following values provide the foundations of the teaching programme are of particular importance to education and practice of social work:

- Acknowledgement of the dignity, value and uniqueness of all human beings;
- The terms 'racial' and 'race' are cited inside quotation marks to stress that they are socio-structural and political constructs while biological differences are used by dominant groups with the aim of oppressing, excluding and marginalising minority groups;
- The importance of advocacy and changing the socio-structural, political and economic conditions that marginalise and exclude people;

- Appreciation and respect for difference in terms of 'race', culture, religion, ethnic origin, mother tongue, gender, sexual preferences and differentiated skills (*Globalne standardy...* 2004, 4).

Development of its methods, techniques and methods of practice responds to the professional expectations of social work. Turning to the practice and form of social work in the Roma community, however, there are additional points to make. Social work is identified as a professional activity, at the moment, a highly specialist one. Therefore the currently used forms of social work are developed within social workers' professional activity, located in social agencies. In the Polish reality, such agencies are most frequently connected with the public system of social aid, being part of the system itself or through carrying out tasks required by the system. Nevertheless, the Polish tradition of social work pays a lot of attention to the specific, national and Polish context of social work. In particular, the significant influence of Helena Radlińska, nowadays considered a pioneer of social work in Poland, is important. She did not use this notion and favoured the term 'praca społeczna' ('society's work rather than social work'). This is almost identical with the currently used one ('praca socjalna' – 'social work'), the difference being virtually unrecognizable in many modern languages. Radlińska saw 'society's work' as processing the social environment by means of forces that existed within that environment. The social worker is, according to this concept, a social activist, a leader of a community, a natural leader. This model of social work focuses on stimulating the community so that it could solve its own problems. As Dąbrowska-Jabłońska (2005: 290) writes, stimulating social forces 'can be an engine to activate strengths and values that lie dormant in individuals, groups and agencies in order to make the most of their potential for the fullest possible development of themselves and their surrounding reality". This context of social work is still strongly present in the life of Polish local communities, in social work education and activity on this issue. With this focus, developing social work means developing ways of inspiring, animating and organising communities towards actions for social inclusion of the Roma people, as well as actions aimed at activating their own participation.

The system of social aid
Social assistance from *Miejski Ośrodek Pomocy Rodzinie* (the Municipal Family Aid Centre - MCAF) based in Opole extends over 34 Roma families comprising 88 people. Since September 2007, the co-author of this paper has been responsible for six Roma families consisting of 25 Roma people. The available forms of assistance in social aid agencies can be divided into material and non-material ones. Social aid benefits are financial allowances (fixed allowances, temporary benefits, benefit for special purposes, special

needs allowance, loan for economic independence, aid for foster families, aid for becoming independent in or continuing education, financial allowances for refugees for maintenance and expenses in learning Polish) and non-material ones (social work, vouchers, premiums for health insurance, social security contribution, material aid, including economic self-sufficiency, funeral arrangements, specialist counselling, crisis intervention, providing shelter, meals, necessary clothing, domiciliary nursing and care services, support centres or family-run homes offering assistance, specialist domiciliary care and support centres, supported housing, residence and services at the social aid centre, foster care and residential child care, assistance in securing suitable living conditions, including supported accommodation, assistance in finding employment, aid for settling down – in the material form for self-sufficient people, training, family-oriented counselling and therapy run by adoption agencies).

The Roma people who are beneficiaries of the MCAF in Opole, most often receive financial aid; this kind of assistance is granted to all families who are clients of the Centre. The most frequent forms of the aid include a temporary allowance received for typically between three and six months, together with financial aid to purchase food. Another fairly-frequently provided form of assistance is extra financial help to purchase medicines. Roma seniors obtain aid in the form of fixed allowances, since they have not acquired rights to receive old age pensions during their lives and at present can maintain themselves relying solely on social aid benefits.

In Polish social aid, the Roma people are seen as a group taking advantage of the regulations concerning foster families. Such a family receives allowances of PLN 900 (about €220) for one child under seven, one of the highest social benefits. Using family connections, the Roma entrust their children to their cousins or grandparents, exclusively with the aim of obtaining a material benefit, which improves their standard of living significantly.

The forms of social work within the system of public assistance are poorly developed, the whole intervention being based on a personal contact between the social worker and the Roma family, which aims to obtain the highest possible benefits. The higher the benefit, the better the social worker is in the eyes of the client. The co-author of the paper, working with Roma families has not witnessed a case of such a family becoming financially independent.

Table 8.1 *Practice methods for working with the client or client's family*

Explaining	Mainly focuses on legal and formal questions on benefits received – an area for cooperation;
Self-understanding	Social workers do not undertake this form of intervention due to the fact that they do not feel confident in the inter-cultural space. It is mostly junior workers with limited work experience who are allocated work with Roma families. Typically, such young practitioners have not achieved a stable image of their own personalities yet and do not have rational and stable world-views. In this context, helping others achieve a stable picture of themselves, when they are experiencing an immense cultural divergence, is impossible – lack of cooperation.
Informing	This is one of the key forms of cooperation. A number of pieces of information are prepared and presented in a form comprehensible to clients. Left to themselves with this information, clients would not be able to understand it fully – an area open to cooperation;
Material aid	The basic form of assistance – an area for cooperation;
Rearing-related activities	The social worker becomes an advocate for the Roma family's interests in the education system. This creates an opportunity to influence, to a limited extent, the behaviour of children and also parents' attitudes – an area of cooperation within a restricted scope. On the other hand, this is potentially a significant area to develop the relationship between the social worker and the family.
Counselling	To a limited extent counselling related to health-promoting behaviours, but also possible initial work orientation and help in finding employment; classical family counselling is generally not available – an area of cooperation of a very limited range;
Confrontation	Social workers do not undertake this form of work – no area for cooperation

Persuasion	Social workers do not undertake this form of work – no area for cooperation
Imposing requirements and restrictions	Imposition of restrictions takes place solely in a formal way as it turns out to be an area of potential conflicts. Restrictions are treated as a negative factor, limiting freedom, as too much interference in the functioning of the traditional family and puts the social worker in the position of confrontation; for this reason social workers are afraid of imposing restrictions – no area for cooperation;
Supervision	As with requirements and restrictions: the social worker wanting to end the intervention agrees even to resign from supervising and controlling the client thus taking the opportunity of closing the case – no area for cooperation;
Broadening social contacts	Parents are encouraged to cooperate with the school, to use the health care services, to participate in religious congregations, to be active in the field of art, to pursue education on a higher level for younger people, to integrate with labour market agencies – an area for limited cooperation;
Revealing possibilities	Social workers do not undertake this form of work – no area for cooperation
Forming structures in the environment and making use of them	Social workers do not undertake this form of work – no area for cooperation
Social contract	A contract constitutes the basis of starting an intervention; its essence should be less formal and more a process of negotiating conditions and listing obligations on both sides towards each other; however, in practice, this never develops; thus, a contract has usually become a formal attachment to the documentation and has not become an autonomous aspect of social work practice - no area for cooperation;

Source: Co-author's analysis.

Developing forms of social work with Roma people within projects in local communities in the Opole Region

Public social assistance is relatively slow at reacting towards social changes, working out new forms of social work with difficulty and being an administrative structure granting allowances rather than a creator of effective solutions that achieve practical results. Communities take on such roles themselves in a variety of ways. The rise in the concern about issues about the Roma people is undoubtedly influenced by the fact that, at present, it is possible to apply for grants to develop projects involving this ethnic group using external sources of finance, such as government subsidies or European Social Fund grants. This possibility has motivated local community activity and in a short time has yielded the first effects in the form of new projects in which new approaches towards working with the Roma people are sought.

Roma work to clear debts

The programme was established in Głubczyce, where the Roma community is 167 people, including 92 children and young people below 18 years of age. In recent years a few Roma families have settled in Głubczyce. The starting point of the project was the Roma community relying on the commune's resources had serious difficulty in paying rents. Unemployment in this group reaches almost 70% and therefore using the concept of an earlier programme on working to pay off debts, the project 'Roma work to clear debts' was launched. The programme has been operating since 2005 and has almost become part of the Roma people's life there. Monthly, three to six people, representatives of the indebted families, are employed to do simple maintenance and tidying jobs or working on construction sites. Both men and women can do the jobs. The people agree to transfer 50% of the wages to pay overdue rents. If one of the Roma people, who is a member of the indebted family, cannot come to work, then someone who has already cleared their debt agrees to work instead. This neighbourly exchange within the system of mutual support has been functioning effectively. At the beginning, as the programme was being developed, it was fairly hard to persuade Roma men to take up jobs; they would leave after two or three days. At present such situations never occur and it is clear that the programme has been accepted by the Roma community, and is yielding improving outcomes. Those who clear their debts start feeling like residents with full rights and often demand to be treated respectfully (Protokół 2007: 1-14).

Let us get to know each other better

Since 2004 there has been another project run in Głubczyce, which involves the Roma community, under the name 'Let us get to know each other better'. It was the first project developed in the Opole Region to be approved by the

Ministry of Interior Affairs and Administration in Warsaw. The subsequent developments of the project in later years made it possible to employ Roma assistants at a primary and junior high school, including, among others, one Roma woman, who was one of the few Roma people in the Region to complete higher education. She worked as a teacher at school for two years, being a model for the children. At the moment there are also other Roma assistants working in schools and they provide a useful link between the school and the Roma community. The broadly-conceived educational, social and therapeutic work aims at equity in educational possibilities. Also, it seeks to promote understanding of the Roma tradition and culture in the local community as a vital element of overcoming barriers to tolerance and appreciation of spiritual and material values. The project has brought about positive results: a considerable increase in the attendance rate among the Roma children at school has been observed (in 2007, 93% in contrast with lows of 50% recorded earlier), a decrease in the number of low grades and a drop in lateness for lessons. Also, Roma children successfully completed successive years of primary school, participated in remedial classes, special needs teaching, speech therapy, and corrective gymnastics and took part in computer, mathematics or natural science interest groups. Other positive results include development of sports skills, taking part in sports contests and competitions, reaching top places in football tournaments or athletics events on the commune or county level and setting up Roma dance groups. Moreover, in collaboration with Roma parents and assistants, a census of Roma people has been carried out; similarly, stimulating and integrating surrounding schools and the Roma community through cooperation with the Social-Cultural Society of Głubczyce have been achieved (Protokół 2007: 1-14).

Roma people in the labour market
The programme is addressed to adult Roma people who are long-term unemployed, but want to actively search for work. It is run in Nysa, a city in the southern part of Opole Province. There are 204 people belonging to the Roma community living in the city. 76 people are of working age. The unemployment rate among the Roma community of Nysa was 98%. There are no jobs even for those registered at the Job Centre. The only form of employment available is 'intervention' jobs organised by *Ośrodek Pomocy Społecznej* (Social Aid Centre) for a maximum amount of two hours daily. Trying to increase the opportunities for this group of citizens of finding work, the programme 'The Roma people in the labour market' was launched, part of which was developing, in collaboration with the local authorities, an information guide covering basic procedures used in looking for a job, such as drawing up a cv and preparing for a job interview. An innovative feature of the guide is that is was created in consultation with a representative of the

Roma community and was adjusted to the abilities of likely recipients of it. The information guide was written using a very simple language so Roma people use it effectively.

Courses designed for the Roma community in Nysa are run as another element of the programme. On the average there are 17 people who complete training courses every year. So far, course have been organised in computer literacy, operating cash registers, safety at work, and getting a driving licence. The programme actively involved *Stowarzyszenie Romów* (Association of the Roma people) in Nysa, which has already led to participation in the programme of people from neighbouring counties, especially the county of Prudnik. As a result of the courses three people from that county found employment. At the moment an analysis of demand in the local job market is being carried out. It appears that in the years to come the biggest demand for workers is expected to be in construction industry so further investment is being considered in educating Roma people in relevant trades, which will allow them to find good employment. At the same time, work in the community is being conducted, to encourage the Roma to take jobs in trades in which they have not worked so far (Protokół 2007: 1-14).

Conclusion
Social work in multicultural practice is, due to the fairly uniform nature of Polish society in as its national, religious and racial character, a new and developing area. The activity of many public agencies still favours exclusion of the 'alien' who belongs to a different ethnic group rather than inclusion. In practice with the Roma people, their families and whole communities, social workers have used only basic interventions and a limited catalogue of forms of social work. Being driven by fears, apprehensions for their own safety and stereotypes, they restrict the contacts to the essential minimum and can even avoid carrying out interventions required by the agency procedures, everything to free themselves from the necessity of dealing with Roma people. Such a situation, obviously, calls for searching for models, methods and forms of social work with the Roma community, both in professional practice in social work education.

However, there has been a rise in the social activity of local communities and a series of projects and programmes addressed to the Roma community. Despite the fact that they are mainly stimulated by the inflow of external financial means, they have, in many cases, become an integral part of the life of local communities, bringing about permanent changes in their functioning. The programmes are of great significance also for the following reason: they prepare us materially and professionally for work in the conditions of society which is becoming more and more multi-cultural with each coming generation.

Bibliography

Dąbrowska-Jabłońska, I. (2005) Świetlica środowiskowa jako forma pracy socjalno-wychowawczej Ośrodka Pomocy Społecznej. (The local day-centre as a form of social and child development work of the Social Aid Centre"). In: J. Brągiel and P. Sikora (eds), *Praca socjalna – wielość perspektyw. Rodzina – Multikulturowość – Edukacja* (*A Multiplicity of Perspectives in Social Work – Family work, Multicultural work, Education*), Opole: Wydawnictwo Uniwersytetu Opolskiego: 281-289.

Gerlich, M.G. (1997) *Raport: Romowie o edukacji swoich dzieci (na przykładzie Cyganów Karpackich)* (*A Report: The Roma About Education of Their Children (a case study of the Carpathisn Gypsies)*), Oświęcim.

Globalne standardy edukacji i szkolenia do pracy socjalnej (2004) Trans. By J. Szmagalski. [Original version: *Global Qualifying Standards for Social Work Education and Training*, http://www.iassw-aiets.org/en/About_IASSW/globalstandards.htm_].

Lister, R. (2007) *Bieda* (*Poverty*), Warszawa: SIC!,.

Kwadrans, Ł. (2007) Charakterystyka sytuacji edukacyjnej Romów w Czechach, Polsce i Słowacji. (Characteristics of the educational situation of the Roma people in the Czech Republic, Poland and Slovakia). In: Borek P. (ed), *Romowie w Polsce i Europie. Historia, prawo, kultura* (*The Roma in Poland and in Europe. The History, Law, Culture*), Kraków: Wydawnictwo Naukowe Akademii Pedagogicznej: 233-248.

Merton, R.K. (1982) *Teoria socjologiczna i struktura społeczna* (*Social Theory and Social Structure*), Warszawa: PWN.

Nowicka, E. (2007) Romowie i współczesny świat. (The Roma and the contemporary world). In: Borek P. (ed), *Romowie w Polsce i Europie. Historia, prawo, kultura* (*The Roma in Poland and in Europe. The History, Law, Culture*), Kraków: Wydawnictwo Naukowe Akademii Pedagogicznej: 124-147.

Protokół nr PK/9/07 z posiedzenia Plenarnego Wojewódzkiej Komisji Dialogu Społecznego w Opolu w dniu 23 kwietnia 2007 roku, Opole 2007 (dokument w archiwum Urzędu Wojewódzkiego w Opolu) (Minutes No. PK/9/07 of the plenary session of the Regional Commission for Social Dialogue held in Opole on 23rd April 2007).

Ustawa z dnia 12 marca 2004r o pomocy społecznej (DzU nr 64 poz 153 z późn. zm.) (The Act on social aid of 12 March, 2004. *Journal of Laws* No. 64, entry 153 with subsequent amendments).

Znaniecki, F. (1990) *Współczesne narody* (*Contemporary Nations*). Warszawa: PWN.

Weissbrot-Koziarska, A. (2007) Pomoc koleżeńska dziecku niepełnosprawnemu w klasie integracyjnej. (Friendly help offered to the disabled child in an integration class). In: Sikora P. (ed.) *Wolontariat i samopomoc – podstawowe wymiary solidarności w społeczeństwie ryzyka* (*Voluntary Work and Self-Help – the Basic Dimensions of Solidarity in Society*), Opole: Instytut Nauk Pedagogicznych Uniwersytetu Opolskiego oraz Regionalny Ośrodek Polityki Społecznej: 105-114.

9   Aspects of social work with foster families

Alicja Kurcz
Opole University, Poland

Origins and trends in family-based foster care in Poland

The pioneer of creating foster families in Poland was the Reverend Gabriel Baudouin, who, in 1736, established a hospital for abandoned infants in Warsaw. To reduce the high mortality rate among children, he entrusted the infants to the care of rural women, who, in return for feeding and bringing up the children until they were eight years of age, were given modest payment (Kulpiński 2000: 24-25). The experience of the family-based foster care was not always positive and that there were periods when its development was held back, mainly because of foster parents neglecting and abusing children. However, the approach survived and its breakthrough came in 1925, with the 'experiment' started in Łódź, resolving problems with orphans by placing them in foster families who were not related to them by blood. The success of this social experiment was achieved by careful selection and assessment of both potential foster carers and the children, establishment of detailed regulations and organisation, provision of appropriate support and control of foster family care. Outcomes showed that foster families' care proved, not only cheaper but also, more beneficial in providing care than institutional provision. Thus, in 1938, foster care provided for 10,617 children across the country. During the Second World War, a period of universal threat, the process of establishing foster families was generally spontaneous and available data suggests that there were 74,000 children cared for in foster families at that time (Winogrodzka 2007: 69-71).

In the early years after the War, foster families provided care to over 70 thousand children (68 thousand in 1946, and 73 thousand in 1949), yet because of a policy shift by the then government towards centralization of care services, and a preference for institutional care, there was twenty-year-long setback in developing family-based foster care (Badora 2005: 273). A renewed rise in the number of foster families, which occurred at the beginning of the 1970s, was brought about by a change in the policy favouring family-based foster care (*Monitor Polski 1971*, No. 56, entry 364) and greater financial support to cover the costs of maintaining children in foster families. Subsequent legislation and numerous initiatives increased the number of foster families and children placed in this form of care (in 1995,

46,101 children were brought up in 35,038 foster families, and in 2005, 49,667 children were brought up in 36,510 families).

The year 1999 is regarded as the boundary between 'the old and the new model of foster care' (Karczmarek 2006: 16), since implementing the reform of the child and family care system was delegated to local government, counties (*poviats*) and the Family Aid Centres (*Powiatowe Centra Pomocy Rodzinie)* established within their structures. Another significant moment for the reform was the transfer of the department of child care from the Ministry of Education to Social Policy, which took place in 2000.

Prior to the care system reform, the main focus for meeting children's rights to have proper care where they were at risk because of family problems was 'taking away' children from their parents and placing them into a care institutions. This removed parental responsibility for the child's future, since the child's future upbringing remained the sole focus of the care system, action to maintain children's bonds with parents were neglected and generally the natural family was not helped to regain their ability to care for their children (Brągiel 2004: 12). The main reason for placing children in institutions was the belief that children with severe problems needed help that was available only in appropriate specialist centres that secured comprehensive care. However, studies of consequences of excluding the child from its family setting and deficiencies in the institutional care system identified negative consequences of that approach. These were mainly signs of institutionalisation ('orphan's disease') and difficulties in young adult care-leavers achieving independent functioning. In numerous debates on the future development of the child and family care system, the advantage of family-based forms of foster care over the institutional ones were emphasised, and the need for dynamic development of family-based foster care was increasingly endorsed. Moreover, a more effective action aimed at maintaining the child's bond with its natural parents was stressed, and improved involvement with the child's family and relatives. Changes in foster care have also been influenced by theory focusing on an ecological approach towards the family and parenthood, espousing the view that effective help to children is not possible without taking into account their family relationships and cultural background (Hellinckx, 1999: 122).

Regulation on social and care work with families currently in force in Poland fits with international trends and with the constitutional principle of subsidiarity in providing help, which requires family problem-solving to be carried out as close as possible to the family, at the lowest level of local government, without depriving the parents of responsibility (Andrzejewski 2003: 193-212). The approach of thefamily and child care system, in particular, sought to maintain the family, re-integrate children with it and normalise the child's life situation (Kwak 2006: 35). Re-integration of the family is understood as a planned process of developing liaison between children placed in any form of care and their families through support provided to them and various contacts which confirm children's connections with their families. Following this approach, people providing care in a foster family do not replace parents, but are expected to complement natural parents and to make every effort to keep up and strengthen any bonds that exist, or to rebuild them where they have been broken. Normalisation of the child's life situation is defined as creating conditions for children similar to those in which most of their peers live, and establishing a network of interpersonal relations similar to those possessed by the majority of children of the same age (Colton 2000: 173; Kwak 2006: 37).

The foster family as an area of social work practice
According to Social Aid Act of 12th March 2004 (*Journal of Laws* No. 64, entry 593 as amended), local authority tasks in securing care and upbringing for children who are partly or completely deprived of their parents' care, include: organising and running specialist counselling for both natural and foster families, offering family therapy, running a crisis intervention centre, organising foster care, granting financial assistance to cover part of the living costs of children placed in foster families, and assisting care leavers from any care setting to integrate with their community (including granting material aid to become self-reliant and continue with education).

Including in the social assistance system responsibilities for managing institutions providing good standards of care for orphans, care and support to families in achieving successful care and upbringing of their children is a significant broadening of the social work role. It has been accepted that social workers are to have responsibilities in each part of the child and family care system, ranging from preventive work, running family-based care to working in specialist institutions designed for children with special needs. Managing personnel to cover such broad areas, with only very broadly defined responsibilities, has led County and District Family Aid Centres (*Miejskie Ośrodki Pomocy Rodzinie*) to develop a variety of service strategies, assigning social workers a range of responsibilities within fostering practice, from tasks focusing only on inquiries into the background of potential foster families to those where a social worker becomes a coordinator or an active participant in working out an individual plan for the young person. These might include education, becoming self-reliant (see Chapter 10) and planning work with the foster and natural families aimed at re-integrating the biological family. Working on such issues often requires cooperation with other professionals such as psychologists, educators, lawyers, guardians, medical doctors, or representatives of non-governmental organisations and the police.

Informed by a comparative review analysing international trends in foster care and the practical experience of many countries in the search for optimal provision of care to orphans and a reliable definition of foster families (Colton and Williams 1999: 230) an appropriate definition relevant to Poland is: 'A foster family is a permanent or temporary form of complex care for children deprived of the possibility of care by its natural family, achieved in the setting of another family related or not related by blood with the child, formally established to complement or replace the biological parents' care until the obstacles that make it impossible for them to provide care to the child themselves are removed" (Brągiel, Kurcz 2007: 78).

Children's caring needs and the organisational systems for foster family care in Poland, have led to the evolution of different models of foster families. One distinction is between families related or unrelated by blood to the child. Professional foster families are a distinct category with several sub-types: families for large numbers of children, families for children with special needs and foster families providing care in emergencies. Professional foster carers are a comparatively new form of provision in the Polish system, and they differ from the more commonplace related or unrelated foster families in that the foster carers enter into a civil legal agreement to offer foster care to a child or children, for which they receive a salary. Professional foster families for multiple children host not fewer than three and not more than six children, unless the number of the siblings is higher, in which case a principle of not separating siblings holds. 'Specialist' families provide care to not more than three children with special needs for care and upbringing, such as where there are developmental disabilities, health problems, indications of disturbed socialisation or emotional and behavioural disorders. Emergency professional foster carers accept not more than three children at a time for a temporary stay, until their life situation stabilises, for not longer than twelve months, which in exceptional circumstances may be extended by a further three months. Such families are prepared to accept children at risk, for example where they have been abandoned or ill-treated. Emergency foster carers cannot refuse to accept a child of under ten years where the child has been taken into police care without the consent of the child's guardians. In practice emergency foster families may perform treatment interventions but mainly provide care in early childhood.

Foster carers in foster families of each type are required to meet successfully formal qualification criteria and to possess an appropriate personal psychological temperament and physical capacity. For professional foster parents, the criteria include completing training courses that offer an extended programme of preparation for managing and resolving problems of care and upbringing, depending on the type of professional foster care they will be involved with. This includes skills of working with other adult participants in the care process, for example, building appropriate relationships with social workers or participating in support groups that facilitate foster families and natural parents who want to regain their children.

All foster families of whatever type constitute a unique family structure (Kwak 1994: 91); they are 'an open system' allowing 'sometimes intensive' contacts with people from outside the family, for example, the involvement of biological parents, natural siblings, relatives, or representatives of public services. The most important function of foster families is undertaking, together with natural parents, co-responsibility for the children's future. Consequently, the number of children returning to their natural families is regarded as a measure of effectiveness of the 'institution' of the foster family, or the foster care system as a whole. This also represents the effectiveness of assistance in the biological family's regaining its fundamental functions (Legat 2004: 14). Being in a foster family is one of the most difficult services in social assistance and is a specialist service, with a goal of re-integrating children with their natural families through maintaining bonds, or, if the child's return to the natural family is not possible, successfully leading the child towards becoming self-reliant (Legat 2004: 13).

Accomplishing these outcomes of foster families forms a vital criterion in evaluation of effectiveness of this form of care provision. However, the main task of foster families is their current care role with children, who have mostly been affected by consequences of problems within their natural families and have experienced trauma related to this. As a result, they run the risk of developing emotional disturbances, and having difficulty in establishing relationships with their peers and adults, learning at school and absorbing and respecting norms and values. Very often, before children were removed from the setting of their biological families, they experienced violence, neglect, serious illnesses or demoralising influences. Among the children put into foster families there are also those who have already changed their carers several times, temporarily been in care in various institutions providing complex care incorporating intervention and attempts at socialisation, such as emergency care centres, children's /homes, family group homes and family-based emergency care. Alternatively, they may have experienced a failed foster family placement. |Therefore, foster families

86

will be living with children who have directly experienced the effects of multiple rejection and real social bereavement (Kurcz 2006: 732-737).

Therefore, the most important role for social workers working directly with foster families is to normalise children's situations. This involves acting to protect children, to eliminate the risk of their being left in a setting that is unfavourable for their future development and to prevent circumstances arising where the child's needs might be marginalised, experiencing the stigma of a life situation leading to their experiencing all the negative effects of bereavement. In most regions, social workers have been involved in work with the foster family during its acceptance. They collaborate directly with adoption-care centres, which run courses and workshops to prepare adoptive parents and foster parents for their new social roles. Among more practical tasks in foster care practice are placing children into foster family care and helping the family gain financial benefits, material support, and maintaining up-to-date documentation about the child's situation and work with the family, including the questionnaire about the child's environment required by the Minister of Labour and Social Policy. They are must also assist care leavers from foster care (see Chapter 10). Social workers also participate with educators, psychologists and foster carers in deciding on the child's care needs, identifying real and potential threats to development, and also in supporting foster parents in overcoming difficulties of adaptation, learning, upbringing, health, emotions, or moving acting successful preparation for leaving care.

A qualitatively new task for children's social services results from the newly-accepted model of care provision in which the objective is reintegration with the biological family. This involves assessing difficulties in the biological families of children in family-based foster care, and deciding on the likelihood of re-integration and the scope of contacts with the foster family.

Barriers and requirements in foster family social work practice
Achieving the tasks arising from the organisational and legal structures and policy goals behind social work with foster families connects with the need to overcome many obstacles. A report of *Instytut Spraw Publicznych* (Institute of Public Matters) (Kaczmarek 2004: 3-13) and empirical research (Giermanowska and Racław–Markowska 2004: 103-108) show that the difficulties appear as early as at the first stage of formation of a foster family and manifest themselves with barriers in the process of recruiting applicants for unrelated families and in managing professional foster families. As a result, there are problems in securing care for children already needing to be placed in unrelated and professional foster families. This, in turn, means the

use of temporary solutions or placing it in a care home, an outcome that is not always favourable for the child. The shortage of candidates for unrelated foster care also leads to the process of professionalization of care services, which was taken for granted in the reform of the system, and has therefore slowed the process of gradual closure of children's homes.

Too many children are placed in foster families related by blood with the child, despite reservations about the quality of care and upbringing that will be provided. The research to date conducted by Kolankiewicz (1997), Kawula (1998), Jamrożek, (2005), Brągiel and Kurcz (2007), and Holewińska-Łapińska (2008) has shown that in Poland foster families related to the child by blood are in the majority (nearly 85%). They are mostly families of medium or low educational status, unstable employment, and lower levels of wealth and health, in many cases they are incomplete families. The role of the foster carers most frequently taken by people over 55 years (mainly the child's grandparents). The significance, needs and the scope of social work within such foster families are of unusual nature, concerned not only with the child's care and emotional development, but also with work with the foster parents themselves. This consists of concurrently monitoring how they function in the roles of parents, supporting and shaping their coping skills with care and upbringing, material and personal problems.

Foster families in Poland bring up children whose natural parents are alive, yet upon decisions of courts, the parents are deprived of parental rights (40%) or have limited rights (30%). Such a situation influences, to a considerable extent, the new areas of activity for social workers, for instance carrying out tasks in reintegrating children into biological families and overcoming difficulties that occur on the road. The studies show that over half the foster carers (53%) are convinced that contacts between the child and its biological parents should be restricted, another 66% express equally strong worries about the child's future on return to the natural parents. Such attitudes result from a number of factors: their altruistic motivation to take on the role of foster carer, their attachment to the child and the child's acceptance of them as sole carers. Also relevant is information on continuing difficulties in the child's home situation, and a passive attitude, on the part of the natural parents, towards creating conditions which would enable them to regain their child (Brągiel and Kurcz 2007: 84-86). This aspect of practice with foster parents evokes the greatest controversy among social workers, being an ethical dilemma.

Another barrier that makes it difficult to delineate the scope of tasks in social work with foster families are fixed patterns in which their needs are perceived. According to social workers, not all foster families that receive formal supervision expect them to organise systematic, intensive assistance or social support, although such expectations are very high. Inquiries with social workers confirm the results of a study conducted a few years ago (Kurcz 2005: 407-413), which show that almost half the families seek assistance regularly and one in four family sporadically. Additional financial allowances are the dominant form of help requested mainly because of specific health and education needs of the children, as well as material aid in the form of medicaments, clothes, toys, books, sports equipment, or funds to organise summer and winter leisure activities. In addition to material aid, foster carers expect social workers to support them in resolving upbringing and education problems, mainly finding help to overcome learning difficulties and in referral to agencies able to offer, for example, psychological and teaching assistance. Foster parents often turn to social workers for help in sorting out official matters and problems connected with the child's legal situation of, the foster family and the biological one. An important reason for foster parents expecting assistance from social workers is an activity with the aim of involving the latter in regulating the manner in which contacts between the child and its biological parents are arranged, as well as in helping to protect the child from possible demoralising influences. Another area of expected assistance that a few social workers draw attention to is the need to offer emotional support to foster carers and to raise their level of self-worth in taking on the difficult role of a foster parent they have to play, particularly they are elderly person or isolated. The increased scope of the help that foster parents expected and obtained causes them to be perceived by social workers as clients and not partners on providing care. Assuming such attitudes leads to a lack of cooperation, builds communication barriers and on occasions leads social workers to assess families' self-sufficiency. In some cases open conflicts or too much focus on helping activities limits families' self-reliance.

Some social workers consider that the extended responsibilities of social work with foster families reaches beyond current expectations of social workers, current realities and their competence. Nearly 40% of respondents evaluated their theoretical and practice preparation in supporting the care, upbringing and compensatory responsibilities of foster families as insufficient, 30% as sufficient and only 6% felt that they had a very good preparation to carry out social work with foster families (Kurcz 2995: 410). According to social workers, raising the quality of social work in this field will not be possible until increased financial resources are provided for this work, the number of the personnel employed in social service agencies increases, specialisation develops in particular aspects of the work and systematic professional development is available. These developments are needed so that social work intervention may be strongest during the period of establishing the foster family, in cases where it is necessary to issue an opinion justifying the child's stay in the foster family and when the care leaver's plan for self-reliance is being prepared (see Chapter 10). Social worker respondents confirmed that after the process of forming the foster family has taken place, it is too often left 'to itself'. This happens despite their awareness that without systematic support through counselling, strengthening and raising the level of self-esteem, without providing legal and material aid, assistance from voluntary workers, or forming support groups, an accumulation of difficult situations, mistakes in upbringing, which burdens children and parents excessively. Sometimes a failure results in dissolving the foster family and transferring the children to another less beneficial form of institutional care.

Conclusion
In summary, the current stage of implementing reforms of the child and family care system, and social policy is not so much a completed, standardised area of social aid as one that is being formed and is rather at the planning stage. This is because at the currently available level of financing, with the current state of employment and professional competence of social workers, social work with foster families is still to develop fully. Among fundamental conclusions from various analyses of the present situation is that a higher standard of social work with foster families can only be achieved with a professionalization of its adult participants, advancing professional specialisation, for example by developing a family pedagogue, and promoting interdisciplinary teams to coordinate work from different service providers of educational, social and criminal justice agencies. A change in the perception of foster parents is required to treat them not as clients of the social aid system, but as partners in working towards a better care system.

High hopes for favourable changes in family aid system are tied to the proposals for a foster care act, which has already been submitted in the Polish Parliament/ This seeks to pick up trends in European care services and successful experience in the field, as well as the principles that lie behind social work with foster families.

Bibliography

Andrzejewski, M. (2003) *Ochrona praw dziecka w rodzinie dysfunkcjonalnej. Dziecko-Rodzina-Państwo* (*Protection of Children's Rights in a Dysfunctional Family. Child-Family-State*) Kraków: Zakamycze Publishing House.

Badora, S. (2005) Rodzina zastępcza. (The foster family). In: J. Brągiel and S. Badora (eds) *Formy opieki, wychowania i wsparcia w zreformowanym systemie pomocy społecznej* (*Forms of Care, Rearing and Support in the Reformed System of Social Aid*), Opole: University of Opole Publishing House: 272-287.

Brągiel, J. (2004) Rodzina obszarem pracy socjalnej. (The family as an area of social work). In: J. Brągiel and P. Sikora (eds), *Praca socjalna – wielość perspektyw. Rodzina-Multikuturowość-Edukacja* (*Social Work – Multiplicity of Perspectives. Family-Multiculture-Education*), Opole: University of Opole Publishing House: 25-36.

Brągiel, J. and Kurcz, A. (2002) *Pracownik socjalny: Wybrane problemy zawodu w okresie transformacji społecznej* (*The Social Worker: Some Problems of the Profession in the Period of Social Transformation*) Opole: University of Opole Publishing House.

Brągiel, J. and Kurcz A. (2007) Oblicza rodzin zastępczych na Opolszczyźnie. (The faces of foster families in Opole Region). In: W. Jacher and A. Klasik, (eds), *Zmieniające się oblicza regionu górnośląskiego* (*The Changing Faces of the Region of Upper Silesia*), Katowice: 'Gnome' Publishing House, Polish Academy of Sciences:: 78-89.

Brągiel, J. and Kurcz, A. (2008) Rodzina zastępcza a sytuacja szkolna dziecka. (The foster family and the school situation of the child). In: A.W. Janke (ed.), *Wychowanie rodzinne w teorii i praktyce. Rozwój pedagogicznej orientacji familiologicznej* (*Family-based Upbringing in Theory and Practice. Development of the Pedagogical Famiologic Orientation*), ToruńL 'Akapit' Educational Publishing House: 131-144.

Colton, M. and Williams, M.,(1999) Światowe kierunki w opiece zastępczej (International trends in the foster care system). In: Z. W. Stelmaszuk (ed.) *Współczesne kierunki w opiece nad dzieckiem* (*Contemporary Trends in Child Care*), Warszawa: 'Żak' Publishing House: 217-132.

Colton, M. (2000) Tendencje w opiece zastępczej. (Trends in the foster care system). In: Z. W. Stelmaszuk (ed.), *Zmiany w systemie opieki nad dziećmi i młodzieżą. Perspektywa europejska* (*The Changes in the Care System for*

Children and Yound People. The European Perspective), Social Worker Library, Katowice: 'Śląsk' Publishing House: 170-183.

Giermanowska, E. and Racław–Markowska, M. (2004) Instytucjonalne i rodzinne formy opieki zastępczej nad dziećmi i młodzieżą – raport z badań. (Institutional and family-based forms of foster care for children and young people). In: M. Racław–Markowska and S. Legat (eds) *Opieka zastępcza nad dzieckiem i młodzieżą – od form instytucjonalnych do rodzinnych* (*Foster Care for Children and Young People – from Institutional to Family-Based Forms*), Warszawa: Institute of Public Affairs: 95-136.

Hellinckx W., (1999). Opieka instytucjonalna i jej alternatywy w krajach unii Europejskiej. (Institutional care and its alternatives in the countries of the EU"). In: Z. W. Stelmaszuk (ed.) *Współczesne kierunki w opiece nad dzieckiem* (*Contemporary Trends in Child Care*), Warszawa: 'Żak' Academic Publishing House: 115-143.

Holewińska-Łapińskiej, E. (2008). Orzekanie o umieszczeniu dziecka w rodzinie zastępczej. (Rulings in placing the child into a foster family) *Problemy Opiekuńczo-Wychowawcze* (*Care and Upbrining Issues*) Vol. 9: 3-10.

Jamrożek, M. (2005). *Rodzina zastępcza jako środowisko wychowawcze* (*The Foster Family as a Rearing Environment*), Kielce: Świętokrzyska Academy.

Kaczmarek, M. (2006). Reforma systemu opieki zastępczej (The reform of the foster care system). In: A. Kwak (ed.), *Z opieki zastępczej w dorosłe życie. Założenia a rzeczywistość* (*From the Foster Care Into the Adult Life. Assumptions and the Reality*), Warszawa: Institute of Public Affairs: 15-32.

Kawula, S. (1998). *Studia z Pedagogiki Społecznej* (*Studies in Social Pedagogy*), Olsztyn: The Higher School of Pedagogy Publishing House.

Kolankiewicz, M. (1998) Rodziny zastępcze (Foster families). In: M. Kolankiewicz (ed.) *Zagrożone dzieciństwo. Rodzinne i instytucjonalne formy opieki* (*An Endangered Childhood. Family-Based and Institutional Forms of Care*), Warszawa: School and Pedagogical Publishing House SA: 259-291.

Kulpiński , F. (2000) Początki opieki w Polsce (The beginnings of care provision in Poland). In: Z. Dąbrowski and F. Kulpiński (eds), *Pedagogika opiekuńcza: historia, teoria, terminologia* (*Pedagogy of Care: the History, Theory and Terminology*), Olsztyn: University of Warmia and Mazury Publishing House: 17-97.

Kurcz, A. (2004) Przygotowanie pracowników socjalnych do udzielania wsparcia społecznego rodzinom zastępczym (Preparation of social workers to offer social support to foster families). In: J. Brągiel and P. Sikora (eds) *Praca socjalna – wielość perspektyw. Rodzina– Multikulturowość–Edukacja* (*Social Work – Multiplicity of Perspectives. Family-Multiculture-Education*), Opole: University of Opole Publishing House: 25-36.

Kurcz, A. (2005) Rodziny zastępcze jako obszar działania pracowników socjalnych (Foster families as an area of social workers' activity). In: K. Marzec-Holka (ed.), *Marginalizacja w problematyce pedagogiki społecznej i praktyce pracy socjalnej* (*Marginalisation in the Problem Area of Social Pedagogy and Practice of Social Work*), Bydgoszcz: Academy of Bydgoszcz Publishing House: 402-414.

Kurcz, A. (2001) Kompetencje pracowników socjalnych do wypełniania zadań 'systemu pomocy dziecku i rodzinie' (Competences of social workers to fulfil tasks of 'child and family care system'). In: A. Olubiński (ed.) *Tożsamość oraz dylematy pedagogiki opiekuńczej* (*The Identity and Dilemmas of Pedagogy of Care*), Toruń: 'Akapit' Publishing House: 141-149.

Kurcz A., (2006). Sieroctwo rodzinne (Family bereavementIn: T. Pilch (ed.), *Encyklopedia Pedagogiczna XXI w.* (*The Pedagogical Encyclopedia of the 21st Century*), Volume V. Warszawa: 'Żak Publishing House: 732-737.

Kwak, A. (1994) *Rodzina i jej przemiany* (*The Family and Its Transformations*), Warszawa: University of Warsaw Publishing House:.

Kwak, A. (2006) Zmiany założeń opieki zastępczej – zwrot w kierunku rodziny (Changes in the assumptions of foster care – a turn towards the family). In: A. Kwak (ed.) *Z opieki zastępczej w dorosłe życie. Założenia a rzeczywistość* (*From the Foster Care Into the Adult Life. Assumptions and the Reality*), Warszawa: Institute of Public Affairs: 33-49.

Legat, S. (2004) Rodziny zastępcze a wybrane aspekty polityki społecznej państwa (Foster families and selected aspects of social policy of the state). In: M. Racław-Markowska and S. Legat (eds) *Opieka zastępcza nad dzieckiem i młodzieżą – od form instytucjonalnych do rodzinnych* (*The Foster Care Over the Child and Youth – from the Institutional to Family-Based Forms*) Warszawa: Institute of Public Affairs: 9-26.

Winogrodzka, L. (2007) *Rodziny zastępcze i ich rodziny* (*Foster Families and Their Families*) Lublin: The Maria Curie-Skłodowska University of Lublin Publishing House.

10   Social work with people brought up in foster care becoming self-reliant

Józefa Brągiel and Małgorzata Kozak
Opole University

1   The main assumptions behind the reform of the care system in Poland

Studies carried out by many pedagogues and psychologists have clearly shown that living in a family setting, cared for by biological parents, offers children the best developmental environment. Despite this and the fact that it has been widely publicised in the media, each year a large number of children, cannot be brought up in their natural families and must be looked after within the child care system, since remaining at their family homes is harmful to them for many reasons. Until 1990, securing foster care for a child had been displaced because most care was provided in institutions. Chapter 9 gives a fuller account of the foster care system, but in summary, children whose parents were declared unable to secure appropriate care, for whatever reasons, were separated from their natural background and put in institutions specialising in providing care for children. The basic form of care for neglected, abandoned or orphaned children until 1990, had almost exclusively been in children's houses financed by the state. In those institutions, care work concentrated on the child's development. There was almost no work with the family. For decades, the child had been seen as 'saved' from the family and the limiting environment, and the parents had been 'relieved' of the responsibility for the fate of their child.

The main change leading to the development of foster care for the child is connected with the transformation in the socioeconomic system that took place in Poland in 1989. This resulted in the introduction of several significant reforms. The most important for the care system was the boundary-reform of administrative areas in 1990. This introduced a new devolved government structure: the county (*poviat*). *Powiatowe Centra Pomocy Rodzinie* (County Family Aid Centres) were established in counties and entrusted with the task of organising foster care for orphaned and neglected children in ordinary families. At the same time, legislation charged local government with responsibility for developing family-based forms of foster care and transforming large care institutions (children's homes) into small centres with specialised functions. In 2000, foster-care agencies were transferred from the Ministry of Education to the Ministry of Social Policy.

Implementing foster-care-related activities was based on *Ustawa o pomocy społecznej* (Social Assistance Act) which was reformed in 2000 and to which the new section *Opieka nad rodziną i dzieckiem* (Care for the family and the child) was added. The Act established a preference for a new approach to child care provision, which may be described as follows: the family as a whole is the focus of assistance, and it needs to be supported in fulfilling its functions. Separating children from their families and placing them in foster care is the last resort and ought to be temporary. Social workers should undertake work with the family to remove any difficulties and reintegrate the child with the biological family. Reintegration should be a goal of the intervention whenever children are placed in care outside their natural home (Stelmaszuk 1998: 108). Thus, intervention for the benefit of the child ought to focus on the whole family. The child is inside the family, and resources should be sought within its closest relationships, that might be activated to avoid the need to take children permanently away from their home. If, however, this proves unavoidable, then foster care ought to be of short duration, since reintegration of the child with its natural family should be incorporated into the aims of the intervention whenever children are received into care outside their homes (Stelmaszuk 1998: 108). Implementing reintegration starts from the process of rebuilding bonds within the family where, due to a crisis, they have been broken or strained. At the next stage, the work consists of maintaining contacts between the child and the family they can be rejoined.

Despite all these honourable assumptions, it has turned out, in practice, that the period of the socioeconomic transformation proved an extremely difficult one for many families. Often, parents have not been able to cope with the challenges of the new reality: they have lost jobs, fallen into poverty and been unable to take care of their own children. As a result, the number of children received into care has grown considerably. Decisions of family courts have led to such children being received into the care of foster families, children's homes or family-based children's homes, or being sent to stay in children's villages. The scale of the phenomenon can be illustrated with the following data: in 1990, there were 31,881 children who were taken into these forms of care. In 1997, the number rose to 37,341, and in 2006, it amounted to as many as 49,667. Looking at particular forms of care, in 1990, there were 16,279 children in children's homes, in 1997, 16,719, with the number dropping to 11,772 in 2005. Family-based children's homes and children's villages accommodated 1,161 children in 1990, 1,155 in 1997, while in 2005, 1,859 were accommodated in this way. These statistical data not only show the rise in the number of children included in the care system, but also point to the growing number of children in foster families. Family-based foster care has been acknowledged to be the closest in character to that of the natural family and has become the intervention of choice in our country. Stelmaszuk, in her research (1989: 123), sought to answer the question whether the children concerned were given a real chance of rapid reintegration with their biological families, following the assumptions of the reform. It turned out, however, that, to the extent that relevant educators and tutors were able to assess it, this was viable in only 22% of those staying in children's homes and 17% of those foster families. In the case of the others, foster care must be extended over the rest of the period until they come of age. Obviously, foster care is where they prepare themselves to live their adult independent lives; the group of children entering the latter stage is considerable, and, as Kolankiewicz states (2005: 40), every fourth person leaving foster care is of adult age. As Kwak observes (2006: 68), leaving the foster care system and attaining the status of an adult person, with relevant rights and duties, as well as starting out in ordinary life in society without 'the protective umbrella' can be as hard as entering the foster care system itself.

2 General principles behind the process of building self-reliance in foster care

The reform of the care system of 1990 has altered the approach towards the process of building self-reliance among people in foster care. 'Instead of becoming self-reliant being understood as a one-off activity of paying out a benefit due and granting what might be termed an "outfit" to the person leaving the agency's responsibility, an attempt was made to understand the process of building self-reliance as achievement – together with the individual concerned – of a learning plan' (Andrzejewski 2001: 25). People in foster care must be active and conscious participants in the process of building their own self-reliance, that is to be subjects who are able to construct, on their own or together with tutors, an individual plan for becoming self-reliant.

The person who has achieved self-reliance, that is, who has come of age in a foster family or in residential care is entitled to receive various forms of support and assistance in the process. They are as follows:

- financial assistance to become self-reliant;
- financial assistance to continue education;
- help to find suitable housing;
- help in obtaining employment;
- material aid to furnish the home.

To be eligible for these forms of support, various requirements have to be met. First, the County Family Aid Centre must receive relevant information from the head of the residential care home or from foster parents not later than three months before the individual leaving the place that provides care. The relevant County Centre then has to be notified and sent documents relating to the individual achieving self-reliance not later than one month prior to the leaving.

In turn, the person starting out on the process of becoming self-reliant needs to choose a tutor. This needs to be someone who engages in the process through offering advice and support, yet who does not do things instead of the young person concerned. They should have good relations with the young person and share a sense of responsibility for them. The chosen 'building self-reliance' tutor must agree in writing to perform this role. The tasks of such a counsellor include the following:

- becoming familiar with the documentation and the 'life-line' of the young person concerned;
- elaborating, together with the person moving towards self-reliance, a programme for this process;
- evaluating the implementation of this programme and introducing modifications as required;
- assessing applications for financial assistance to facilitate self-reliance and for continuing in education;

People building self-reliance ought, on their own or with help from their tutor, to work out an individual programme which should include a concise plan of actions to be undertaken and time schedule for their achievement. This individual programme, signed by the individual concerned and the tutor, should be approved by the manager of the relevant County Centre. In this way, people achieving self-reliance take it upon themselves to reach the goals included in the individual programme a month prior to coming of age. The programme contains items relevant to material and non-material issues and forms of support like the following:

- cooperation in contacts with the family;
- gaining education suitable for the abilities and aspirations of the person achieving self-reliance;
- gaining professional qualifications;
- assistance in establishing entitlement to health insurance;
- settling of the individual in a different county from that where they lived before coming into foster care;
- assistance in achieving reasonable standards of housing;
- taking up employment;

- assistance in obtaining benefits the individual is eligible for (Orders of the Minister of Social Policy of 23 December, 2004).

In the course of carrying out the process of achieving self-reliance, some changes can be made to the approved programme (provided there are sensible reasons for this), but such changes must be agreed by the manager of the County Family Aid Centre. When the individual self-reliance programme comes to an end, the individuals, their tutors and the manager of the County Centre, assess its outcomes.

3   The process of achieving self-reliance: views of people involved

We have only had a relatively short period of experience of enabling people in foster care to achieve self-reliance, achieved according to the new principles of the reformed care system. What is happening has been of interest to people who are responsible in practice for achieving it rather than to researchers (Rostocka 2002). Thus, there has been not much research conducted that attempts to investigate this issue and what is available focuses mainly on formal indexes of effectiveness in helping people become self-reliant. The results of the study which we would like to present, have been based on evaluation of the self-reliance process provided by the participants in the process themselves, that is, former beneficiaries of care. They aim at answering the following questions:

- How do people in care evaluate their preparation for living a self-reliant life and the development of the process itself?
- Are the opinions on the course of the self-reliance process and preparation for self-reliance differentiated by the form of care provided?

The research was carried out in 2008 and covered 45 people in care who became self-reliant (fifteen in children's homes and thirty in foster families). All of them had been in foster care for at least two years. The research was a study of a series of individual cases.

It is important to remember that rendering persons self-reliant is the final phase of the foster care system. People over 19 years of age are legally adults and are granted full citizen's rights. The regulations require people of this age to leave the children's centre or foster family where they have stayed until then. Only people continuing education have the right to stay on until graduating from the school attended before coming of age.

The real beginning of the self-reliance process begins with the moment of admission of the child to foster care, because preparation of children to live a self-reliant life is the target goal. Therefore, we asked the respondents if they felt prepared by their care unit to live such a life. The decisive majority (93.4%) claimed that care had prepared them well to be independent in life. Only 6.6% were not convinced they had this capacity, mainly those from children's homes. However, a more detailed analysis of the preparation to function in a self-reliant way in specific walks of life did not confirm the optimism (Table 1).

Table 10.1 *The sense of competence to function in a self-reliant way (percent distribution)*

Area of functioning	Capacity to:	People from children's homes	People from foster families	Total
		Sense of being well prepared	Sense of being well prepared	
Performing family-related roles	Play husband's/wife's role	20.8	100.0	73.3
	Play father's/mother's role	20.0	86.6	64.4
	Take care of children	20.0	86.6	64.4
Managing money	Spend money	80.0	93.3	88.8
	Save money	40.0	93.3	68.8
	Pay bills	20.0	93.3	68.8
	Plan shopping	60.0	93.3	82.2
	Do shopping	80.0	93.3	88.8
	Open a bank account	40.0	80.6	71.1
	Open a savings account	20.0	73.3	55.5
Practical arrangements	Apply for a flat	60.0	73.3	68.8
	Sort out matters at offices	40.0	93.3	75.5
	Apply for work	80.0	86.6	84.4
	Self-reliant use of health care services	80.0	93.3	88.8

	Furnish the flat	60.0	93.3	82.2
Self-care	Do washing	60.0	93.3	82.2
	Do ironing	60.0	93.3	82.2
	Do tidying	80.0	93.3	88.8
	Prepare meals	100.0	93.3	95.5
Preparation to live with others	Maintain contacts with peers	100.0	93.3	95.5
	Express own needs	100.0	93.3	95.5
	Express feelings	100.0	93.3	95.5
	Solve conflicts	100.0	93.3	95.5
	Take on responsibility for own actions	80.0	93.3	95.5

It follows from the study that the sense of competence of living a self-reliant life is the lowest in the area of 'fulfilling family roles': 64.4% of the subjects felt well-prepared to perform the parental roles and to take care of their children, whereas 73.3% were positive about their ability to perform the roles of spouses. To a degree, this is understandable, since the subjects had had no opportunity to test their skills in this sphere of life before. Still, there is a striking difference between the sense of competence in playing parental roles in persons cared for in children's homes (merely 20% of them claimed they felt well-prepared in this aspect of life) and those from foster families, 86.6% of the studied cases in this category. The difference can be explained by the lack of opportunity to observe adults performing these roles in children's homes. Competence in the other areas: managing money, self-care and coping with various practical needs in ordinary living, appeared slightly higher than those related to the parental roles. Again, the people from foster families showed a stronger sense of being properly prepared. For example, 40% of the respondents from children's homes expressed a sense of being well-prepared in the sphere of saving money, whereas 93.3% of those from foster families felt this; the skill of paying bills was familiar to 20% of those from children's homes, while 93.3% of the people from foster care were able to do so. In almost all the aspects of preparation for adult life explored, people in foster families scored much higher on the sense of self-reliance. It is only in the sphere of living with people, such as skills in maintaining personal contacts with peers and solving conflict situations that people from children's homes displayed a stronger sense of competence than those from foster families (see Table 1).

That the feeling of being well-prepared for living independent lives was less strong among people from children's homes confirms the fairly widespread opinion that institutional forms of care create fewer natural situations of life, which prepare young people to carry out tasks in their independent lives than foster families. The quality of outcomes that can be achieved by a children's centre in helping people to become self-reliant is limited.

When the completion of the formal requirements of the self-reliance process was checked, it was found that the requirements laid down in individual plans were satisfied, since the plans had been completed within the set time. Most often tutors in charge of the process in foster families were foster parents (63.3%), and those at children's homes were social workers (80%). The respondents always spoke favourably of them, as the following responses illustrate:

My tutor is a social worker who helps me sort out formal issues connected with getting a place to live and support to continue my education. He advises me effectively and I can confide in him.

My cooperation with the tutor is developing smoothly. It is necessary, because this is often the closest person you can talk to.

I think that the self-reliance tutor is necessary, because I can count on his assistance.

Nevertheless, people in foster care asked what the individual self-reliance plan was, did not know what it meant. Some saw it as a programme of continuing education or for gaining qualifications, which indicates that the element of self-reliance was missing while working out such plans, or that tutors had completed the plans for the young people in their charge. It was thus quite a frequent occurrence that respondents said something like the following:

I am signing the programme. I think it is necessary. I am doing this so that I can receive financial support and to acquire a trade.

To all the respondents, the most important goal in their individual self-reliance plans was gaining education related to their potential and, consequently, gaining professional qualifications. This is a vital aim for a person's independent functioning in the future, but also for the very process of becoming self-reliant as it is a prerequisite to receiving financial support.

The self-reliance programme is connected with graduating from school and finding employment. The programme is important because it is tied to gaining professional qualifications. It helps plan education.

Analysing measurable benefits of the self-reliance process, showed that the respondents had been able to implement the basic aims contained in the plan of support, the biggest accomplishment being achieving successive stages of education, finishing school or pursuing education at a higher level. Also, finding an interesting job and obtaining a flat were treated as the most significant accomplishments, which can be illustrated as follows:

Achieving the programme consists in my attending school and doing my best there.

Thanks to the programme I am staying in a protected flat. I am glad of it as the programme allows me also to finish my school.

To complete my school and start an independent life are my paramount goals.

The biggest success of mine in implementing the programme has been passing my [school leaving examinations].

The most important thing was that I was able to get money which enabled me to pursue further education.

The biggest help is the financial support and the County Family Aid Centre helped me a lot with that. Basically, it was only the financial support. I would be happy to stay in my centre. I'm afraid of having to be self-reliant.

These comments from people brought up in care who were helped towards self-reliance confirm the fact that the process meets the formal requirements. The people concerned are most frequently passive participants in creating the individual self-reliance plans, the results of which can, primarily, be boiled down to being granted financial aid that enables them to exist and continue education. They do not perceive the process as giving them opportunities to gain self-reliance in other spheres of life.

Conclusion
These differences disclosed in the extent of preparation for independent life between young people brought up at children's homes and in foster families confirm the appropriately popularised need for developing family-based

forms of foster care. Apart from that, analyses of the implementation of the self-reliance process suggest the necessity of advancing more effective work with young people so that they could be involved in a more conscious way in the self-reliance process. It should not be limited merely to the financial sphere and obtaining a trade.

Bibliography

Andrzejewski, M. (2001) Prawne aspekty reformy opieki nad rodziną i dzieckiem (The legal aspects of the reform of care of the family and the child). In: Stelmaszuk, Z. W. (ed.) *Zmiany w systemie opieki nad dziećmi i młodzieżą: Perspektywa europejska (Changes in the Care System for Children and Youth: European Perspectives)*, Katowice: Wydawnictwo Naukowe Śląsk: 16-21.

Bieńko A. (2006) Proces usamodzielnienia wychowanków domów dziecka (The self-reliance process for people in children's homes). *Problemy Opiekuńczo-Wychowawcze (Care and Development Issues)* 4:15-22.

Bieńko A. (2006) Proces usamodzielnienia wychowanków domów dziecka. Część druga, The self-reliance process for people in children's homes: Part two). *Problemy Opiekuńczo-Wychowawcze (Care and Development Issues)* 5: 21-30.

Gwizdek B. (2003) Przygotowanie do usamodzielnienia (Preparation for self-reliance). *Problemy Opiekuńczo-Wychowawcze. (Care and Development Issues)* 4:. 35-38.

Hryniewicz J. (2006) *Odrzuceni. Analiza procesu umieszczania dzieci w placówkach opieki (The Rejected: An Analysis of the Process of Placing Children in Care Centres)*. Warszawa: Instytut Spraw Publicznych.

Kolankiewicz, M. (2005) Szanse i zagrożenia instytucjonalnej opieki nad dzieckiem (Opportunities and threats to the institutional care of the child). In: Racław-Markowska, M. (ed.) *Pomoc dzieciom i rodzinie w środowisku lokalnym (Aid to Children and the Family in the Local Environment)*, Warszawa: Instytut Spraw Publicznych: 12-17.

Kwak A. (2006) Kreatorzy procesu usamodzielnienia (Creators of the self-reliance process). In: Kwak A. (ed.), *Z opieki zastępczej w dorosłe życie: Założenia a rzeczywistość (From the Foster Care into the Adult Life: Assumptions and Reality)*, Warszawa: Fundacja Instytutu Spraw Publicznych: 67-115.

Lewandowska M. (2004) Czy placówka opiekuńczo-wychowawcza może przygotowywać swoich wychowanków do samodzielności? (Can a care institution prepare its residents to be self-reliant?). *Wychowanie na Co Dzień (Everyday Child Development)* 6: 25-26.

Stelmaszuk, Z. W. (1998) Szanse reintegracji rodziny w systemie opieki nad dzieckiem (Opportunities for re-integration of the family in the children's care system). In: Kolankiewicz, M. (ed.) *Zagrożone dzieciństwo: Rodzinne i instytucjonalne formy opieki* (*The Threatened Childhood: Family-Based and Institutional Forms of Care*), Warszawa: Wydawnictwa Szkolne i Pedagogiczne: 108-136.

Stelmaszuk, Z. W. (1999) Nowe spojrzenie na rodzinę (A new look at the family). In Stelmaszuk, Z. W. (ed.) *Współczesne kierunki w opiece nad dzieckiem* (*Contemporary Directions in Care of the Child*), Warszawa: Wydawnictwo Akademickie 'Żak': 172-173.

Rostocka B. (2002) Usamodzielnianie wychowanków (Making people in foster care self-reliant). *Problemy Opiekuńczo-Wychowawcze* (*Care and Development Issues*) 9: 38-40.

Wachowicz J. (2003) 'Pomoc usamodzielnianym wychowankom (Help for looked-after children achieving self-reliance). *Problemy Opiekuńczo-Wychowawcze* (*Care and Development Issues*) 6: 20-24.

Świtka M. (2003) 'Rodziny zastępcze i ich wychowankowie kontynuujący naukę u progu trzeciego tysiąclecia (Foster families and their looked-after children continuing education on the threshold of the third millennium"). *Nauczyciel i Szkoła* (*The Teacher and the School*) 3/4: 149-158.

Ustawa o pomocy społecznej z dnia 12 marca 2004 r. (Social Aid Act, 12 March, 2004).

Rozporządzenia Ministra Pracy i Polityki Społecznej z 2004, z 2003, z 2005 (Ordinances of the Minister of Labour and Social Policy 2004, 2003, 2005).

11   Homelessness and employment

Ole Meldgaard
Kofoed's School, Denmark

Introduction: homeless people as an excluded group
Homelessness is an extreme situation of exclusion. It means that the whole life of a person is destabilised. In general, the term homelessness goes beyond not having a home or rough sleeping in the streets. It is often used as an umbrella term to define people facing multiple disadvantages.

This extreme situation consists of different areas and inter-related factors. Homelessness and unemployment, for instance, are closely interlinked. Loss of a home affects negatively the ability of a person to keep a job or gain a job. Many homeless people are long term unemployed. Unemployment is one of the main trigger factors that can lead to homelessness. The frustration of being unemployed can contribute to the disempowerment of a person and negatively affect the individual's physical and mental health, that also are main factors in homelessness. It is a fact that many homeless people have difficulties in actively seeking work, in writing applications or in registering with the employment office.

Homeless people often face more than one problem; they face multiple barriers in society. The accumulation of problems is often the key issue. Society is not particularly good at solving accumulated problems. That is why homeless people often start to develop their own strategies to survive outside mainstream society. They start to beg in the streets or they sell street papers, they start to live on garbage or collect bottles and other kinds of rubbish, they start to steal, to burgle, to sell drugs, and women prostitute themselves. Very few homeless people live on earned income from the ordinary labour market. If they are not entitled to social security benefits, they start to work in a kind of alternative market. This way, the cliché arises of homeless people as tramps, who do not want to work or who do illegal work.

Some of the barriers to society could be termed personal barriers. Many personal barriers are linked to the direct experiences of homelessness, such as physical appearance and hygiene. It is difficult for homeless people to keep their clothes clean and ensure sufficient personal hygiene. A chaotic lifestyle is another barrier affecting, for instance, the ability to respect the specific time schedules of working hours. Their organisation of life and time structure is simply not in line with mainstream society. Often they live in social isolation with no supporting social network. They lack the skills to function in society, for instance communication skills, the ability to deal with conflicts and the respect of certain behaviour rules in society. They often suffer from addiction and mental problems that are not taken care of because they are outside of the treatment system. They have debt and they have poor budgeting skills. Their family relations and network might have broken up. A kind of loneliness and feeling of powerlessness might contribute to their further disintegration in society. In short, people experiencing homelessness often lack core life skills that enable a person to function in society.

However, such personal barriers are closely linked to general social structures that reinforce exclusion. A homeless person needs a stable place to live. Housing is an important structural factor for all people, also for homeless people, but because of homelessness and lifestyle, homeless people are not welcomed in the normal housing system. And without a decent place to live it is difficult to convince an employer that a person is able to sustain employment. Without an address it is complicated to write applications for a job and open a bank account; these things are necessary for taking up a job. Also it is almost impossible to engage in education. Living rough or in overcrowded shelters is in itself a barrier to integration often leading to stigmatisation and discrimination against the homeless.

Homelessness often leads to health problems which affect opportunities to engage in employment, training or education. Once people are in a situation of homelessness, a variety of health problems may result, such as exposure to infectious illness, development of mental health problems or aggravation of substance-abuse and addiction, or health problems resulting from an unsanitary or overcrowded environment. Homelessness often implies a greater risk of bad nutrition and poor diet leading to poor physical health. Another barrier to integration is dental problems.

There is also a link between homelessness and education. The majority of homeless people has a significantly poorer education than the general population and homeless people are over-represented among people with poor literacy skills.

There are also barriers related to the services society provides – or doesn't provide. Access to public services may be particularly difficult for homeless people. Only a few homeless people are registered with the employment office because they have very limited access to internet or a telephone. The same applies other kind of services. The services offered are mainly emergency service with the risk of 'shelterisation' of homeless people in institutions for homeless people, in psychiatric hospitals or in prisons.

The result of homelessness is poverty and exclusion. The process of becoming homeless is often described as a spiral or as a chain of events. There is a very complex interplay between causes and consequences of multiple and interrelated factors often set off by some form of crisis or breakdown in personal and family relationships followed by negative consequences, for instance alcohol or drug misuse, depression, loss of confidence and motivation, loss of housing or social network.

However, one of the main barriers to integration is lack of government attention to homeless people's issues and needs. Lack of specific integration strategies and welfare provision is a significant problem that leads to perpetuating the state of homelessness so that rehabilitation into mainstream society becomes a more difficult and long term challenge.

A holistic approach to the needs of homeless people
To break the chain of events and the spiral of homelessness it is necessary to use a holistic and tailored approach addressing all the problems or issues faced by the homeless person, including housing, employment and health, also mental health and treatment for addiction. Most people who are homeless require support in more than one area, and support has to be linked and co-ordinated. It also means that public agencies and NGOs must co-ordinate their efforts and work in partnership linking the different areas of provision. Specialist services are important in terms of support in crisis situations but important as well is the possibility for entry into mainstream services because this helps inclusion and integration into the service of the wider society.

What does a sustainable model look like, that provides a route for homeless people to move from homelessness to integration and employability? Such a model must allow for variation according to individual needs, type of support and the length of time. The model must also allow for two linked outcomes: access to education and the labour market, and personal development; This emphasis on personal development and entry to mainstream services is a crucial aspect other provision for many exclude groups discussed in this book, for example unemployed people in Chapter 7, Roma people in Chapter 8; young people leaving care in Chapter 10; and drug addicts in Chapter 12.

The entry into mainstream services must be given a direction. In all European countries, greater independence of homeless people, empowerment, employability and finally employment are seen as the main routes out of homelessness, poverty and social exclusion. Education and employment play a crucial role for social inclusion as well as personal fulfilment of an individual – and employment also contributes to the economy and social cohesion of society as a whole.

However, it is important to understand that inclusion into employment must go beyond the mainstream labour market. For most homeless people the immediate solution will not be to find a full-time job in the mainstream labour market. Inclusion into employment aims to improve the overall situation of an individual by improving the employability of the person.

The multiple obstacles to mainstream society and employment require multiple solutions to make homeless people integrated and employable. One of the main components is education. Homeless people must gain skills, competencies and motivation. The focus must be on improving the employability of homeless people to connect with the labour market and favour their social inclusion through an approach that is adapted to their individual needs. This approach must include the engagement of a person in all kinds of occupational activities that help the person to connect with working life and the labour market in general. Policies are ineffective if they are not tailored to the multiple needs of the homeless.

A European model of employment services for homeless people
One of the key findings in a recent European research on homelessness, employment and learning was the importance of a combined holistic and tailored approach that is adapted to the individual needs of the homeless (OSW, 2007). This means addressing all the problems or issues faced by the individual, doing this as an individual process for each individual homeless person. A highly personalised approach is most effective in producing long-term results. Homeless people should not be treated as a homogenous category. The important element of a holistic approach is integration and partnership between specialists and general providers. Secondly, there should be linkages between areas of provision, primarily education, employment, housing, health and psychological support. The potential benefits of the tailored approach are sustainable outcomes and effectiveness in tackling chronic homelessness and multiple needs. A tailored approach that addresses individual needs is a potentially effective way to tackle chronic homelessness and to prevent people from becoming institutionalised, which is the pitfall of more traditional, general provision.

The research on homelessness, employment and learning was carried out in nine European countries and the report recommended a stage strategy from homelessness to sustainable employment, a kind of a journey from homelessness towards greater independence, empowerment and employability.

The first stage is to meet homeless people and engage with them. This meeting can take place as outreach in the street or in drop-in centres or in institutions for homeless people. Engaging involves listening to the personal issues of the homeless person and gaining his or her trust in the helper and the organisation; as Sikorski suggests in Chapter 13, these interpersonal skills are crucial in social work. This first meeting is basically about making the homeless believe they can change, to recreate the self-confidence and self-esteem to develop a basis for a longer-term programme. A general finding of the research was that confidence, self-belief and motivation are crucial to achieving a change.

The second stage is an assessment of the needs of the homeless person, using the assessment as a platform for the development of the next stages and tailoring the support to the individual according to an individual action plan. This includes an initial as well as an ongoing assessment of the needs and aspiration of the person. Many homeless people may require extra time and support before being able to or ready to take up a job.

The third stage is setting up an individual action plan to meet the individual's needs. This action plan must involve the homeless person in setting the overall goal and finding ways to reach this and interim goals. It must be the homeless person's own action plan, but it must also be an action plan that connects with the mainstream services of society.

The fourth stage is the main stage of holistic, joined-up delivery of support by different agencies, support to housing, to education, financial support, health support and emotional support encouraging people to move forward. But it is also the stage of life-skills building, re-socialisation, training and job search support to make the homeless employable, for instance CV-writing, it-training, personal support or more specialised vocational training. Also basic skills in literacy and numeracy are important. Of course this fourth stage can be organised in different ways, but the setting should be of such a kind that it can generate a feeling of participation and belonging and a joined-up delivery of services. This points to a kind of community setting, a centre or an institution with broad competencies and provisions and dynamism with a sufficient level of financial and human resources, a variety of programmes and a strong communication and partnership with specialist providers and mainstream agencies.

The fifth stage is a preparation for the labour market through work placement or supported employment schemes. Here it is important that the homeless person is supported by a mentor in the workplace or other setting to establish social contacts in the workplace.

The sixth stage is in-work support, supported employment, in-work financial advice etc. before the seventh stage of employment.

Here is must be stressed that there should be incentives for employers to target the most vulnerable groups and to promote the transition into the labour market for whose who are ready to do so.

How should these holistic efforts for homeless people be organised? The best way is through casework. It means each individual homeless has his/her own case worker. The case worker is the one who gathers all the information on the steps to be taken; it is the case worker the client can turn to with any type of problems. The case worker is the one who takes the person through the process of change. This is a base on which holistic social support may be organised. This, of course, does not mean the case worker takes over responsibility from the homeless person. An important element of casework is to empower homeless people to act themselves to respond to their problems.

Another important element in the organisation is the agency for homeless people. As part of the service and caring job, agencies for homeless people should also be educational institutions to include socially excluded groups into the general trends within education and learning and in doing so improve the social prospects for excluded groups. The conclusion is that it is no longer just a matter of service but of acquiring new skills and competencies. Personal development programmes, training programmes, education and activation are all important elements in the work among homeless people.

Conclusion
I would like to finish with a quotation from the Polish brother Albert, who in 1892 said: 'There is a confirmed requirement, especially in the big cities, to have shelters open for every poor person. A human being who for some reason has to live without a jacket, a roof over his head, without even a piece of bread, who is reduced to stealing to stay alive, will be unable to find work or even simply to work. But this same person would, if he is has been guided

in the right direction by a helping hand, be in a much better position to make progress. A person already retrieved from poverty must be educated to a level where he can find hope in his independent ability to work, his honesty, and his diligence. These three elements can become a motor for his progress. Without his further education, the initial effort to take him from the streets was futile'. (Source unknown).

Acknowledgement
The article draws on the findings and results of an analysis carried out by the Employment Group of Feantsa of which the writer of this article was an active member.

Bibliography

FEANTSA (2007) *Multiple Barriers, Multiple Solutions: Inclusion into and through Employment for People who are Homeless*. Brussels: European Federation of National Organisations working with the Homeless.

Notes
On www.feantsa.org see national reports on Employment and Homelessness 2007 from Austria, Belgium, Czech Republic, Denmark, Estonia, Finland, France, Hungary, Italy, Ireland, Luxembourg, Netherlands, Poland, Portugal, Spain, United Kingdom

Ole Meldgaard is the author of "Kofoed's School: The History 1928 – 2005". Copenhagen 2005; "Activation: Kofoed's School's Basic Methods". Copenhagen 2003.

About Kofoed's School, see: www.kofoedsskole.dk

12 Approaches to therapeutic work with chronic drug addicts in Blue Cross centres in Wuppertal

Stefan Ligus
Blue Cross in Wuppertal, Germany

Introduction

Blue Cross is an organisation which has been active in Europe and all over the world for 130 years. Centres of the organisation operate on each continent and the location of the headquarters of the International Blue Cross is in Bern, Switzerland. It comprises member organisations from 54 countries. The Blue Cross is a Christian organisation with roots stemming from the Evangelical Church. Nowadays, it functions as a Christian organisation which is supra-denominational, and which specialises in rendering adaptable assistance to people addicted to alcohol, medication and other drugs. We also deal with addictions that are not only connected with ingested substances, such as addiction to gambling, the Internet, or uncontrolled eating. We offer help not only to the addicted themselves, but to members of their families as well. We run extensive programmes with the aim of explaining and preventing addiction in schools, companies, denominational communities and other environments.

In Germany, the network of centres belonging to our organisation is extensive and covers all the *lander* (the regions of the Republic). The basic form of the work relies on self-help groups: over 1,100 groups of this type comprise about 25,000 addicts and members of their families, who come to meetings every week. We run a number of specialist counselling centres, a detoxification clinic, adaptation centres, socio-therapeutic centres for chronically addicted people, protected flats, cultural centres for young people, a publishing house and a bookshop.

In the present paper, I focus on the activity of the Blue Cross Centre based in Wuppertal, which is designed for people chronically addicted to alcohol and drugs. Wuppertal is a city with 370,000 inhabitants, situated in Northern Rheinland-Westfallen (Rhineland-Westphalia). Until 1968, alcoholism had not been regarded as an illness; it was not until the German Federal Social Court acknowledged alcoholism to be an illness that clinics and outpatient departments treating people addicted to alcohol started to be established and developed quickly. In the new institutions providing treatment to the group in question, alcohol addicts at a chronic and severe phase of the illness were neglected. They were called people depraved psychically and physically, irrevocably disturbed, incapable of going successfully through any form of therapy (Heide 1994: 11). People with the illness whose development was advanced to that extent were placed exclusively in psychiatric clinics and nursing institutions. They could also be found in shelters for homeless people, on the street or in prison, where they were serving terms for minor offences. Today some continue to be treated in psychiatric wards or remain in prison; however, many take advantage of the assistance provided by centres specialising in this kind of social therapy. The number of people suffering from chronic addiction in Germany is estimated at 400,000.

The first attempts at providing professional help to alcoholics at the severe stage of the illness were made at the end of the 1970s. Blue Cross is among the pioneers in this sphere of activity, with its centres established in Hagen and Wuppertal.

The main assumptions behind the work with chronically addicted alcoholics accepted by the Blue Cross in Wuppertal
The Blue Cross Centre in Wuppertal includes the following units:

- The municipal circle of the Blue Cross comprising about 120 members of the organisation; there are 20 self-help groups for people addicted to alcohol, medication and other drugs that run their activity under its auspices; family members of addicted people take active part in the work of the groups; there are also specialist groups for women, for children and one for young people;
- The outpatient clinic that deals with treatment, counselling and prevention of addictions;
- Two residential socio-therapeutic centres designed for people chronically addicted to alcohol or other drugs;
- External groups for people who leave our residential centres but are not able to live with full self-dependence;
- A set of supported flats for people whose physical and psychological health and social competence permit to move them into a self-contained flat, but who need professional support in solving life problems in the period of adapting to their new surroundings.

Blue Cross, and our Centre in particular, has a great deal of experience of working with people who are chronically addicted: the first institution which was established more than 35 years ago was a centre with places for 12 women; today we have 80 residential places for women and men at our disposal.

Work with chronically addicted people requires practitioners to hold suitable professional qualifications and having special personalities. Therefore, in our centres, there are interdisciplinary teams that work with the patients, the core of the team recruiting from social pedagogues and social workers. Depending on the size of the institution, there are between two and five specialists from these disciplines employed in it. Some, in addition to their academic education, have a specialist training in working with addicted people, that is a specialist certificate in treating addictions. The second group of specialists in the team are occupational therapists who are responsible for running therapies through work and creative therapy. The centres employ between one and three occupational therapists. The other members of the team are teachers of sports and rehabilitation, nurses, dieticians, employees responsible for supplies, accountants and workers on night duty.

The majority of people admitted to the centre are sent to specialist clinics for addicted people where clinic doctors decide that a four-month treatment will not be sufficient for the patient to undertake to live without alcohol. The costs of stay at the centre are the responsibility of the national office of social affairs. The resources allotted to patients are time-limited, but where there is a lack of visible progress, they are allotted to specific people for longer periods of time. Our statistical data show that the average patient's stay at the centre lasts two years. In individual cases, the period extends to more than 10 years (Blaues Kreuz 2007).

The overwhelming majority of people staying at the centre do not only suffer from a type of addiction. Almost all of them develop different kinds of disturbance or psychological problems such as schizophrenia, hallucination, depression or dementia. Most have serious chronic organic illnesses, among others, different types of jaundice, diabetes, cirrhosis of liver, AIDS, etc. Despite the intensive medical and psychotherapeutic efforts, frequently the patient's health condition cannot be improved. In such cases, our activities are limited to stabilising the status quo and to slowing the process of deterioration of health. Nevertheless, each year we deal with premature deaths of our patients due to abuse of alcohol or drugs over many years. In many cases, too, we are forced to put our patients in nursing homes when they are not able to participate in a therapeutic programme.

Improvement of the health condition is often preceded with a number of relapses into drinking alcohol. In quite a few cases the improvement is minimal and it is only sporadically possible to accomplish full recovery and

116

return to full social integration. Most of our patients, on leaving the centre, require further social support for many years, resulting from the fact that their brains or other parts of the nervous system, or organs (liver, heart, pancreas, alimentary canal) have been damaged irreversibly.

Due to heavy psychological burden connected with the character of the work at the Centre and the very slow process of patients' recovery, employees are required to have special personality traits. Thus, it is necessary for the management of the Centre to, among others, possess the skill of selecting appropriate team members: competent professionals with suitable qualifications and appropriate personality. The management are also expected constantly to care for staff and create good psychologically healthy work conditions.

To achieve this, we pursue the following principles:

- Regular supervision (generally every two months) of each team of employees;
- Planned, regular individual talks to the employees;
- Sending the employees to participate in seminars developing their professional skills and personalities;
- Organising excursions and other cultural events for the employees.

The main task and goal of our work is to enable the patient, through psychotherapy, occupational therapy, medical help and social activities, to reach their maximum social integration (re-integration) and to take over responsibility for their own lives with the support of supportive services.

Therapeutic processes
Reaching the basic goal of work with the patient requires going together with them through a series of essential stages, achieving minor aims on the way. The most important of those are described below:

Raising awareness about the illness
A considerable proportion of patients finding their way to our centres are not aware of how advanced their illness is. Very often they do not realise the course, significance and effects of the addiction; they do not know what addiction is, although they have been 'developing' the illness for many years. Beginning with the assumption that the patient cannot cope with something they do not know, we bring the problem closer to them through, initially, theoretical description of its course and all other related aspects of the addiction-based illness. At the next phase of the process of work this is

carried forward through confronting the patient with their own state of health. We undertake this task in two forms: individual talks and group therapy. The individualised part of this process secures the protection of privacy that makes it possible to develop trust in the therapist, as well as working through topics that could not be dealt with (yet) in a group of patients. Group work, on the other hand, makes it possible to use experience of other patients, especially those who have stayed in the Centre for a longer time.

Acceptance of oneself in the present situation

Our patients avoid conscious confrontation with the situation in which they find themselves – they do not want to accept themselves as they are. Their image of themselves is one of what they would like to be, but not what they really are like. The patients aim, generally, at transforming their lives, a proof of which is their presence in our Centre. They want to somehow leap over one stage of life, that is without recognising and accepting themselves in the present reality, they wish to find themselves, healthy, in the future. A well-known American psychiatrist and therapist, Gestalt, wrote: 'A change will follow when someone is who they are, and not when they try to be someone they are not' (quoted in Beisser 1997: 144). Acceptance of oneself, despite the illness, the ability to say, with confidence: 'I am a seriously sick alcoholic who must give up many aims and dreams' is not easy. Yet, reaching this acceptance is absolutely necessary for further therapy to be successful.

Inducing motivation – exercising perception – finding the sense of life

The most effective method of motivating patients to work on themselves is facilitating them to enjoy new experiences in situations that are forgotten or unknown and also teaching them self-awareness, to recognise their feelings and their reactions to theory surroundings. In addicted people these abilities are always disturbed and require a series of therapeutic actions in order to stimulate or reactivate them (de Rock 1995: 25).

Medical treatment

As patients arrive at the Centre, it is necessary, at the outset, to begin treatment of the illnesses which they have. Due to extreme neglect they often suffer from various physical illnesses. An experienced nurse is employed at the Centre, who coordinates the treatment of patients. The Centre cooperates with a number of trusted physicians, specialists in the areas of particular importance to addicted people. We have also signed an agreement on collaboration with specialist clinics (hospitals running detoxification treatment, psychiatric and neurological clinics, wards for diabetes, diseases of liver and similar conditions).

Therapeutic working through the past

Achieving this step consists of 'working through' the past from the early childhood up to the current stage. This serves the purpose of getting to know the sources of the addiction, learning about the development of the individual's phases of becoming addicted, as well as about the replacement function which the addiction has performed in the life of the patient so far. Where the patient has a damaged central nervous system, we do not work on their past, but, with the help of relevant methods within the scope of behavioural and cognitive therapy, we aim to obtain desired changes in their behaviour.

Structuring behaviours – the rhythm of the day and the week – hygiene

The alcohol addict does not live a systematic life, mostly because of frequent states of intoxication; they act on the principle of chance. For example, they consume a meal when they are relatively sober, not when the time is right to do so, they get up not in the morning, but when they want to satisfy some necessity like buying alcohol. Somebody finding themselves at a severe phase of addiction ceases to differentiate between a working day and a holiday, between day and night. They neglect hygiene of both their body and soul, they do not take care of the places in which they live. They neglect and lose contact with their family and circle of friends, their lives concentrating solely on alcohol. Admission to a centre breaks up this evil pattern of life and our aim is to begin a process of slow return to natural, healthy structures and rhythm in the patient's life by applying relevant therapeutic and pedagogical strategies (Blaues Kreuz 1998). Patients being admitted to the Centre are requested to sign a few documents, which an a formal basis, impose on them the necessity of abiding by the life rhythm established at the institution. The documents include, among others, the following:

- Operational procedures of the institution;
- Therapy programme;
- Timetables of activities during the day and in the week.

To get better acquainted with the rhythm, at the first stage of their stay at the Centre, patients are given support from the staff responsible for individual departments of the institution, for example, while getting accustomed to activities connected with bodily hygiene, the patients are assisted by nurses, while tidying their rooms daily they are helped by staff members responsible for maintenance of the Centre or young men doing their substitute military service, or while preparing meals, the patients are supported by a dietician. Certain support tasks for new patients are taken over by selected patients who have stayed at the Centre for a longer time, the very activity itself serving the purpose of developing the skill of structuring the day in new patients and developing social competence in those who have reached a higher degree of integration at the Centre and are able to help newly-admitted residents.

External contacts

Social contacts of people who are chronically addicted are usually limited to a circle of people who drink alcohol with them. Therefore, after reaching the state of integration inside the Centre, we help our patients restore contacts, for instance with their family, and make new contacts, especially with members of a self-help group. Such a group is an indispensible factor that supports persons who leave centres. For this reason, making and strengthening this contact at the stage of the patient's stay at the therapeutic centre is vital. Where individuals were connected with a church, we consider, together with them, the sense and possibilities of renewing this connection. The aim of the action is creation, together with the patient and already during their stay at the institution, a network of social contacts which will enable them to maintain abstinence from alcohol upon leaving (Blaues Kreuz 1998).

Strategies of self-dependent existence

Many of those staying at the socio-therapeutic institutions designed for chronically addicted people have never lived fully self-dependent lives, have never taken full responsibility for their existence. Serious disturbance to developmental processes led to very early addiction and lives on the so-called social margin. We run activities of a socialising nature for this group of patients to make up for the neglect of education during their childhood and youth. Another group of our patients consists of people who had gone through a relatively full cycle of socialising, yet despite this in their adult lives got addicted to alcohol or drugs because of various crises. At this stage of therapy, both groups work out strategies for living their lives after leaving the institution. About 40% of the patients leaving the Centre, before entering the next stage of their fully-independent lives, remain in an external group for a few months or make use of support within the system of protected flats. Those who, after their leaving the institution, develop the addiction again have the opportunity to return to the Centre.

Methods and techniques of work

Work with people chronically addicted to alcohol requires application of various methods and techniques. Below there are discussed those which are the most frequently used in our Centre.

Group therapy

This yields the possibility of learning appropriate behaviour in making contacts and communicating with other people. Ways of relating to other people used before admission to the centre are slowly becoming regarded as inadequate and are being replaced with new ones. Patients learn through experience and through observation of both principles of solidarity-oriented behaviour towards others and skills of criticising, discussing, refusing and attempting to have their needs satisfied. In the group, patients' positive and negative behaviours are discussed. The participants learn to plan their actions and to assess what has been achieved between the meetings (Heide 1994: 14). By getting to know the course of life and development of the illness in other patients, the group helps its members to comprehend themselves, their own illnesses and ways out of them. To a number of patients who had never lived in a healthy family the group provides the possibility of partial compensation for this loss and experiencing a sense of safety, warmth and belonging.

Individual talks

These are conducted on a regular basis once a week with each patient. During the first period of stay at the Centre or in a crisis situation, the patient can be offered an additional session to have an extra talk with the therapist. All the personal problems, both those of the past and the ones relating to the present which the patient cannot or does not want to talk about within the group, are worked through in an individual talk. Open discussion of difficult, painful or shameful matters requires creating a special atmosphere of trust and support. For this reason each patient has one therapist assigned to them, with whom they work during the whole stay at the institution.

Occupational therapy

This serves the purpose of reactivating neglected or forgotten skills, as well as developing interest in work and creativity. Under the guidance of an occupational therapist, patients keep the Centre tidy, carry out renovation work, work in the garden and in the kitchen. The acquired skills of, for example, wallpapering, room-painting, cooking meals, baking cakes, prove very useful to them after leaving the institution. The Centre has workshops and rooms where the patients acquire skills in various forms of creativity: drawing, painting, sculpting, working with wood. They create, among other things, Christmas stables, breeding houses for birds, garden furnishing and pieces of furniture. By accomplishing a task or an idea, by successful reaching a goal, patients' sense of self-worth and motivation to work on themselves rise considerably.

Memory training

This form of therapeutic work is particularly important at centres for chronically addicted people. Nearly all of our patients develop problems with effective memory functioning and logical thinking. Memory training is run on the basis of modern scientific methods and the therapists are trained to perform this task in special seminars.

Sports-movement classes

These are carried out in connection with the forms of therapy described above, which brings unexpectedly good results, including improvement in physical and psychic health. The classes are run by sports teachers experienced in physical rehabilitation. The activities are adjusted to the needs, interests and capabilities of the patient, as each of them has an individual sports programme worked out; a specialist doctor acts as consultant to the programme. The range of sports activities used is relatively broad and includes jogging, working out at the gym, rehabilitation gymnastics, swimming, table tennis and bicycle riding.

Free time

If leisure time is not planned, it offers a strong temptation to return to drinking alcohol. Therefore, we pay a lot of attention to this item, working on a change of old habits and development of new ways of spending spare time. The Centre has at its disposal a café that is run by the patients. In the afternoon and in the evening it is also accessible to people from outside the Centre, which helps in making contacts with local residents. Cooperation with Christian communes, allows our patients take part in activities organised by different interest circles and in services. Every year we make it possible for our patients to participate in courses in preparation for obtaining fishing licences. Apart from this, together with our patients, we organise visits to the cinema, museums, concert halls, bicycle rides, cruises on ships, etc. The main aim of these activities is accustoming patients to an interesting and relaxing manner of spending their free time, one that is, crucially, different from that they were used to in the time of abusing alcohol or drugs.

Conclusion

Achieving positive effects that favour regaining health and social integration of the patients chronically dependent on alcohol is possible not only thanks to an excellently equipped institution, but primarily thanks to a good atmosphere and full acceptance on the part of patients striving against their illnesses and imperfections.

Bibliography

Beisser, A. (1997) *Wozu braucht man Fuegel*. Wuppertal: Peter Hammer Verlag.

Blaues Kreuz (1998) *Koncepcja pracy Ośrodka BK Wuppertal-Beyenburg (Blue Cross*. Concept of the work of the BK Wuppertal-Beyenburg Centre), Wuppertal: Blaues Kreuz.

Blaues Kreuz (2007) *Sprawozdanie z działalności Ośrodka BK Wuppertal-Beyenburg* (Blue Cross. Report on the activity of the BK Wuppertal-Beyenburg Centre), Wuppertal: Blaues Kreuz.

De Rock, B-P. (1995) Gras *unter meinen Fuessen*, Reinbek: Rowohlt.

Heide, M. (1994) Nichts geht mehr!?, in: Fachausschuss Soziotherapie des Wissenschaftsrats der AHG (Hrsg.), *'Nichts geht mehr!? - Aspekte der Soziotherapie Alkoholabhängiger*, Hilden: Verhaltensmedizin-Heut: Bd. 3: 10-22.

13 The therapeutic skills of a social worker

Wiesław Sikorski[6]
Opole University, Poland

Introduction

In practising their profession, social workers should contribute to achieving a number of specific goals related to social work. Rybczyńska and Olszak-Krzyżanowski (1999: 32) distinguish six goals of this type:

- Securing basic living conditions for those who are deprived of them – life-saving aim.
- Satisfying needs that cannot be achieved by people themselves within the framework of other agencies– compensatory aim.
- Minimizing the negative influence of factors that cannot be diminished or removed – protective aim.
- Reaching a more satisfying level and quality of living through offering support in solving problems, overcoming difficulties – empowerment aim.
- Strengthening the ability of groups and local communities to develop and solve their own problems in a self-reliant way.
- Effective organisation of various forms of assistance and their management.

Wódz (1998: 24) suggests that the above-mentioned goals are achieved in the everyday professional activity of social workers, manifesting itself in their undertaking such tasks as:

- Analysing and evaluating phenomena that give rise to the need for social benefits;
- Providing information, offering advice and aid in resolving life problems to individuals or groups;
- Inducing social activity and inspiring self-help generating tasks;
- Joint participation in inspiring, working out, implementing and developing social programmes;
- Revealing, analysing and interpreting social needs and problems that exert an influence on shaping appropriate interpersonal relations;

---

[6] Email: sikorski@uni.opole.pl

- Cooperation with other professionals, institutions and organisations that aim at improving existing approaches to social work;
- Participation in developing and raising the level of professional qualifications;
- Initiating new forms of providing help;
- Initiating and participating in studies of social problems (identifying needs).

Irrespective of the ways formal theory frames social work tasks, it is useful to consider those that are part of everyday professional work by representatives of social work. The most important tasks that social workers carry out include the following:

- Very good knowledge of the geographical area of practice and of the problems and needs of individuals, families and social groups living there;
- Designing and carrying out social interventions;
- Elaborating social strategies, mainly to meet the needs of local communities;
- Managing and foreseeing outcomes of help provided or declined;
- Early prevention and deducing unfortunate effects of social issues;
- Seeking and selecting social settings and individuals that need help;
- Providing various forms of help, making use of social work;
- Inspiring the client to be active;
- Facilitating people that require it self-reliant;
- Mediation and negotiation on clients' behalves;
- Proper policy in the scope of granting benefits;
- Self-fulfilment in the profession;
- Active participation in different forms of professional development;
- Promoting social work in the local area.

Among the skills that a social worker should possess, one can list functional skills, that is, those used directly in practice and instrumental skills, that is, those that contribute to the personal capacity to practise effectively. The first group includes the following: selflessness and honesty, respecting the dignity of other people, displaying helpful attitudes, self-control, being able to evaluate critically one's own conduct, communicative skills, empathy and being objective. The instrumental skills, on the other hand, include such skills as: diligence, conscientiousness, inner discipline, decisiveness and consistency, truthfulness, responsibility, personal culture and tactfulness, discretion and organisational skills. With respect to the tasks that are carried out, each social worker should also master the following skills: a) methods of social work, b) social and interpersonal skills c) application of law, d) referring to specialist agencies able to deal with particular needs; e) managerial, f) taking decisions and carrying out rapid social interventions, g) applying research knowledge in practice, h) making use of technology in practice situations (Kwaśniewski 1998: 65).

For social workers to carry out these tasks and goals effectively, developing the necessary skills, achieving personal satisfaction, and practising to other people's satisfaction, it is crucial that they should additionally possess therapeutic skills. As Dąbrowska-Jabłońska says (2002: 67) 'continuing education, perfecting professional skills and updating knowledge ought to be written into the role of social workers as inseparable elements of the profession'. In the same way, therapeutic skills should be developed both during qualifying studies and post-qualifying training courses or workshops. While a social worker will not become a professional therapist in this way, the quality of their work with clients will be advanced as a result. Going further, Sikora (2007: 37-38) argues that voluntary workers who decide to help 'others' by taking up social work tasks should also have professional knowledge and skills.

The therapeutic skills valuable to social workers (see Figure 1) are mainly those of careful observation, listening and speaking, and reacting. These are directed towards improved understanding of clients, their expectations and problems, in order to enable people in need to find ways of overcoming difficulties on their own, offering support to them as they do so or doing a broadly understood social work. The therapeutic skills of social workers can make it easier for clients themselves to respond appropriately emotions, thoughts and behaviours that they display. They also contribute to the ability to understand and comfort others, as well as to make use of crises and to turn them into positive actions.

The skill of reacting
The specific process of helping clients or resolving their problems requires social workers to react appropriately, especially that they should act in a genuine manner (being congruent, true to themselves), be caring and accepting, as well as empathic.

Figure 13.1 *The therapeutic skills of social workers*

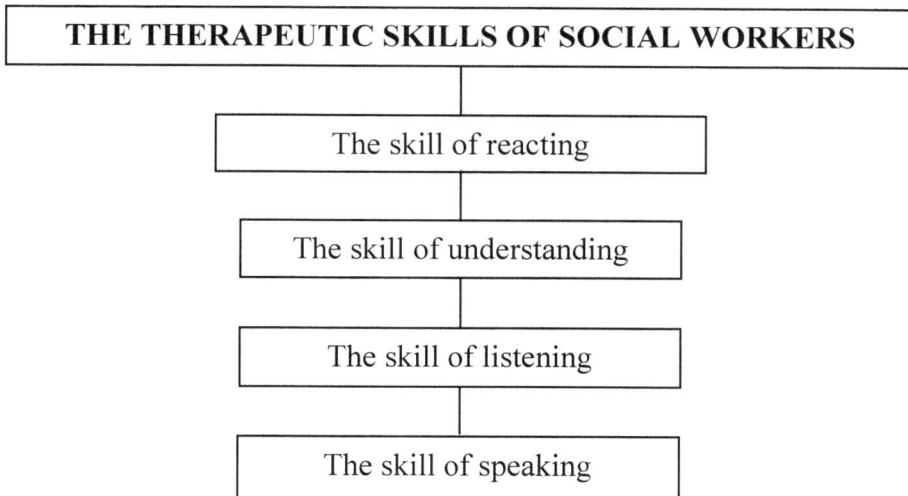

THE THERAPEUTIC SKILLS OF SOCIAL WORKERS

The skill of reacting

The skill of understanding

The skill of listening

The skill of speaking

Genuineness

This aspect of reacting appropriately should make it easier for social workers to communicate accurately feelings and emotions that they are experiencing at any moment in an interaction with clients. As a result, their actions accord with what they are saying. Messages passed through the verbal channel and the non-verbal one ('body language') are highly consistent, and, because of that, much more credible. At the same time, all the steps that a social worker makes are perceived to be sincere, and. this is of paramount importance, to be based on their actual beliefs. All in all, this leads to the situation where their authority grows visibly stronger and so does their status of being not only social workers, but also being efficient and convincing communicators. The social worker's conduct, understood to be truly genuine, free from unclear and critical remarks or implications, causes all their actions to be recognized as appropriate, aiming it serve fully clients' purposes. Also, judgements or suggestions resulting from them are more readily and enthusiastically accepted and applied, within the family environment, as well as outside it (Aleksandrowicz, 2000: 112).

Social workers, who are in this genuine contact with their clients, are able to achieve a lot by using 'themselves', that is not only as an official who meets the formal requirements of their job, but also as a person who can be readily contacted by people in need, without apprehension or lack of trust. Openness in expressing motives, responding to the clients' concerns, which results from social workers' genuineness may make the 'official' more communicative leading to their commitment becoming clearer to people seeking help. Therefore, information circulates more quickly in both directions, from social worker to client and vice versa. Clients, realising that their social workers openly expresses feelings and attitudes, normally respond by taking the same approach, the more so as the object of their mutual relationship is dealing with their own difficulties. Thus, the social worker's genuineness is further strengthened and treated in a more direct and profound way.

The attitude of genuineness on the part of a social worker should result from their readiness to express significant feelings and experiences, when these are called upon in contacts with clients. It is also essential that practitioners should accept their personal responses irrespective of whether they are positive or negative. It is particularly important in the case of the latter, when the social worker does not experience full acceptance or empathy, that they are aware of the feelings and are able to express them. If they do otherwise, for example by thinking of negative feelings about clients as 'unprofessional', this may compromise practitioners as social workers. Similarly where they feel elements of effusiveness, straightforwardness, or unfairness, they may give in to the temptation of putting on a 'mask' of a professional who is infallible, omniscient and who reacts with a cool distancing approach of a professional (Rogers 1991: 53).

Solicitude and acceptance
An important therapeutic skill that is helpful to social workers' reacting skills is the ability to form an emotional attitude towards clients based on solicitude and acceptance, yet, simultaneously, being free from entering into closer intimacy. Social workers can be more effective when they extend a genuine, warm feeling towards their clients and offer sincere, deep, human kindness.

Solicitude is understood here as conduct that avoids excessive interference in the client's right to be independent, negating their own ways of thinking, experiencing and reacting. Building on this, practitioners can attain the state of acceptance, the attitude of approving of clients' good and bad sides, or all the features they possess. It is unacceptable to appreciate some features and deprecate others, to praise some feelings and to question others. At the same time, it is much easier for most social workers to accept negative feelings rather than positive ones, since, focusing on problems, it may become to believe that people with often serious problems in life are capable of developing positive emotions.

Empathic understanding

The third factor that can determine the effectiveness of social workers' reacting skills is their focus on understanding what clients feel and means if they express themselves unclearly or uncertainly. It is hard to imagine doing the social worker's job without possessing the ability to understand emotional states displayed by the client in a penetrating and sensitive manner, or being unable to read the messages behind them. It is only then that social workers are able to help clients concentrate on what they are going through at any particular moment.

Empathy, in social work, means both a readiness to react sensitively to changes in clients' meanings and feelings, and also expressing the feelings which practitioners' experiences of clients' expressions evoke. The social worker must both know how to react in an appropriate way to the client's emotions and also be able to use them effectively in the helping process. Social workers must avoid letting clients realise (for example, through their own behaviour) that they are worried by what the client communicates to them; they must be able to perceive clients' fears without any prejudices or apprehensions. Moreover, they must, at the same time, point out possibilities of coping with the situations which give rise to their worries, controlling reactions in such a way that the clients are able to arrive at a fuller awareness of the meaning of their conduct, or experience it in a more profound manner; as a result, practitioners may achieve an influence on clients' behaviour. The expectation here is that clients, helped by social workers to explore possible meanings contained in their experiences or expressed feelings, would be able to dig deeper into how they feel about the issues they are facing. By doing so, they would develop the skill of concentrating on what they are feeling at the any particular moment and, thus, could, with openness and ease, explore their experiences in a fuller way. In this understanding, empathy to achieve such a good level of identification between social worker and client, that it provides practitioners with better opportunities to know and understand clients, and to enable practitioners to achieve a stronger and more direct experience of what clients are going through.

Because of this, the growing potential to understand the client can considerably raise the level and effectiveness of the social worker's influence. Empathic understanding of what clients say may, at the same time, be a non-specific factor that exerts influence that will assist the process of overcoming their problems. This is because empathic understanding may enable the practitioners to approach the task of building models of clients' problematic behaviour, and also demonstrates acceptance, kindness and warmth. Because it achieves open communication between the parties, it can accelerate and make the process of removing difficulties more dynamic. It can also contribute significantly to counteracting and removing any aversion that clients may experience of sorting out their own problems (Rogers 1991: 66).

Social workers, in the role of therapists, must possess some role-specific personality traits, developing greater maturity, inclined, as Horney (1978: 108) puts it, 'towards people', sensitive to clients' needs, being able to respect values required of social workers, that offer principles preventing them from harming clients and from denying and ignoring their rights.

The skill of observation
Observation serves both the social worker and also the client equally as a process for each continuing to verify the other's progress in overcoming problems raised by the client. This observational mutuality leads to the situation in which communication about can go on without words: an exchange of gestures, a non-verbal code worked out during individual meetings encourage the client to share his/her problems in a freer way. This is particularly valuable in the case of the so-called 'psychological idioms', that is inner states, which cannot be expressed by words. This is most important where the 'psychological idioms' are responsible for situations developing call for social work intervention. Observing a non-verbal message may become the key moment in overcoming difficulties (Gail 2003: 81).

Therapeutic observation serves the purpose of thinking through and describing specific aspects that may be seen in the client's behaviour. This means that practitioners should avoid making any assumptions in advance that might restrict further observation or modify its content. It is inadvisable, or even harmful, to categorise too firmly clients' behaviours, for example classifying the client as sociable, conceited or cynical. Such judgements are very often erroneous and may result from casual, improvised or inadequate observations. Practitioners should avoid generalised judgements about features and qualities, especially during early stages of observation; the beginning focus is on identifying facts information. While carrying out an observation, practitioners should concentrate on both negative and positive behaviours. Only such an approach can make certain that the observation will prove an effective technique in delivering many-sided, clear-headed and objective data on the client (Czabała 2007: 184).

Observation carried out by a social worker cannot be restricted to learning about behaviours only; it should be aimed at discovering relations and regularities that concern connections between particular reactions or groups of reactions and the content of mental experience, physiological processes going on in the client's body, previous life experience, and currently present circumstances in the client's environment. Observation directed towards making the most of these relations and regularities enables practitioners to recognise possible patterns in the client's behaviour, including factors influencing them, in a more effective and comprehensive way. Understanding the behaviour, supported by comprehensive observation, is important practically in analysing the causes of problems, especially those that are presented by clients, which they are aware of to a greater or lesser extent. This principle also seeks to prevent social workers from inappropriate use of formal assessment tools to assess (non-verbal) messages from observation.

A social worker carrying out observation skilfully can, to a considerable degree, make sessions with the client more effective; in particular, it can contribute to strengthening the maintenance of the effects of change over time. Taking into account the principles of therapeutic observation, as well as using of non-verbal messages, such as those expressed with a gesture or a touch, which result from it, favours the client's having a longer-lasting recollection of the social worker's suggestions. Stressing statements with a well-chosen tone of voice, or backing them up with suitable movement of the hands are much more valuable than a raw verbal message. This brings us to the phenomenon of a mutual observation, with the client and the social worker observing each other. This is an element that distinguishes the therapeutic observation from classical, psychological or teaching observations; the two other types being designed to be one-sided explorations (Sikorski 2002: 216).

Being conscious of carrying out observation leads social workers to take greater care and therefore have closer control of the choice of means of non-verbal communication. In this way, they avoid making accidental non-verbal reactions, which may frequently disturb dialogue with clients. Simultaneously, the social worker comes across as more reliable and pragmatic, since the client is a sensitive observer, particularly at the stage of getting acquainted with and 'getting used to' the social worker.

The skill of listening
The skill of interpreting vocal signals (the vocal features of someone's voice) may prove helpful to obtain fairly firm information about clients' personalities. The natural voice is a valuable pointer to a person's personality. G.W. Allport and H. Centril – the pioneers of research into the relationship between the paralanguage and personality – unanimously agree that the voice clearly transmits apt and exact content about clients' internal and external characteristics. They add, at the same time, that the features of

the sound, which contain vocal signals, are fairly precise measures of significant aspects of personality such as: dominance-submission and introversion-extraversion. In the case of the first dimension, it has been shown that voice is more expressive than copies in forming evaluations concerning dominance of a given person; in turn, the face plays a more important role (than vocal signals) in forming evaluations about attachment (Leathers 2007: 279). Therefore, a social worker who listens carefully to the client's paralanguage can, with high probability, establish whether they show tendencies towards being dominating, or submissive.

A social worker who listens carefully to clients' ways of accentuating certain words can fairly precisely recognise true intentions or thoughts. A sentence that sounds the same can express totally different things, depending which word is stressed. For example: *"I don't identify myself with my husband's problems"* changes its meanings as the placement of accents changes. When the first part is emphasised (*"I don't identify ..."*), the meaning can be read as follows: "Somebody else may identify with them but not me." When the accent is shifted and laid on the word *"my"*, the reading can be as follows: "I do understand problems of others, but not those of my husband." In turn, stressing the word *"problems"* suggests the following message: "I don't identify myself only with his problems." It is easy to notice that each change in the accent is accompanied by semantic re-formulation of the message.

Research into medical doctors' communication showed that the more anger there was felt in the voice of a doctor commenting on their work with patients with drinking problems, the harder it was for them to get their patients to stick to the regime of the therapy. Additionally, it was also noticed that doctors whose vocal signals contained the lowest level of boredom, proved the most faithful and professional, as regards the standards of the profession (fuller assessment, precise diagnosis, etc.) and were found to be the most reliable at informing their patients about the illness and the course of the treatment. It was found as well that the patient's satisfaction from doctors' treatment is the highest when their statements are perceived to be kind and warm, while the components of the paralanguage, especially the tone of voice, are explicitly associated with anger and boredom. A simple yet perhaps surprising conclusion follows: a mixture of positive verbal content and more negative features of the voice appear to fit the suitable degree of engagement and concern on the part of the doctor that is expected by the patient (Argyle 1999: 88). In the same way, a social worker might display their care by creating such a combination: to attract verbally and to set against it a vocal signals carrying a negative sound. It is most vital here that this kind of inconsistency arising between the verbal expression and the para-verbal one should be practised suitably and only when there are clear reasons of social work practice for doing so. For example, such moments might arise when some kind of impasse occurs in the course of the work, and the client wishes to break contact with the social worker.

On the other hand, a social worker who wants to read their clients' emotions from paralinguistic messages must make allowances for the fact that certain emotions are easier to recognise and others are much harder to work out. For example, it was experimentally established that anger is identified accurately in 63% of the cases, whereas pride only in 20%. Some other emotions that are relatively easy to identify are the following: vexation, grief, happiness, liking, joy and hatred. On the contrary, it turns out much harder to recognise emotions such as: satisfaction, fear, jealousy, love and shame. In typical situations, those resulting from everyday contacts, joy, grief and anger are identified with less difficulty than fear and repulsion. Some difficulties with identifying successfully underlying meanings to given vocal signals may derive from similarities between some emotional states. This leads to mistaking, for example, fear for irritation, pride for satisfaction, or love for sadness. Among many reasons why there appears a similar pattern of errors, learning to differentiate emotional states that are close to one another on the basis of the context is of the individual's development. Therefore, the receiver of a message could have problems identifying particular emotional states where a particular signal is outside its situational context (Argyle 1999: 96).

The skill of speaking
The manner in which vocal signals are presented is of huge importance to the effectiveness of interaction in social work and may be a considerable factor in the growth of social workers' credibility in their clients' eyes. Moreover, it can positively influence the amount of content that clients remember, as well as the scale of attitude change achieved with them. Most research into these issues convincingly suggests that a poor manner of speaking decreases the probability of reaching intended goal. However, a high standard of presentation does not, of itself, induce expected changes in the attitudes, but raises the possibility of their occurring.

The following paralinguistic behaviours support a proper presentation of messages:

- Taking care to speak fluently;
- Proper choice of voice parameters (intensity, speed, articulation and tone of utterance) suited to the communication skills of a particular client; they have to be adjusted both to the client and also to the circumstances of social work;

- Frequent changes loudness, speed, tone and articulation of the voice; otherwise, if the parameters are kept on the same level, the client may perceive, in the social worker's voice, monotony and boredom with what they are talking about;
- Changes of the voice should not be rhythmical or run according to some fixed pattern, since the client can stop perceiving them as changes, which can weaken the message;
- Hyper-correctness of the paralanguage should be avoided, since too precise an articulation is as harmful to presentation as poor speech;
- While trying to change voice parameters (*e.g.* broaden its range, vary its sound and force) one has to remember to relax one's body; if a social worker speaks too quietly, it can be helped just by relaxing the body as it aids in opening the throat and the upper part of the chest, as well as improves the working of the vocal cords (Leathers 2007: 227).

A social worker and a therapist
Like a therapist, a social worker needs to be a sensitive observer recording changes occurring in the client's behaviour, at least those that are connected with the problems which are being discussed or worked on. They must then be able to detect more significant changes appearing in the client's reactions, ways of communicating – including both 'the language of the face', gestures, interactive distancing oneself and 'paralanguage'. Like a therapist, again, a social worker should be able to recognise the quality of clients' internal mental lives, reach for their past, and also penetrate their current experiences and understand them appropriately; they ought to influence the client not only verbally, but also with a direct, cheerful and kind mode of behaviour, where communication with clients is full of openness, warmth, a smiling manner, a variety of gestures and looks that confirm acceptance, or express an acceptable level of criticism, genuineness of good intentions and understanding.

Using these skills, associated with therapy, contributes helpfully to achieving the objectives of social work.

Bibliography

Aleksandrowicz J.W. (2000) *Psychoterapia* (*Psychotherapy*), Warszawa: PWN.

Argyle M. (1999) *Psychologia stosunków międzyludzkich* (*The Psychology of Inter-human Relations*), Warszawa: PWN.

Czabała J. Cz. (2007)*Czynniki leczące w psychoterapii* (*The Healing Factors in Psychotherapy*), Warszawa: PWN.

Dąbrowska-Jabłońska I. (2002) 'Kształcenie i doskonalenie zawodowe pracowników socjalnych' (The education and professional accomplishments of social workers). In: J. Brągiel, A. Kurcz (eds), *Pracownik socjalny. Wybrane problemy zawodu w okresie transformacji społecznej* (*The Social Worker. Some Issues for the Profession in the Transformation Period*), Opole: Uniwersytet Opolski: 57-68.

Gail K. (2003)*Umiejętności terapeutyczne nauczyciela* (*The Therapeutic Skills of a Teacher*), Gdańsk: GWP.

Horney K. (1978) *Nerwica a rozwój człowieka* (*Neurosis and the Development of Man*), Warszawa: PWN.

Kwaśniewski J. (ed.) (1998) *Praca socjalna – pomoc społeczna* (*Social Work – Social Assistance*), Katowice: Wydawnictwo Uniwersytetu Śląskiego.

Leathers D.G. (2007) *Komunikacja niewerbalna* (*Non-Verbal Communication*), Warszawa: PWN.

Rogers C. R. (1991) *Terapia nastawiona na klienta. Grupy spotkaniowe* (*Client-Centred Therapy: Meeting Groups*) , Wrocław: Thesaurus-Press.

Rybczyńska D. and Olszak-Krzyżanowski B. (1999) *Aksjologia pracy socjalnej* (*Basic Principles of Social Work*), Katowice: Wydawnictwo Uniwersytetu Śląskiego.

Sikora P., (2007) 'Wolontariat istotnym elementem kształcenia pracowników socjalnych na poziomie akademickim – między służbą a egocentryzmem' (Voluntary work as a vital factor in educating social workers on the university level – between a service and egocentrism). In: P. Sikora (ed.), *Wolontariat i samopomoc – podstawowe wymiary solidarności w społeczeństwie ryzyka* (*Voluntary Work and Self-help– Basic Dimensions of Solidarity in a Risk Society*), Opole: Uniwersytet Opolski, Regionalny Ośrodek Polityki Społecznej w Opolu: 7-18.

Sikorski W. (2002)*Psychoterapia grupowa różnych pokoleń* (*Group Psychotherapy of Different Generations*), Warszawa: Wydawnictwo Akademickie „Żak".

Wódz K. (1998) *Praca socjalna w środowisku zamieszkania* (*Social Work in the Home Environment*) Katowice: Wydawnictwo Uniwersytetu Śląskiego.

14 The applications of social facilitation in social work

Martina Špániková and Emília Janigová
The Catholic University in Ružomberok, Slovak Republic

Introduction
Impulses (internal factors) and incentives (external influences) activate the motivated behaviour of a people in their social enviroment. Distinguishing between these two sets of factors as we examine any particular human action is very difficult. Despite this, the most common social incentive influencing the course, intensity and other aspects of human behaviour is the presence of other people. They motivate individuals, changing their experiences and behaviours, either in a positive way, though tactfulness, tolerance, reduction in their own communication, or in a negative way through for example acts of aggression. Individuals who feel included among another people are prepared to respond and their sensitivity to others tends to increase.

The four most commonly described processes of social influence connected with the groups of people are:

- social facilitation
- social idleness
- group polarization
- deindividualization

The authors deal with the first of these, which was first described in 1898. The paper briefly characterises the basic terms, a history of the development of basic and applied research in this field and selected experiments accomplished in the last few years.

Definition of basic terms
The group
The group is defined as two or more people affecting each other (Shaw, In: Výrost et al., 1993: 140)[7]. Social groups constitute the social environment of

---

[7] This definition of group was chosen from the wide range of definitions in order to emphasize the influence of individuals included in a group. Other definitions describing this term in similar ways may be found in such authors as Belz, Siegrist (2001: 38, 43), Oravcová (2005: 216).

human beings from birth, during all their life. They influence individuals' minds, feeling and actions without their realising it. We define small groups as having a membership of between two and 45 members); larger memberships are considered social groups (Oravcová, 2005: 216).

Social facilitation
Social facilitation arises when groups influence individuals. It describes the process by which the individual's functioning is increased because of the presence of other people. They might be present either as a audience or be involved in performing the same activity. Improvement of functioning arises where tasks are easy, well-known and within the competence of the individual. In this situation, the presence of other people is enough to lead to development and increases in individual effort. On the other hand, when difficult or easily-managed activities are performed by individuals in the presence of other people, this can lead to a decline or reduction in success. Michaels (1982) observed billiards players playing alone or before an audience. Good players improved before the audience from 71% to 80% of their capability, but poor players' functioning declined from 36% to 25%. The explanation of social facilitation is that there is an increase in activity because of the presence of other people (Zajonc, 1965). Improved functioning is positively influenced by tasks within the individual's competence, but complicated tasks inhibit efforts (Vaculík et al, 2006: 20). According to Striežnec (1996: 61), social facilitation is a manifestation of interpersonal relations in groups, which makes interaction among human beings easier. It works by removing psychological barriers and increases both individual activity and functioning in shared activities involving several people. Inhibition works in the opposite way. Social facilitation acts by making tasks easier and eventually automatic. With more difficult tasks, group synergy has a negative impact, rather than being facilitating (Krýsl, 2006).

Research in social facilitation
The historical development of the research in social facilitation
The issue of the influence of other people's presence on human behaviour has a long tradition in psychology. An experiment, regarded as the first in social psychology was devised by Triplett in 1898[8], dealing with these issues. He studied cyclists, observing that many rode faster when competing among themselves or following a leader than is they did when cycling alone. Based on these observations, he devised research; children aged 10-12

---

[8] Affirmations of this experiment's innovation by Výrost et al (1993: 183), Blascovich et al. (1999: 68) and Guerin (1993: 7), are questioned by more tentative writers who consider it to be among the first experiments, such as Feinberg and Aiello (2006: 1088), Atkinson et al. (2003: 750) and Hayesová (1998: 48).

performed a task alone and then with others. They achieved better results completing the task with other children who were doing the same task, competitively. (Guerin, 1993: 11).

Since this research, many researchers found similar effects in which co-action either among humans or animals was facilitative (Addessi and Visalberghi, 2001: 297-303). Guerin (1993: 7) suggests that Triplett (1898) and Allport (1920, 1924) defined the term social facilitation and differentiated it from the phenomenon of competition. Zajonc (1965) identified the dependence of social facilitation on the character of the task and in 1980, brought together the most important information from the basic research. Guerin (1993: 8) argues that research in this field has continued to expand.

Several experiments explored the factors involved in social facilitation during this period. Atkinsonová and collective (2003: 750), describe studies where students solved more multiplication problems by co-action than individually (Allport, 1920, 1924)[9], and where the presence of a passive viewer facilitated achievements (Dashiell, 1930). Zajonc (1965, 1980), demonstrated that easy, well-established or instinctive behaviour (such as eating food) was facilitated in the presence of an audience. Where tasks were complex or newly-learned, research subjects were distracted and their effort decreased. This finding was supported both with people and animals (Zajonc et al, 1969), in experiments in which they used cockroaches running on straight or complicated routes in light into a dark box. The presence of other individuals of the same species, even if only as an audience, facilitates achievement when the dominant reaction was correct (running on a straight route), and led to worse achievement if the dominant reaction was incorrect (the complicated route).

Hunt and Hillery's study found that people in the presence of an audience are able to remember a simple maze better than a complicated one without an audience. Cottrell et al (1967) found the same results in a task of memorising a list of simple or complex words. A variety of texts offer brief descriptions of other similar studies (Atkinsonová and collective, 2003: 750-

---

[9] Another situation is where students work together on a common task. In such situations, a different process of social influence, social idleness, has an impact. The author surveyed 302 full-time students, finding that in groups of four students only three on average participated in a dissertation. 95% of students considered themselves extroverts and 91% preferred teamwork in spite of the risk that some members of a group would be unable to work together. It can be assumed that proportion of passive group members is higher among part-time students, even though they may behave responsibly as employees. In these situations, the presence of other people in a group may decrease individual effort.

753; Hayesová, 1998: 48-52; Výrost et al (1993: 182-189) and Guerin (1993). Applied research in this field increased during and after the 1990s.

Experiments investigating social facilitation in social work
A number of studies on social facilitation are relevant to a variety of activities in social work. This may be exemplified by Australian research on problem gamblers and US/Canadian studies on stereotypes of people from of other ethnicities.

Testing the influence of social facilitation on the behaviour of problem gamblers
The previous experiments
The Australian researchers Rockloff and Dyer (2007) devised their study to resolve issues with two previous experiments, which dealt with the influence of the team-mates on the behaviour of an individual player. Hardoon and Derevensky (2001) studied the influence of children between the age of 9 and 13 playing roulette. Firstly, all children played separately, then in groups (in twos or threes) and, finally, were separated again. The level of bets by girls increased between the first separate game and the second group game, and this trend continued when they were separated again. Unfortunately, the experiment did not extend to further games, so it did not uncover any regularities seen during more games. The level of bet will probably increase as players gain experience. Another problem with this experiment was that the analysis of variance (anova), the statistical method used for data analysis, requires independent observers, this condition was not fulfilled.

In another experiment, Martinez et al (2005) used simulated roulette to identify the influence of information about the success or otherwise of other players' bets. During the experiment, some players were falsely informed about the performance of previous player. The incorrectly informed players made higher profits or losses because they made bets that were more risky, compared with uninformed players. This study did not test the concrete impact of the actual presence of successful team-mates on the player's behaviour. In spite of that, it is likely that information about the performance of other players has direct influence on increasing the risky activity of the player.

Roscoff and Dyer's (2007) experiment
Research and theory about the influence of social facilitation led the researchers to expect that the presence of other players or team-mates in a playing room would increase the activity and financial loss of an individual player; hence it has a negative influence on the player. Fifty men and sixty-

six women (aged 18-67 years)[10] played on gaming machines programmed with a fixed winning sequence, after players had experienced an undefined number of failures. The researchers measured the activities of players based on their financial losses, average level of bets, amount of checking games and tempo of play. During the game, some of the players were falsely informed of the wins of other players in the next room who otherwise had the same visual and acoustic information as players who were not misled. The experiment confirmed that the players who had been misled about the success of the fictitious players increased their bets and made higher losses than players who were not misled.

The research on stereotypes as the dominant reactions

The previous experiment

Lambert et al's (2003) study followed up previous research by Lambert et al (1996). In the earlier study, the researchers gathered information about the attitude of white subjects to racism. Two months later, the subjects were invited to express their impressions of particular individuals. The answers of half of participants were confidential but the second half of the subjects had to discuss their ideas with others. In the last part of the study all answers were confidential. All subjects received short biographies of black males with specified information. Subsequently, they read an account of psychology of behaviour orientated to emphasise two opposite poles, intelligence and hostility, which are known in the field of studies of stereotypes of black people. Subsequently, the participants expressed their opinions based on this acquired information. The authors investigated the participants' changes of attitudes to racism. During the research most of the participants transformed their opinions.

The most recent experiment of American-Canadian researchers

The participants completed a questionnaire separately two months before the main research. In compiling the questionnaire, the researchers took into account more instruments for measuring the level of racism:

---

[10] The researchers classified subjects using the 'Problem Gambling Severity Index' (for detail on PGSI, see Ferris and Wynne, 2001; McCready and Adlaf, 2006), and succeeded in recruiting a relatively high proportion of participants with no or minimal gambling problems (47% or 55 subjects) compared with previous experiments (Ladouceuret al., 1997). The study included proportions of subjects with PGSI levels of problem gambling: as follows: 23% (27) players with a minimal ris, 14% middle risk and 9% players with difficulties.

A, **Modern Racism Scale** (MRS[11]), 7 items, scaled from -4 (strong disagreement) to 4 (strong agreement).

B, **Social Dominance Orientation Scale** (SDO[12]), 16 items, scaled from 1 (most negative) to 7 (most positive).

C, **Humanism-Egalitarianism Scale** (HE[13]), 8 items, scaled from 0 (strong disagreement) to 10 (strong agreement).

About two months later, the subjects visited the laboratory again and participated in the research which seemed to be disconnected from their previous contact. The procedure was similar to that of the 1996 study; the difference was in using more instruments exploring the influence of making decisions in public on participants' stereotypes. This experiment is comparable with the previous one, benefiting the application of the research.

Discussion and conclusions
Social facilitation, one of the most frequently described processes of social influence occurring in groups, has a long history as a subject of psychology; the basic, commonly-used definition of social facilitation was formulated in 1880s. After the early research in 1898 and its extension in 1924, applied research in this field and also in social work has continued to develop up to the present time. Developing understanding of relationships with national minorities, clients in groups and volunteers is practically useful in current practice and research.

For example, Allport (2004: 89) studied variations in the acceptance of abuse of national and ethnic minorities, and found that this has the potential to create the negative social facilitation. Allport (2004: 80) found that most people accept verbal or grudging rejection of alien groups, but never go further. Some would accept behaviour that extends to active discrimination, including segregation, and some would physically attack members of minorities and carry out vandalism, take part in public disturbances and lynch mob behaviour. Allport formulated nine steps by which in certain circumstances verbal attacks shift towards violence. Social facilitation plays the active role.

If violence strikes, the following reasons for this situation are evident:

---

[11] From English original 'Modern Racism Scale' (McConahay, 1986)
[12] From English original 'Social Dominance Orientation Scale'(Sidanius, Pratto, Bobo, 1996)
[13] From English original 'Humanism-Egalitarianism Scale' (HE, Katz, Hass, 1988)

1   Previous long-term experience of categorical condemnation. The group is targeted for long term. The people start to lose the ability to think of members of a strange group as the individuals.
2   Long-term verbal complaints about oppressed minority. Suspicion and accusation become customary, with fixed roots.
3   Increasing discrimination occurs.
4   There is concrete external pressure on group members. The group suffers from deprivation, feeling of low living standards, group members were nervous about political progress – examples are restrictions during the war or fear of losing jobs.
5   People are constantly aggrieved by their own inhibitions, there are outbursts of anger. They feel unable to accept unemployment, increases in prices, degradation and confusion. Irrational thinking becomes very attractive. People lose their belief in science, democracy, freedom. They agree with statement that 'somebody who enhances the level of understanding, also enhances the suffering. Down with intellectuals! Down with minorities!'
6   These dissatisfied individuals are attracted to organized movements. If formal organizations are not available, they may use less formal organization – the herd.
7   Individuals belonging to formal or informal organizations gain courage and support. They can observe that irritation and indignation are socially established. The group rules compensate for strained values.
8   Accidents may speeds up the situation. Matters that seem trivial provocations may activate an outburst. Accidents may not happen or may be 'inflated' by backstage manoeuvres.
9   If violence becomes real, social facilitation plays an important role in keeping destructive activity going. When people can observe a mass psychological reactions around themselves, emotions grow and incite further action. The impulse generally becomes strong and personal inhibitons decrease.

These are conditions necessary to unblock the brakes between a verbal attack and open violence (Allport, 2004: 89).

This knowledge may be applied in practice in social work with national or ethnic minorities and in work with groups in psychology (for example, Žiaková, 2005: 105-115). Also, in working with volunteers and dealing with the problems of volunteer management, research on social facilitation could helpfully influence the volunteer recruitment process and also make a contribution to volunteer management theory (see e.g. Mydlíková, 2002).

Bibliography

Addessi, E., Visalberghi, E. (2001) Social facilitation of eating novel food in tufted capuchin monkeys (Cebus apella) : input provided by group members and responses affected in the observer. *Anim Cogn*, 78 (56) : 297-303.

Allport, G. W. (2004) *O povaze předsudků. (About bias character.)* Praha: Prostor: 89.

Atkinson, R.L., Atkinson, R.C., Smith, E.E., Bem, D.J. and Hoeksema,S.N. (2003) *Psychologie. (Psychology).* Praha: Portál, 750-753.

Belz, H. and Siegrist, M. (2001) *Klíčové kompetence a jejich rozvíjení. (Key Competences and their Development).* Praha : Portál, 2001: 38, 43.

Blascovich, J., Mendes, W.B., Hunter, S.B. and Salomon, K. (1999) Social 'facilitation' as challenge and threat. *Journal of Personality and Social Psychology.* 77(1): 68-77.

Ferris, J. and Wynne, H. (2001) *The Canadian Problem Gambling Index : Final Report.* Ottawa: Canadian Centre on Substance Abuse.

Feinberg, J.M. and Aiello, J.R. (2006) Social facilitation : a test of competing theories. *Journal of Applied Social Psychology* 36(5): 1087-1109.

Guerin, B. (1993) *Social facilitation.* Cambridge: Cambridge University Press.

Hayesová, N. (1998) *Základy sociální psychologie. (Essentials of Social Psychology).* Praha: Portál: 48-52.

Henningsen, D.D., Henningsen, M.L., Broz, M. (2007) A Test of Social Facilitation as a Predictor of Home Performance Advantage. *Journal of Sports & Recreation Research and Education*, 1(1): 25-30. Available at : www.scientificjournals.org/journals2007/articles/1012.htm (accessed: 12th January 2008).

Krýsl, D. (2006). *Týmové role a jejich výkonová motivace. (Team Roles and Executive Motivation).* Brno: Filozofická fakulta Masarikovy univerzity v Brně, Psychologický ústav.

Lambert, A. J., Jacoby, L.L., Shaffer, L.M., Payne, B.K., Chasteen, A.L. and Khan, A.L. (2003) Stereotypes as Dominant Responses : On the „Social Facilitation" of Prejudice in Anticipated Public Contexts. *Journal of Personality and Social Psychology* 84(2): 277-295.

Mccready, J. and Adlaf E. (2006) *Performance and Enhancement of the Canadian Problem Gambling Index (CPGI): Report and Recommendations: Final Report.* Winnipeg : Healthy Horizons Consulting. Available at: www.mgcc.mb.ca/pdf/cpgi2006.pdf (accessed: 2nd February 2008).

Mydlíková, E. et al. (2002) *Dobrovoľníctvo na Slovensku alebo 'Čo si počať s dobrovoľníkom'. (Volunteering in the Slovak Republic or 'What to do with a volunteer').*Bratislava: ASSP: 55.

Oravcová, J. (2005) *Sociálna psychológia. (Social Psychology).* Banská Bystrica: Univerzita Mateja Bela v Banskej Bystrici: 165.

Rockloff, M., Dyer, V. (2007) An Experiment on the Social Facilitation of Gambling Behavior. *Journal of Gambling Studies*, 23(1): 1-12.

Strieženec, Š. (1996) *Slovník sociálneho pracovníka. (Social Work Vocabulary)* Trnava: AD Trnava, 1996: 61.

Vaculík, M. et al. (2006) *Vybrané pojmy ze sociální psychologie. (Selected Concepts in Social Psychology).* Brno: Katedra psychologie, Fakulta sociálních studií MU: 20.

Výrost, J., Lovaš, L., Bačová, V. (1993) *Vybrané kapitoly zo sociálnej psychológie II. (Selected Chapters of Social Psychology II).* Bratislava: VEDA: 182-189.

Žiaková, E. (2005) *Psychosociálne aspekty sociálnej práce.* (Psycho-Social Aspects of Social Work). Prešov: Pavol Šídelský – AKCENT PRINT.

15 Principles and practice for alternative punishment: a social work perspective

Emília Janigová and Martina Špániková
The Catholic University in Ružombero, Slovak Republic

Introduction
Imprisonment often leads to offenders developing an environment and culture characterised by behaviours such as intolerance, negation of all positive development, exploitation, criminal values, symbols and patterns. Involuntary incarceration in a relatively isolated social situation is connected with the development of these behaviours. Furthermore, such behaviours influence not only the offender but also social groups such as their family, neighbours and co-workers. The negative effects of prison sentences on people is called prisonisation[14]. According to Kette, Donald Clemmer's project 'The prison community' was published more than 60 years ago, and his studies of resocialization processes are still relevant today (Bačík, 2007). The improvement of alternative punishments is likely to be one of the most appropriate and effective techniques of resocialization.

Basic characteristics of alternative punishment
On 1st January 2006, two precepts of law came into force in Slovakia which supply the criminal code, namely Criminal Law No. 300/2005 and Criminal Order No. 301/2005, which implement new kinds of punishments – alternative punishments:

---

[14] Offenders being incarcerated together creates the opportunity for interaction and leads to confirmation of criminal inclinations and anti-social attitudes. This is often discussed as an important aspect of the process of *prisonisation*, mental adaptation to prison life. Prisonisation causes a loss of initiative, preference for 'line of least resistance', acceptance of values characteristic of prison sub-cultures, adaptation to an artificial prison environment, thereby decreasing adaptability to civil life outside prison. Prisoners' criminal inclinations are confirmed and they become immunised against conventional social norms. The effect of prison sub-culture can be enormous especially during long-term punishment. The longer offenders are incarcerated, the greater the likelihood that they will return to criminal activities. (Matoušek and Kroftová, 2003). The prisonisation process considerably decreases the probability of integration of incarcerated individuals within society after discharge. (Netík et al, 1997).

- imprisonment with suspension, conditional upon probation supervision, § 51 - § 52 of Criminal Law
- home confinement, § 53 of Criminal Law
- compulsory work, § 54 and § 55 of Criminal Law, law No. 528/2005 about obligatory working punishment.

The philosophy of alternative punishments is simple – let offenders free and impose responsibilities or restrictions that function preventively against violation, save public finance and rediect offenders' habits and attitudes towards ordinary life. Alternative punishments emphasise an individual attitude to the solution of criminal activities and point to the importance of preventive work with offneders (Rizman et al, 1997).

Historically, the most important source of alternative punishment in the criminal justice systems is the Meeting of the Secretariat of the Council of Europe in 1976 which adopted resolution No. 10 'Some alternative punishments'.

In 1991, the Council of Europe published 'Alternative punishment versus imprisonment' in which they divided the alternative punishments into three groups depending on the impact on offenders and consequently in 1992 they adopted recommendations on punishments and outcomes achieved in a society. These recommendations offer 90 items of guidance, which parallel European imprisonment guidance and constitute the complex of recommendations to member states for creating new legislative provisions. Among the most significant guidance is:

- the need for external regulation of the activities of authorities responsible for carrying out sentencing and punishment,
- offenders' rights to defence, including the existing social welfare,
- rights of appeal against the verdict and sentence,
- provision for implementing punishments in the most meaningful way that contributes to the personal and social development of offenders,
- special attention to compulsory work which should be socially relevant and increase the skills of offenders (Marešová and Valková, 1994).

The process for arramging complulsory work punishment (CWP)
This paper deals with the CWP in Slovakia. After the sentence of CWP and any subsequent appeal to the chief justice, the offender reports to the probation officer, for a term stipulated by the court. The probation officer's actions are as follows:

- discuss the conditions of CWP with convicted offender

This is crucial, since probation officers should not underestimate offenders, especially as they acquire information about health factors that will produce limitations that will be disadvantageous in the search for a job provider; essential information must be checked with medical advice. Even more important are offenders' financial situations, for example whether it will be possible for offenders living in rural areas to participate, and their level of education, for example their capabilities, qualifications, or any special skills. It is important that the job provider gets an effective worker. Also useful is information about whether the offender is or is not employed, is a student, can travel to work, and if he can work abroad.

- selecting an appropriate job provider

Based on the information about the offender, the officer looks actively for a job provider, providing information about the offender in order to meet the needs of the provider.

- agreement in writing between the job provider and court

At this point, a job provider is selected who is able to match the offender's skills with a suitable job.

- report for chief justice involving:
    outcomes of the discussion about the conditions with the offender,
    the kind, amount and place of CWP requirements
- the chief justice of the district court makes the order for the requirements of the offender's CWP

Based on the report provided, the judge delivers 'The order of the court for implementing the sentence' in which the kind, place and amount of work for the offender is specified. During the period of the sentence, a suspended prison sentence is made, conditional on probation supervision, under § 51 and § 52 of the Criminal Law.

- CWP begins

Practice during this period may be divided into:

    the probation officer's supervision of the CWP

the job provider meeting the requirements of the order

there is a minimum working time each month (20 hours),

the offender meets the rules and limits (§ 51, Criminal Law).

- CWP ends: final report for the chief justice

If there is good cooperation between the job provider and offender and the outcome of the punishment was helpful, the contract with the offender can be closed. (Cehlár, 2007).

Job providers
The beginnings of CWP were difficult. On one hand, the judges did not make this kind of sentence because there was a lack of job providers. On the other hand, job providers did not present themselves with satisfactory information and adequate proficiency in doing this job. With respect to the nature of the challenge that Slovakia was facing in this area a more likely option is cooperation with self-government.

One of the most significant problems with CWP is poor communication among agencies involved, the Department of Work, Social Services and the Family (DWSSF) and the courts, when DWSSF are required to provide a list of job vacancies. Another practical problem is the prejudice of other employees, who do not agree with work for offenders.

CWP was suggested as an appropriate sentence for robbery, battery, disorderliness, causing damage to other people's property, promoting fascicm and similar offences.

Alternative punishments might be thought helpful for people who have made efforts to change themselves, but failed and have shown evidence of accepting their responsibility for finding ways of avoiding offending behaviour. Thus, through offering them 'a second chance' the public participates in their re-socialization, their efforts bring a positive response and by remaining with their everyday family or working enviroment they continue to fulfil their own responsibilities.

Although unemployment in Slovakia is declining, statistics point to the high proportion among long-term unemployed people who belong to the minority group of offenders find it more difficult in the employment market compared with most unemployed people. This target group for CWP is affected by higher barriers preventing them from smooth access to the employment market:

- low educational level,
- inefficient work habits and motivation,
- low self-confidence, self-esteem,
- fear of failure in relationships with relatives or co-workers,
- other people's scepticism and doubts.

The present state of punishment in EU countries

The following part of our project concerns theoretical and practical experience of the IS EQUAL Project 'Chances for Offenders' set up in 2005 to 2008 through the 'Developing Partnerships with Multinational Cooperation and Experience Exchange'.

The main aim of the project 'Chances for Offeders' is to eliminate bias and discrimination against offenders and former offenders and help them reintegrate into society or the employment market. The outcome of the project was to deal with problems with re-education, resocialisation but also reintegration nationally. The main emphasis is on an individual approach to the offender's participation on training and educational programmes the the aim of re-integrating them succesfully into society and increasing their chances of engaging in an ordinary daily life.

The international meetings dealt with identifying problems with prisons and after-care services and also with participation of employers and society in social and work integration of offenders and former offenders.

During the joint meetings in the individual countries, we had opportunities to explore ways of employing offenders in and after a period in prison. The main aim of the meetings is to exchange experiences with such problems in a way to reach compatibility among EU countries in alternative punishments, and post-prison after-care. Slovak practitioners in contact with the target group of offenders and from minority groups reviewed their experience and results achieved with this group, which included education, preparation for the employment market, job creation and employment and social integration. The programme was divided thematically in two topics: 'Preparation of offenders for the employment market during imprisonment and after discharge' and 'Job creation by public companies'.

Volunteers are concerned with the project 'Opportunities for Offenders'. They provide models for clients with the aim of positively influencing the socialization and motivation of offenders and preventing further offending. The importance of voluntary work is mainly in maintaining contact during imprisonment, achieving confidence and motivation with offenders for cooperation after discharge in the first critical year. In this way, the project helps volunteers to move towards the role of social workers, acquire practical skills and educate them as potentional social work pracititoners.

This experience shows that issues with offenders and employument can be resolved through public companies. However, it is equally important to:

- create for offenders conditions that enable them to manage their personal life, both short-term and longer-term problems of living,
- involve the offenders effectively in resolving problems, through useful activities that connect with their special interests,
- involve the public in the elimination of discriminiation,
- create the background and conditions for increasing qualifications or training for particular jobs,
- establish agencies for personal support of and consulting about employment.

We have also worked on difficulties of offenders' employment in prisons in Poland, towns Zakopane and Krakow in March, 2006. Our approach was to build cooperation and eliminate barriers to employment. In Zakopane, clients had the opportunity to exhibit products such as paintings, plastics at the exposition in Szturm, Poland. These will be presented in a catalogue and customers can order them. The profit will be divided between the creators and charitable projects.

Employment practice with offenders in France
We visited the France twice as part of the international cooperative project, in October, 2006 in Bayonne, Anglet and Biarritz and in October, 2007 in Montpellier and Toulouse.

The first topic 'Interests of companies in professional integration of offenders' dealt with the help after discharge. The project is based on partnership between young offenders, society and the criminal justice system with the aim of porposing new visions of social representation. Partnership is considered to be one of the methods of improving the quality of provision for allagencies involved. The partners developed new version of cooperation their shared involvement in resolving difficulties.

The most frequently disscused issue was the importance of work as a key factor in the process of re-integration; this is influenced by the state of the employment market. Following the project, this reliance on availability of jobs is balanced by with creating direct relationships with companies, solving not only working but also other problems that arise for offenders alongside work, for example, accommodation. In this way, young offenders can be more motivated and this is one of the ways of influencing their future life plans and increasing their feeling of responsibility for what happens to them. Dealing with unemployment by itself is not such a motivation for young offenders as working with a range of personal, mostly housing, problems alongside this.

In the south of France, the partners introduced a system of employment in prisons. The prison Maison d'Arrét de Villeneuve les Maguelone is 60 kilometres from Montpellier, situated in upland near the Mediterranean Sea. Young offenders are also placed in this prison, mainly to achieve the activities related to education, gaining practical life routines and creative work attitudes are achieved. There are well-equipped workshops for woodwork and weaving.

A useful experience was to the factory for production of the A380 airbus in Blagnac near Toulouse. Over 17 000 workers are employed there. The employers, mostly the Airbus company, the largest aeroplane manufacturer in Europe, established factories directly in prison and allowed offenders to gain not only technical education through the state educational bodies but also practical skills. By doing this, offenders' preparation for the employment market and post-discharge life is able to be more systematic. Longer-term prisoners have more opportunities to acquire technical qualification and positive working habits. The best qualified are prepared for specific qualifications in their firld of employment. Their preparation focuses on discharge. They are financially rewarded for work and are able to buy equipment such as computers and work clothing.

Employment practice with offenders in Italy
In Bologna, prisoners also make amends for their crimes through social services, in a similar way to CWP Slovakia. Many of them are imprisoned for a short time (three months). The partners introduced one of the most significant projects in Italy, with a gross expenditure of €650 000. Three town councils, several government and non-government agencies and the University of Bologna all participate in this project. They aim to work on the following issues: supporting prisoners, maintaining non-offending behaviour, stimulating offendes'development, help them to integrate into daily life and decreasing recidivism. The social workers cooperate closely with prisons, public authorities involved and private sector conmapnies to re-socialize offenders. In the Bologna area, 45 workers are employed in this work.

Ferrara, where the prison is situated, cooperates closely with the chemical factory Basell. The company helps by re-education and re-integration of offenders into everyday life through employment for a period of time, offering them jobs and certificated education to help the offenders' future work prospects after discharge. The Mareco Luce srl. company also employs four offenders installing garden lighting. We spent all day in the Basell factory at Ferrara, the factory manager Claudio Mingocci demonstrating involvement of senior staff by welcoming us in a big congress hall and describing the history of the company. The company is one of the most significant companies in the production of polypropylene, polymers, variable catalysers and synthetic fertilisers. It operates in 120 countries across the world, with over 7000 employees and annual turnover more than €11.5m. The company was established in 1953 by two chemists – Giulio Natta and Karl Ziegler who achieved Nobel Prizes in 1963; the company is now part of Lyondellbasell, an international plastics, chemical and refining company. Our visit included laboratories, research and training centres. We discussed the work of ten offenders who were trained and subsequently worked in various roles. The partners explained that among the complications of concluding business between the members of the partnership is the need for all employees of the factory to agree with employing offenders in their company.

Conclusion
Because of the different circumstances, historical development, tradition and legislation, it is hard to compare employment work with offenders in and out of prison in EU countries. It requires the courage, good partners and enthusiastic workers in supporting new ideas in each different context and projects for helping people who significant needs. We should not argue that progress is impossible because we have difficulties in our particular system and legislation.

Bibliography

Bačík, J. (2007) *Kultúrna diverzita väzenského prostredia.*(*Cultural differentiations of penitentiary enviroment.*) In: Zborník príspevkov zo VII. doktorandskej konferencie Aplikovaná antropologie 2007. Olomouc: Univerzita Palackého v Olomouci: 76-81.

Cehlár, V. (2007) *Uplatňovanie trestu povinnej práce na Okresnom súde v Žiline.* (*Applying of obligatory work punishment in District Court in Žilina.*)In: Zborník zo seminára Alternatívne tresty v praxi. Dolný Kubín: Konzultačné a informačné centrum EDUKOS v Dolnom Kubíne: 41-49.

Marešová, A. and Válková, J. (1994) *K problematice alternatívních trestu. (To the problems of alternative punishments.)* Praha: Institut pro kriminologii a sociální prevence.

Matoušek, O. and Kroftová, A.(2003) *Mládež a delikvence. (Young people and crime)* Praha: Portál.

Netík, K., Netíková, D. and Hájek, S. (1997) *Psychologie v právu. (Psychology in justice.)* Praha: C.H.Beck.

Rizman, S., Sotolář, A. and Šámal, P. (1997) *K problematice alternativních trestu. (On the problems of alternative punishments.)* In.: Trestní právo: 7-8/1997.

The Criminal Law No. 300/2005

The Criminal Order No. 301/2005

Law No. 528/2005 on compulsory work punishment.

16   Social work with disabled people

Beata Górnicka
Opole University, Poland

Introduction
Everyday life, presents people in contemporary society with various difficulties. Weaker members of society, such as people who are ill or disabled, or people entangled in social issues which are expanding on a broader scale nowadays such as unemployment, poverty and homelessness, find themselves in particularly difficult situations. They are frequently excluded from society or, at the best, live in danger of social exclusion. Fortunately, at the same time, contemporary societies have developed mechanisms that enable people at crisis points in their lives to receive assistance and support from the society and the state they live in. Social work, which is developing on a greater scale nearly all over the world, plays a significant role here. Both the social worker and the personal assistant working with disabled people occupy a series of roles within the scope of social work aiming to offer social assistance to disabled people, particularly with help and support in overcoming difficulties of life and solving problems.

The present paper deals with important individual issues resulting from disability, as well as with the problem's dealt with through social support. It also attempts to show roles carried out within the social work services with disabled people.

Disability as a determinant of life situation - problems of disabled people
The state of people's health has always had a decisive influence on their life, and the life choices of people who are not fully fit are significantly affected by their disabilities.

The term 'disability', according to the International Index of Physical Damage, Disabilities and Handicaps published by World Health Organisation in Geneva in 1980, applies to all kinds of limitations or incapacities, resulting from physical damage, in performing tasks within the scope that is considered normal for human beings (Dryżałowska 2004: 646). This can be caused by sensory, motor, psychological or somatic damage, occurring at different levels of severity (slight, moderate, or severe). This creates one of the more important problems of contemporary world.

According to the data published by WHO, people with disabilities form around 10% of the world's population, whereas in the economically developed countries of the European Union disabled people make up 15% of the population. In Poland, the number of disabled people is to almost 5.5 million, over 14% of the population of the country (*Rocznik Demograficzny GUS* 2008: 185).

Disabled people, irrespective of the type or degree of their disabilities, have to overcome various difficulties and barriers in their lives. These adversities come not only from physical, sensory or intellectual limitations, but are often a result of inappropriate social interactions orpoor social responses to their difficulties. It is impossible to list all the problems which disabled people might encounter in their lives, but the most important include the following:

- *emotional problems* resulting, among other things, from the sense of 'injustice of fate', a feeling of being wronged, experiencing upset and grief due to the illness or disability, difficulty accepting one's own psychological and physical state, a failure to come to terms with being affected by disability, lacking in self-acceptance, lack of belief in one's own potential, the sense of helplessness, difficulty in determining one's own life identity;
- *physical problems* connected with limitations to self-sufficiency and independence, difficulty in performing daily activities of self-maintenance, handicaps in communication, transport and movement both locally and over longer distances to use public building such as shops, offices, cultural facilities;
- *social problems* mainly difficulties in relationships with others, a frequent lack of acceptance by other people, restrictions in social contacts;
- *professional problems* deriving from limited educational opportunities, which often leads to a lower level of education and professional qualifications than the disabled person might be able to achieve, and this gives rise to problems in gaining employment appropriate to both personal qualities and preferences, and which very often makes it impossible to find employment at all;
- *material problems* connected not only with the low income level, but also with the need to cover the costs of rehabilitation and specialised equipment required for everyday functioning, adaptation of accommodation and furnishings;
- *family problems*, a specific category of social issues, concerned with both difficulties in establishing partner relationships, starting families and participating in family life and in household activities,

such as caring for and bringing up children, spending free time with them, helping them to learn.

Most of these life problems can occur in everyone's lives, but disabled people are more likely to encounter such difficulties to a greater extent and more frequently, because their capacity to function in a self-efficient, independent and effective way is restricted both on the personal and social arena. Their limitations are tied to the fact of being disabled.

On the other hand, disability must not lead to exclusion from life, either in personal developments or social activities, even if it restricts everyday functioning, limits opportunities for gaining knowledge and skills, hampers a professional career and undermines efforts to resolve problems and, very often, determines life choices. Disabled people, irrespective of the kind and degree of their dysfunctions, are entitled to the same rights as any citizen, with guarantees of equal treatment by the Constitution of the Republic of Poland (1997) and the right to live an independent, self-fulfilling and active life, the right to be protected against discrimination (Bill of disabled people's rights, 1997).

The reality of life is not that promising, though: social attitudes still hold a stereotype of disabled people as weak, incompetent and isolated. This leads to negative attitudes among fit people towards disabled people, and, in consequence, such attitudes are responsible for a lack of social acceptance and putting up barriers for disabled people on their roads to self-acceptance, creating a positive picture of themselves, and achieving active participation in their personal and social lives. It is a challenge to our contemporary times to achieve a normalisation od disability in everyday life, a task to which social work contributes.

Social work with disabled people – preventing social exclusion
Even though, in the literature of the subject, social work is defined in a fairly varied manner, what is emphasised in all of the definitions is the fact that it is a professional activity for the benefit of weaker members of society. For instance, Wódz, on the basis of Resolution 16/67 of the Council of Europe, concludes that 'social work is a specific professional activity, whose task is to facilitate mutual adjustment of individuals, families, groups and the social environment in which they live, and also development of the sense of their own individual value through making use of possibilities present in people, in interpersonal relations, as well as in resources made accessible by local communities (1996: 12).

The essence of social work seems well reflected in the definition accepted by the British Central Council of Education and Teaching Within Social Work, according to which, social work is regarded as a professional activity aimed at individuals, families and groups, which makes it possible to identify personal and social factors that affect their functioning and also creating possibilities of overcoming difficulties and solving various problems through maintenance of the preserved potential, securing and corrective, as well as rehabilitation-oriented activities (Wódz 2000: 12; Piekut-Brodzka, 2004: 8).

In Poland, according to the Social Aid Act, 12th March, 2004 (*Journal of Laws* 2004), social work is treated as 'a professional activity with the aim to assist individuals and families in strengthening or regaining the ability to function in society through performing appropriate social roles, and also through creation of conditions favouring this goal' (art. 6.12). This constitutes one of the basic tasks of social work (art. 15.2), which covers individuals and families, among others, because of a disability, long-term or severe illness, needing help because of problems in securing child care and development, running the household, unexpected emergencies, unemployment (art. 7). Thus, disabled persons, independently of the type and degree of the disability, make up one of the most numerous groups of potential beneficiaries of social assistance and social work.

Achieving tasks within the full range of social assistance, therefore including social work, is the responsibility of local government in districts and counties, while some roles are undertaken on the higher level of the province. Many tasks are carried out also by non-governmental organisations, foundations and associations established to develop activity for the benefit of disabled people. These tasks are financed by local government, subsidised from the national budget. In recent years, a considerable proportion of these costs has been covered by EU funds (EFS). The tasks are, to a considerable extent, carried out directly by social workers employed in social assistance who, among others, are responsible for the following:

- assessing events that give rise to the need for social assistance and eligibility cases eligible for assistance;
- providing information, advice and assistance in solving problems of everyday life to people who will then be able to solve their own problems independently,
- assisting people in difficult situations with counselling about options for resolving problems and obtaining help from appropriate state or local-government and non-governmental agencies, supporting people in getting this help;

- stimulating social activity and inspiring mutal support actions to meet needs of people, families, groups and social environments;
- cooperating and working with other professions to prevent and reduce problem behaviour and begative effects of social circumstances;
- initiating new forms of social aid to persons and families experiencing difficult situations and inspiring the establishment of new agencies to meet individual and family needs;
- participating developing regional and local programmes of social assistance aiming at raising the quality of life.

Social workers constitute, thus, a pillar of social assistance, yet because a multitude of tasks assigned to them and because high caseloads, they cannot deal with all these tasks to the highest standard. The most common shortage is time to provide direct support for people receiving care services at home, especially disabled people who because of limitations arising resulting from their disabilities often need accompanying in different everyday situations of life. In recent years, in Poland, this gap has been filled with personal assistants to disabled people, who carries out activities similar to those of the social worker, differing in that the assistant works with only one disabled person and their family.

The position of the assistant to a disabled person is a fairly common service in the majority of the EU member states, and the scope of the service is established by local authorities according to the relevant legislation. Each disabled person is offered a chance to use this kind of assistance and the cost of the assistant is generally covered from the local government budget, social insurance of disabled people or a special fund designed for this purpose. Some disabled people employ their personal assistantsfrom their own resources.

The need for personal assistant services, emerges from increased interest in the social environment of disabled people. Following the experience of European states that took the lead in this area, and responding to the needs of disabled people, new occupational groups were introduced in social assistance. in 2001, upon the request of the Minster of Labour, Ac Ordinance issued by the Minister of National Education on 29th March 2001 changed the ordinance classifying groups in the vocational school system (*Journal of Laws* No. 34, entry 405). This created an occupational group entitled 'assistant to a disabled person', within social assistance and social work, assigned the number 346. It was entered on the list of professions with the number of 346101, in the index of occupations included in the classification of professions and specialisations introduced by the Ordinance of the

Minister of Economy and Labour on 8th December, 2004 (*Journal of Laws* No. 265, entry 2644) amended by Order of the Minister of Labour and Social Policy on 1st June 2007 (*Journal of Laws*, 106, entry 725). The tasks assigned to the assistant to a disabled person are set out in the programme 'foundations for the occupation of assistant to a disabled person' approved of by the Minister of National Education in 2001 (*Journal of Laws* of 2005, No. 66, entry 580). The following are included in them:

- accompanying a disabled person in fulfilling social and professional roles;
- participating in identifying and resolving social problems of disabled people;
- collaboration with social workers and other specialists in improving disabled peoples' quality of life;
- providing assistance to disabled people in obtaining medical and rehabilitation services, and opportunities for professional retraining;
- assistance in making social contacts and organising spare time;
- advocacy for disabled people;
- basic hygienic and nursing activities.

The assistant to a disabled person can bring a completely new quality into the life of disabled people and their families, very often changing their lives totally. The work of the assistant creates a chance of undertaking activity, self-fulfilment and independent functioning for disabled people. Certainly, offers opportunities of support to disabled people and assistance in resolving problems of daily living. However, in Poland, as Stanisławski claims: 'there are only a few assistants who support disabled people. The majority of them are employed by non-governmental organisations (altogether there are about 100 assistants working for such organisations), using the European Social Fund (EFS) programme 'Equal', and the State Fund of Rehabilitation of disabled people */Państwowy Fundusz Rehabilitacji Osób Niepełnosprawnych - PFRON/ - programme 'Partner'''* (2008: 24).

The work of the assistant to a disabled person can be carried out in innovative ways. The literature of the subject describes the following models:

1. Assistant acting **on the instructions of disabled people**. Such a person only carries out the wishes orders of disabled people themeleves, the 'model having been elaborated in the American Centres of Independent Living and then made use of in a number of European countries. The assistant performs only these activities for disabled people that they are not able to do themselves'

(Stanisławski 2008: 25). Hence, while accompanying a blind person, the assistant is the person's reader and guide; being an assistant to a deaf person, they play the role of interpreter. The assistant does not influence the decisions of disabled people, carrying out only these actions which disabled are is not able to performthemelves; the responsibility is taken by disabled people.

2. Assistant as **a mentor and a teacher**. This kind of assistant tries to inspire and encourage disabled people to be active, they advise and teach, offer psychological and emotional support, are companions in making social relationships, can even become friends. This model has been worked out by the Foundation of Help for Children and Young People (*Fundacja Pomocy Młodzieży i Dzieciom 'Hej Koniku'*). It features an assistant supporting disabled persons, who 'without help will never be active, not leaving homes for years and being completely helpless' (Stanisławski 2008: 27).

3. Assistant acting and an **employment coach**. This model of assistant has been worked out by PFRON. 'The assistant to a disabled person is a worker assisting the latter at work and only in relation to that activity, including someone who facilitates disabled people in communicating within the work environment (Stanisławski 2008: 27). The task of the assistant is to find disabled people willing to undertake employment and to prepare them for the job. After the disabled person person is employed, the assistant keeps supporting them in carrying out duties which they cannot deal with on their own, as long as they cannot acquire the skills to perform them independently.

The assistant to a disabled person is an role that can can contribute a considerable amount to overcoming all kinds of barriers in living that affect disabled people and provide crucial help in resolving their life problems. Here, solving emotional issues in disabled people's lives seems the hardest task since it can be achieved only through overcoming the difficulties tyat a disabled person may have in accepting their own psychological and physical condition, that is, coming to terms with the disability and deciding on their own priorities in life. Someone who can offer emotional and spiritual support to a disabled individual in this aspect of their self-fulfilment is an important resource. Personal assistants to disabled people, irrespective of the approach to their role, provides a sense of safety, and being a companion responds to disabled people's sense of loss, loneliness and social rejection. At the same time, by supporting disabled people in everyday life situations, the assistant contributes to maintaining faith in the person's own abilities and avoiding feelings of helplessness.

The physical problems of disabled people are connected with limitations to their independent functioning, affect their potential or cause serious difficulty in carrying out self-care and communication. Solving problems of this type is relatively easy, since personal assistants simply help disabled people do what they are not able to do on their own. If there is such a need, the personal assistant may dress disabled people, help them get up in the morning, prepare meals or tidy their accommodation. However, the assistant is supposed to assist the disable person, but not do all that instead of them (like a kind of social nurse), which means that disabled people does parts of the activities themselves with the assistant's supervision avoiding unnecessary risk. Solving practical problems of this kind, helps disabled people move about both within their close surroundings and in broader areas. Having such support enables disabled people to make use of accessible public spaces, doing shopping, settling official business and going to the cinema or theatre. Consequently, solving practical physical problems means supporting the progress of disabled people in perfecting their skills, which leads greater self-sufficiency and independence. In this way disabled people can 'leave their home' and are prevented from being marginalised in social life.

Solving social problems of disabled people, however, is much harder, since thisarea of practice, including mainly interpersonal relations, requires both the disabled people and those around them should participate. In this case, the assistant's work consists of facilitating disabled people to make contacts with others, assisting with overcoming relationship difficulties through solving problems of physical nature, but also shaping attitudes of others towards disabled people and vice versa. Removing restrictions on socialising helps disabled people to stop 'being afraid of reaching out to other people'. Instead, they can show their real selves, people like anyone else, having their own needs and encountering their own problems, yet coping with reality. In this way, they contribute to raising the level of other people's acceptance of disability and modifying social attitudes towards disabled people.

Disabled people can take part in activities organised in many Polish cities by associations acting for the benefit of disabled people and their families, and also though social aid centres that provide support groups for disabled people. These are groups established with the aim of creating opportunities for disabled people to feel free of the sense of loneliness, raising their own sense of wellbeing and the level of self-worth through contacts with persons with similar problems. They can thus obtain mutual support in resolving issues by exchanging life experience. Meetings of support groups are, then, useful in overcoming both emotional and social problems.

Dealing with disabled people's employment problems requires collaboration among a number of different environments and agencies. The work life of disabled people is affected not only by limitations in their skills and, very often, lower standards of their professional qualifications, although it is also true that disabled people persons' skills and qualifications are simply not valued enough. However, there are also issues with the situation in the labour market. Recently, a great number of people have difficulty in finding work and disabled people are worse off in this respect, even where they are ready to take work and possess appropriate motivation. The 'work coach' personal assistant role consists in. first, reaching out to disabled people, and then finding a potential employer for them. When the connection is made and a job is found, the personal assistant contiues supporting the disabled person,– accompanying them in carrying out the occupational duties until the person becomes fully effectoive in their work role.

Disabled persons find employment, for example, at occupational therapy workshops (*Warsztaty Terapii Zajęciowej*), sheltered workshops (*Zakłady Aktywności Zawodowej*) or in the open work environment. They can obtain work as a result of participation in the program 'work coach-aided employment of disabled people' established by PFRON. They can themselves start their own business activity, among others, through making use of the assistance offered by PFRON (within the project 'Support for employment of disabled people in the open labour market').

The material conditions of disabled people improves as they are more financially independent through having their own incomes, but even then the problems do not disappear completely. This is because disabled people often need to cover costs of rehabilitation, purchase of equipment needed for everyday functioning, adaptations to their living accommodation and furnishings. The assistant to a disabled person, by helping the latter to solve such problems, provides them with information, explores with them options for using various different benefits that disabled people are eligible for, encourages them to use donations and subsidies. In this way, the assistant monitors the activity of organisations and associations and acts for the benefit of disabled people, assisting them to make the best sue of offers of support and help.

It is possible to obtain extra financial support (from the PFRON budget) to cover the costs of rehabilitation and training periods, have physical barriers in living accommodation removed and to provide disabled people with orthopaedic items and auxiliary equipment such as specially adapted computers.

Many disabled persons also have to cope with issues in their family lives, connected with relationship problems or difficulty in bringing up and taking care of their children. The personal assistant supports disabled people in this sphere as well and can offer practical help to carry out tasks which the disabled person cannot deal with on their own. This is mainly about running the household but primarily focuses on support with child care. The assistant accompanies disabled people person in caring activities, in organising and spending spare time with disabled people and their children, for example, going for a walk, to the cinema, or reading books. The assistant might also help the child with schoolwork, directly assisting the child in learning or organising relevant help, accompanies the child to school, to agencies running out-of-school activities or accompanies a disabled parent helping their children participate in these activities.

Conclusion

Contemporary societies commonly belive it to be important that disabled people receive support and assistance from close family members, but also from different government and and non-governmental agencies (Mikulski 2002: 193). It concerns children and youth, but also adult persons at different stages of their lives. It is particularly important to prepare a disabled person for independent functioning in their adult lives, through, for instance, becoming self-caring; this is one of the most important tasks of social work (Górnicka 2004: 146-152). Yet, even people who are prepared for life in the best possible way, being self-caring and able to live independently, must overcome various difficulties in everyday living and solve their own life problems. Disabled persons who need support in this respect nevertheless retain their right to autonomy and self-determination in decisions about their lives. It is a mistake to treat them in an excessively caring way and performing all life-tasks for them. They must be assisted, accompanied and supported only when they cannot carry out a task themselves. Social work is contributing usefully to the needs of disabled people in local settings, among others, through the role of the personal assistant to a disabled person, which is becoming an increasingly popular options in services for disabled people acrisszx the world and is highly valued by disabled people themselves.

In addition, other forms of social work with disabled persons, are not discussed here, such as volunteer support or social and work rehabilitation projects. These are run by non-governmental organisations (*e.g.* 'Good Practices'). Howeverm, the main focus of this paper has been to explore ways of assisting disabled people in resolving their living issues effectively. The more effective thus help is, the greater benefits it yields, not only for disabled people themselves, but also for society. Disabled people must not be socially excluded, since they constitute a valuable part of society: being able to overcome many problems in their lives, they contribute uniquely to raising the quality of life, both their own and those of other people around them. Thus, they are not mere 'receivers' of help, but themselves create social capital and cultural value.

Bibliography

Dryżałowska, G. (2004) Niepełnosprawność (Disability). In: Pilch T. (ed.) *Encyklopedia pedagogiczna XXI wieku* (*A Pedagogical Encyclopaedia of the 21st Century*) Vol. III, Warszawa: Wydawnictwo Akademickie 'Żak': 646-649.

Górnicka, B. (2004) Elementy pracy socjalnej w usamodzielnianiu niepełnosprawnych wychowanków placówek opiekuńczo-wychowawczych (Elements of social work in rendering persons put in care of care-and-rearing centres self-dependent). In: Brągiel J. and Sikora P. (eds) *Praca socjalna – wielość perspektyw. Rodzina – Multikulturowość – Edukacja* (*Social Work – A Multitude of Perspectives. Family-Multiculture-Education*). Opole: Uniwersytet Opolski: 145-153 .

Karta Praw Osób Niepełnosprawnych. Uchwała Sejmu RP z dnia 1.08.1997 (*The Charter of Rights for Disabled People.* Bill of the Polish Parliament of 1st August, 1997). Monitor Polski z dnia 13 sierpnia 1997.

Konstytucja Rzeczpospolitej Polskiej z dnia 2 kwietnia 1997 (*The Constitution of the Republic of Poland* of 2nd April, 1997). *Dziennik Ustaw Nr 78, poz. 483* (*Journal of Laws No. 78, entry 483*).

Mikulski, J. (2002) Praca socjalna wobec osób niepełnosprawnych (Social work with disabled people). In: Frysztacki K. and Piątek K. (eds) *Wielowymiarowość pracy socjalnej* (*The Multidimensional Character of Social Work*). Toruń: Wydawnictwo Edukacyjne 'AKAPIT': 193-211.

Piekut-Brodzka, D. M. (2004) Wiedza z zakresu pedagogiki specjalnej niezbędna w pracy socjalnej (Knowledge in the field of special pedagogy crucial in social work). In: Piekut-Brodzka D. M. and Kuczyńska-Kwapisz J. (eds) *Pedagogika specjalna dla pracowników socjalnych* (*Special Pedagogy For Social Workers*), Warszawa: Wydawnictwo Akademii Pedagogiki Specjalnej: 8-14.

Podstawa programowa dla zawodu asystenta osoby niepełnosprawnej zatwierdzona przez ministra edukacji narodowej w 2001 r. (The programme foundations for the profession of assistant to a disabled person, approved by the Minister of National Education in 2001): *Dziennik Ustaw z 2005r. Nr 66, poz. 580* (*Journal of Laws of 2005, No. 66, entry 580*).

Rocznik Demograficzny GUS (*The Demographic Yearbook of the Chief Statistical Office*), (2008) Zakład Wydawnictw Statystycznych, Warszawa.

Rozporządzenie Ministra Edukacji Narodowej z dnia 29 marca 2001 r. zmieniające rozporządzenie w sprawie klasyfikacji zawodów szkolnictwa zawodowego

(Ordinance of the Minister of National Education of 29 March, 2001, changing the Ordinance concerning the index of professions in the vocational school system): *Dziennik Ustaw z 2001 r. Nr 34, poz. 405* (*Journal of Laws of 2001, No. 34, entry 405*).

Ustawa z dnia 12 marca 2004 r. o pomocy społecznej: *Dziennik Ustaw z 2004 r. Nr 64, poz. 593* (Act on social aid of 12 March, 2004: *Journal of Laws of 2004, No. 64, entry 593*).

Wódz, K. (1996) *Praca socjalna w miejscu zamieszkania* (*Home care social work*). Warszawa: 'Interart'.

17 The higher education institution as a living environment for disabled people – possibilities for social inclusion

Iwona Dąbrowska-Jabłońska
Opole University, Poland

Introduction: disabled people in Poland

Disabled people are a numerous group in Poland, amounting to nearly 5.5 million, about 14.3% of the whole nation. This means that every seventh Pole is disabled. From a broader perspective, we could even say that this group is the largest minority in our country. This is more than whole populations of certain European states, such as Norway, Lithuania or Latvia. Yet, on the other hand, merely 4% of disabled people hold higher education degrees (among the population, it is 10%). This means that human potential is wasted. In this article, I discuss how to prevent the situation from continuing and also suggest a number of practical courses of action to increase the proportion of disabled people in academic communities.

I develop my considerations using systemic approach as it permits a transition from a narrow and restrictinve orientation to taking a wider look at social work, to 'perceiving phenomena on both a macro-social and individual's, micro-social, scale' (Marynowicz-Hetka 2006: 267). What does it mean in practice? For many years, in Poland, a model of disability that focuses on the individual (a medical model) has been preferred. It is founded 'on the assumption that disability is a personal tragedy of the individual and must be dealt with with the help of professional intervention, that is by removing medical complications or functional limitations of the individual through,for example, rehabilitation' (Piasecki and Stępniak 2003: 7). In this framework, the source of disability is found in human beings themselves. This has meant an imdividualised struggle with disability, and the development of social mechanisms that exclude disabled people from everyday life; it also underlies the assumption that care provision and helping actions would be the basis of services. Unfortunately, this model of disability is still widely accepted, supported by the media, which shows disabled people as suffering hardships in a simplified way. Also, public bodies stress the social care system as the most significant service for this group of citizens. The state shapes policy towards disabled people based on protected employment and rehabilitation. A considerable proportion of the group attending day-care centres within the structure of the social care system are people with neurological or musculo-skeletal diseases, and impairment of motor functions. Despite the fact that working with such disabled people towards more active involvement in employment, is frequently discussed, day-care centres mainly organize therapeutic workshops, whose aim is to teach the participants skills that will improve their chance of getting employment in the future (Sikora 2005: 560-561). Although this ,ay be helpful, it is still exceptional for social care institutions to try to provide services to educate disabled people to a higher level, thus confirming the assumption in wider society that the aim of such centres is mainly to prepare their clients to carry out simple activities that do not require formal education. Disabled people themselves mau come to accept such false stereotypes, through passive acceptance of their excluded social status.

A systemic (and ecological) approach towards disability suggests that the behaviour of each individual influences attitudes and behaviours of family members, their peer group and thei community, the individual being modified in turn by their reactions. Disabled people are part of their families, which makes up a system which, while it is composed of other individuals, is also at the same time more than the sum of its members. Any alteration to one part of the system (a subsystem or unit) affects other parts. Since we do not live in isolation, people who are members of a family are also, at the same time, components of another system, within their broader surroundings, or social environment. In this way, it is not only members of the family who influence one another within their social system, but also the environment that exerts a considerable influence on the family system through its individual members. Such an approach leads to some consequences: we may achieve a departure from the thinking focusing on a problem in favour of identifying strengths, resources and opportunities within the individual, in the family and in the environment, from work not only with the individual, but with the family and broader social systems as well. This is not an easy thing, the more so, as Weissbrot-Koziarska writes, there is a strong conviction, ingrained in the society's values, about family autonomy and the privacy of family life (2005: 69).

The systemic approach allows us to shift the model of disability from the individual (medical) one to a social (interactive) one and to a model based on human rights. The social model of disability assumes that 'disability arises as a result of limitations experienced by persons who are touched with it, ranging from individual bias to institutional discrimination, from inaccessible public architecture to inaccessible transport system, from segregation of education to provisions excluding disabled people from the labour market' (Piasecki and Stępniak 2003: 7). In turn, a human rights model demands that the way we perceive disability should be one of an everyday aspect of human life, so as to prevent it from being the basis of discrimination or social exclusion. Here, disability is treated in a dynamic way, as an intervention between disabled people and their environments; it is subject to constant changes and is not treated as a deficit of the individual, but as one of their features. This feature causes a person function in a particular way, but the fact should not pose a problem to the individual experiencing disability. The source of the disability exists beyond the individual, somewhere at the point of interaction between the individual and the environment. In this very mode, the idea of equal opportunities is a key notion around which individual and political solutions are formed (Ochonczenko 2005: 34-35). Such an approach suggests also a need to replace the term 'disabled person' by 'a person with disability'. Therefore, I shall use this term in the remainder of this paper.

A higher education institution as a living environment[15] – experiences of applicants and students

The social and systemic models for understanding disability have significant implications in the way we should think about and approach people with disabilities in higher education institutions. Applying the medical model in such an institution leads to assumptions that only fit people is able to fulfil the obligatory course programme in its standard form can become students. People with disabilities (conceived of in a medical model as 'sick people') should first undergo a medical examination and then take up regular studies following the standard curriculum. On the other hand, applying an interactive and human rights model enables all people, both fit people and those with disabilities, to start education. An individualised approach with people with disabilities means that we would determine the difficulties caused by the disability, and establish ways of overcoming them. Then, appropriate adjustments can be made to create alternative programmes. Progression arrangements can vary just as much as the disabilities experienced by students. They depend on the major subjects chosen by the person with disability. The basic principle, however, remains unchanged, that the alternatives and adjustments must not decrease the essential requirements that students with disabilities are expected to satisfy in the course of their studies.

---

[15] The term 'living environment' refers to the functional environment of an institution or a centre. See: E. Marynowicz-Hetka, "Środowisko życia i jego przetwarzanie w toku pracy społecznej" ('Life environment and its processing in the course of social work'). In: E. Marynowicz-Hetka (ed.), (2006) *Pedagogika społeczna* (*Social Pedagogy*), Warszawa: Wydawnictwo Naukowe PWN: 63.

Dfficulties in responding to the needs of students with disabilities has affected both public and private higher education institutions. Private sector institutions, as Widelak points out, have been actively developing in recent years: 'Among 427 higher education institutions operating in Poland at the year-end of 2004, 321 were non-state institutions compared with 126 state, institutions, with 582,100 students attending the former' (2007: 192).

Becoming part of the academic community poses a serious challenge to people with disabilities. Common difficulties experienced by all students beginning their studies include problems connected with the need to adapt to a new environment, changes in learning and teaching methods. For students ith disabilities, the disability adds to these. People with disabilities fear that they will not be able to carry out their students' responsibilities well enough and that they will meet with a hostile reception in their new surroundings. Below are comments on this issue, which were collected from students of two major higher education institutions in Opole, the University of Opole and Opole University of Technology

> I managed to complete my primary and grammar comprehensive schools without any difficulty. It was then a natural thing to decide to continue my education. So the question was: what school next? Where? In my situation , as a person with hearing difficulty who had no concrete career plans, it was not easy to choose. I remember I was tempted to apply for admission to study computer sciences, but the final argument against taking up that challenge was the awareness of the need to chase continuously after broader knowledge in the field, because of rapid technological progress. And on top of this, you have to have your eyes and ears wide open. The same applied to other majors, like psychology, Polish studies, library studies. I took into account Opole University, obviously, and the Academy of Podlasie based in Siedlce since the latter has a good reputation for integration. In the end, I found myself studying pedagogical therapy with special pedagogy at the University of Opole. (A.F.)

> After finishing secondary school, I was afraid of beginning studies, though I dreamed of continuing. I thought I would not manage. I was afraid that before I could gain my diploma, I would lose my sight completely. I spent over four years at home, losing hope that anything positive could still come my way in life. However, a variety of events led me to decide to take up studies. First of all, I got to know that there is a specialist computer equipment adjusted to the needs of blind and partially

sighted people. Thanks to a computer equipped with a program designed for enlarging and providing sound to the graphic material I have obtained, unlimited access in practice to typed texts, the Internet and other sources of information. Studying requires a lot of effort, devoting most of my spare time, and support from my family and friends, but I have never regretted taking the decision. (I.N.)

Beginnings are always difficult. In my case it was so, too; I did cry on many occasions. Over time, however, it got better. I found that whenever I want to achieve something I have to do it by myself. It was very important for me to see how the new environment would accept me; obviously I didn't want to impose my disability, weaknesses in myself or handicaps on them. I positively remember that I indeed got a lot of support from the lecturers. Here I must make it clear – it didn't consist in being exempt from examinations or that I didn't have to read a book or so; on the contrary – I had to prove that I was as good, or maybe even better, as other students [...]." (D.L.)

Persons with motor disability must additionally take into account the presence of architectural barriers. Below is am excerpt from an email about this issue:

In June I will have finished my second year at comprehensive school, but because of the individualised course of studies I have, I have to decide which subjects I want to take my final exams in and what kind of studies I would like to do later. I use a wheelchair (myelo-meningocele) and I am interested in economics. I don't live in Opole [...] It is vital to know if there are lifts, stairs, what kinds of entrance to the buildings there are and if I could use my wheelchair in classrooms and take part in classes. Is there a difference between extramural studies and regular daytime courses when it comes to the places where the classes are held and conditions for disabled people? It is also important for me to know if there is a restroom available. Could you give me information on students' halls of residence, too? Does any of them have rooms adapted to the needs of disabled people, with an appropriate bathroom?" (M.R.)

And also a list of difficulties faced by students:

My main problems are with moving and everything requiring motor coordination [...] The faculty where I am studying is not adjusted at all to the needs of people with motor impairment: there are plenty of stairs, getting into the premises of the Faculty in a wheelchair is impossible. I am lucky because my disability is visible [...] everybody can see that I have great difficulty getting to the second floor to visit the Dean's office. Sometimes I need help, but I must tell those who would like to study in my University that they can always count on assistance on the part of lecturers, on support at the Dean's office, and – first and foremost – on the help from other students." (E.B.)

A college of higher education, as a public institution, is required to remove, among other restrictions, architectural barriers, to support the functioning and study of persons with seeing and hearing difficulty and other disabilities. It is also crucial to build up social awareness on disability issues constantly, as well as careful 'cherishing' by engaging the whole academic community in this process. The community of a higher education institution has great potential in this respect, both individuals (students, lecturers) and that of collective bodies (the college authorities, students' organisations). Thanks to this, initial difficulties can be transformed into success and satisfaction with what it has been possible to achieve. The quotation given below is an example of such change:

"The beginnings were really hard: new people, new teachers, a new style of studying, more demanding requirements from the academic programme and loneliness in the crowd. A few sessions with a psychologist helped me to raise my spirits a little and adapt to the new place and environment. Luckily, there were some schoolmates from my senior high school studying together with me, who helped me survive the first months. That 'survival' [...] consisted of copying notes made during lectures, information on tests, examinations, assignments to prepare for classes and other equally important matters. Not for a moment did the thought cross my mind that I could resign from studying because of 'not hearing'. Initially it was classes that were a real challenge to me as I realised how much of the knowledge 'slips' past my ears. I informed the teachers of my hearing difficulty, asking them to speak while standing in the front part of the classroom and – if possible – closer to me; still, some of them forgot about that in later classes. It was extremely difficult for me to speak in front of the whole group, and what was really humiliating for me was the fact that I couldn't follow the main thoughts of certain lectures, or when I couldn't hear questions that I was asked to answer, or – still – what the discussion was about. Thus, I often didn't know what and how to answer [...] Yet, with time I grew more confident in contacts with people, including my teachers. Better links with my peers made it possible to cooperate in a more effective way and to get to know one another better. All that was complemented by the specific character of my major – special-care pedagogy – and the notion of disability which is connected with it. Fellow students stopped being afraid of me, weren't afraid of crossing the limits of tolerance – was it assisting or maybe taking pity? Additionally, the courses outside the University and other subjects to study, which were on offer at my institute – and of which I availed myself – strengthened my integration with the group. Despite that I remained an individual until the end of our studies, one that had to rely on myself. I didn't look at others, I didn't compare myself to them – I did what I was required to do and the rest developed naturally. (A.F.)

This student raises another important issue in her comments, the need for psychological support to be extended to people with disabilities. Plenty of valuable information and suggestions concerning organization of support groups for youth are presented by Wiesław Sikorski in the book *Psychoterapia grupowa różnych pokoleń* (*Group Psychotherapy of Different Generations*) (2002: 234-318). On the one hand, what matters is securing professional, psychological support; on the other, organizing support groups for students with disabilities. One female student describes this issue in the following way:

Organising meetings with friends, talks on current problems, exchanging observations and opinions on studying different majors, adaptation meetings for disabled freshmen, access to information necessary to organise everyday living (newways of getting financial support, university-related affairs, 'what's up in your world'), or the most important – mutual personal support. After all not every disabled person can have a strong character and a militant, stubborn attitude towards adversity. What I missed during my studies was a sense of being the only DIFFERENT one. I hope it will change in the future. (A.F.)

The experiences described above show what apprehensions and expectations young persons with disabilities have in relation to higher education institutions. In the following part of the paper, I will try to illustrate the institutional reactions to these needs.

Persons with disabilities in higher education institutions – support opportunities

The majority of students' groups include people with disabilities, which, to a lesser or greater degree, affect their studies. Both at Polish and foreign colleges there are blind students and students with sight impairments, with hearing difficulties and deaf, with motor dysfunctions (able to walk by themselves or unable to do so), with chronic diseases, displaying behaviour disorders and also those who have learning difficulties that results from their disability. Working with them requires a suitable adjustment of ways that they may participate in classes, and the resolutions for the difficulties selected to meet individual needs must relate to the type of disability and the particular student's current condition. What might a higher education institution offer to such people so that they would be able to, and would want to, take up and continue their education? At the same time, how to can we prevent them from being socially excluded?

Blind and partially sighted students should have the chance to use equipment that makes it possible for them to write, read set books, make use of the Internet, print materials in Braille or with enlarged print; a good solution may be a library of digital books. Blind and partially sighted students should be taught foreign languages in courses run using methods that do not exploiting the sense of sight.

Deaf people and those with hearing difficulties should have an opportunity to use specialist sound system, which enhances the quality of hearing, should be provided with sign-language interpreters, and have the opportunity to attend classes in foreign languages, conducted in small groups (even though in this case this would mean learning the written form of the given language). Classes should be arranged in the way that the teacher's face ought to be clearly visible all the time in order to allow deaf people to lip-read. Moreover, the speed of teacher's speaking should be slower than that typical of everyday talk. Exaggerated articulation of sounds is not necessary, because it distorts them.

Students with movement dysfunctions should be provided with an open access to most of the buildings where the teaching is provided and to students' halls of residence. They should also have convenient access to the places where classes are held by means of transport adjusted to their needs, support to use library resources, and, if this proves necessary, help from assistants who will help them carry out activities that are too difficult for people with particular disabilities (*e.g.* taking notes). Also computer desks at libraries and computer rooms should be adjusted to the needs of students with disabled hands assistive technology allows people with almost no hand function to be able to use keyboards. The most common adjustments include transport by suitably adapted university buses, car parks with parking space reserved for disabled people and selection of appropriate classrooms.

There are also persons with mental disorders studying at Polish universities; this includes people with anxiety neurosis, depression and schizophrenia. 'There are more and more students with mental disturbances at Polish higher education institutions. According to statistical data provided by the World Health Organisation (WHO), in Europe, one in eight young people suffers from a mental illness, while mental disorders occur in 10% of the adult population. It has been predicted that by the year 2020 the number of mentally ill people will have increased by 50%. Due to strong stigmatization of these kinds of illnesses, the majority of people suffering from psychiatric problems do not seek specialist help" (http://www.bon.uw.edu.pl/budw/niep_psych.html accessed: 25th July 2008).

Mental disorders is not the same as learning disability, and people with psychiatric illness often display above average intelligence. WHO suggests creating suitable conditions for persons suffering from mental disorders so that they may pursue education on the ordinary and self-reliant basis at any higher education institution that they decide to enter (Charter of Ottawa, 1987). Nevertheless, fears remain: 'The apprehensions on the part of lecturers, with this group of students, concern unpredictability of their reactions. However, unpredictable reactions in people with mental disorders usually occur in severe states that are treated in hospital; the majority of mental disorders is of chronic character; after a severe phase remission follows or at least a decisive improvement of the health. At this stage, taking up studying is possible. In some cases, persons with mental disorders need additional support to be able to complete the curriculum. Mental illnesses still evoke negative connotations in society, which results in the fact that for most of the students suffering from this problem there is a strong fear of discrimination and being stigmatised. Consequently, they often hide the true information on their real health condition" (http://www.bon.uw.edu.pl/budw/niep_psych.html; accesed: 25th July 2008).

The above-quoted excerpts are from the Warsaw University webpage, the University having a very broad experience providing support to persons with disabilities. In the academic year 2006-7 there were over 900 students with disabilities there. The decade-long experience of working with students with disabilities at Warsaw University offers a model, unprecedented in Poland. for other higher education institutions to follow. At the same time, it shows that a higher education institution, as a living environment for disabled people, can give them a good chance of development and worthwhile life, but crucially can include them in the currents of social life. It is worth adding that this is not a one-sided influence: students with disabilities are not mere receivers; on the contrary, many of them actively participate in the academic life of their communities, support the activities of interest groups and organisations promoting a more inclusive social environment.

In parenthesis. It is important to recognise that there are also applicants and students who seek to make use of their disability to win privileges, as if they sought exclusion from society. For example:

> I am a disabled person, how can I benefit from this fact? Some extra money? Some easier treatment while studying? (A.C.)

or

> I believe that, as in other state-run higher education institutions in Poland, at least one place in majors close to the vital interests of disabled people, such as social work, should be reserved for a disabled person (L.D.)

The 'principle' called on by this applicant, in reality, does not exist in Polish higher education institutions, since all applicants are treated in the same way. Implementing such a policy would violate the principle of equal opportunities for all. The quoted statements testify to the fact, however, that in particular situations, the label 'disabled person' is desirable and is not then felt as leading to marginalization.

A similar attitude may be observed during study, which is aptly described by Anna Kobylańska (2003: 352). The author observes that some students with disabilities do not 'use' the fact of their handicap until they have difficulty studying, they do not contact the office concerned with people with disabilities; on the contrary, they identify themselves with the community of the able. When problems resulting from their studies start to appear, they begin to become 'disabled students' and then the group 'us, disabled people' becomes the most important social resources for such students, apart from their families. Then the label 'disabled student' is willingly used, serving the purpose of a helpful explanation and excuse. Thus, on the one hand, persons with disabilities want to be treated like all fit ones, like ordinary students; on the other, at a crisis, they are prepared to identify themselves with the group of disabled people, one that is in danger of social exclusion. This can be defined as voluntary exclusion (Grotowska-Leder 2005: 37). Most students with disabilities do not display such reactions, but I want to mention them here to show that 'belonging' and 'non-belonging' to the group, partial inclusion and partial exclusion can occur simultaneously and do not have to mean a general loss of previous social identities.

Opportunities for support to people with disabilities at higher education institutions, mentioned earlier, should always take into account the principle of reasonable rational adjustments (referred to as *reasonable accommodation* or *reasonable adjustment* in the literature on the subject). It means that the adjustment should come within the limits of the so-called common sense, the costs of the accommodation being not disproportionate to the scale of the problem itself. To illustrate this principle let me make use of a case that occurred at my own university – the University of Opole.

In the academic year 2006-7 we had six students with movement dysfunctions, who had to use wheelchairs (including two intramural and four extramural students). One of them requested to have transport organised to and from the University at agreed times. After talks with the University authorities, we came to the conclusion that the expenses necessary to do that, that is, purchase of a specialist vehicle with an appropriate lift, insurance, maintenance, servicing and employment of a driver, were not reasonable from the point of view of the University. Yet, so as not to leave the problem unsolved, we contacted higher education institutions based in Opole, the Municipal Centre for Aid to the Family, associations integrating people with disabilities, as well as the Vice-President of the City of Opole, who had received representations about this issue by then. We made a joint decision and undertook to act towards finding a solution. As a result, we have had a taxi-van adapted for the purpose, which can be called to get people with disabilities to and from the University, to work, to rehabilitation centres, to the cinema or a restaurant. In this way, the interests of many parties have been met and the satisfaction from achieving successful cooperation is of great importance to many citizens in the local community.

Final reflections –excluding education
Over the centuries, the attitude of societies towards disabled people has undergone changes: beginning with sheer hostility through isolation of individuals departing from accepted norms of ordinary health and development, through their segregation. At last, we have moved towards into bringing to life the idea of the social integration of people with disabilities and the normalisation of their living conditions. Today, the time has come go move even further, to implement the idea of inclusion of persons with disabilities into society, which involves education as well. Inclusion means altering schools so that they can meet the needs of their students in a better way and take into account a wider scope of variety. For this to occur 'the school as a whole needs to change in such a way that it should secure access

to the full range of educational and social opportunities for all learners' (cf. http://www.cmpp.edu.pl/integracja/wlaczajace/: accessed 28th July, 2008), as well as lead to avoiding segregation and isolation.

Table 17.1 below compares the traditional segregation-oriented approach in education and the contrasting inclusion-based one:

Table 17.1 *Traditional and inclusive approaches to the needs of students with disabilities*

Traditional approach	Inclusive approach
Education reserved to some	Education for all
Static approach	Flexible approach
Collective, group learning	Individualized learning
Emphasis on teaching	Emphasis on studying
Concentration on the subject and curriculum	Concentration on the person
A diagnostic-descriptive approach concentrating on deficits	Holistic approach concentrating on abilities and possibilities
Chances limited due to segregation	Equality of chances for all

Source: http://www.cmppp.edu.pl/integracja/wlaczajace/ : accessed: 28th July 2008

This vision of inclusive education is being achieved in different regions of the world to a varying degree, being perceived, inside the European Union, to be an effective tool to reach greater social integration (Kość 2006: 59-61). It seems it is a process developing along a road with no return. Examples reaching us from Canada, the USA, Great Britain and Scandinavia show that even in cases of graver and multiple disabilities, the idea of inclusion is possible to implement and yields helpful effects, both for very disabled people themselves and their peers, teachers and, in a broader perspective, for the whole of society. Nevertheless, it needs to be achieved in a well-thought-through and flexible way, securing relevant legislation, with preparatory learning within institutions on many levels and establishing effective supportive service. A higher education institution is a place where all these principles can be successfully accomplished. It seems that Polish higher education centres realise that fact, since they try, as much as the possibilities permit, to create a more friendly environment for people with disabilities.

Bibliography

Grotowska-Leder J. (2005) 'Ekskluzja społeczna – aspekty teoretyczne i metodologiczne' (Social exclusion – theoretical and methodological aspects). In: Grotowska-Leder J. and Faliszek K. (eds), *Ekskluzja i inkluzja społeczna. Diagnoza – uwarunkowania – kierunki działań* (*Social Exclusion and Inclusion. Diagnosis – Conditions – Directions of Activities*), Toruń: Wydawnictwo Edukacyjne „Akapit": 25-45.

http://www/bon.uw.edu.pl/budw/niep_psych.html, strona internetowa Biura ds. Osób Niepełnosprawnych na Uniwersytecie Warszawskim (webpage of the Office in charge of disabled people at Warsaw University).

http://www.cmppp.edu.pl/integracja.wlaczajace/, strona internetowa, zawierająca tekst Nauczanie włączające (webpage including the text: 'Inclusive Teaching'), Warszawa: A. Wyka, PAN.

Karta Ottawska, 1987 (*Ottawa Charter*).

Kobylańska A. (2000) 'Człowiek z niepełnosprawnością jako student – niepełnosprawny czy student?' (A disabled person as a student – a disabled person or a student?). In: Rzedziecka, K. D. and Kobylańska, A. (eds), *Dorosłość, niepełnosprawność, czas współczesny. Na pograniczach pedagogiki specjalnej* (*Adulthood, Disability, Contemporary Time: On the Frontier of Social Pedagogy*), Kraków: IMPULS: 349-356.

Kość, I. (2006) Przemiany systemu polskiej edukacji w warunkach procesu europeizacji (*The Transformations of the Polish Education System in the Conditions of the Europianisation Process*), Szczecin: Oficyna IN PLUS.

Marynowicz-Hetka, E. (2006) *Pedagogika społeczna* (*Social Pedagogy*), Warszawa: Wydawnictwo Naukowe PWN.

Ochonczenko, H. (2005) 'Od "inwalidy" do "Osoby niepełnosprawnej" – przemiany w definiowaniu osób niepełnosprawnych' (From 'an invalid' to 'a disabled person' – transformations in defining disabled people'). In:Ochonczenko, H. and Miłkowska, G. (eds), *Osoba niepełnosprawna w społeczności akademickiej* (*A Disabled Person Within the Academic Community*), Kraków: IMPULS: 17-38.

Piasecki M. and Stępniak M. (eds)(2003), *Osoby z niepełnosprawnością w Unii Europejskiej. Szanse i zagrożenia* (*People with Disabilities in the European Union. Chances and Threats*), Lublin: Fundacja Fuga Mundi.

Sikora P. (2005) 'Ośrodki wsparcia dziennego' (Centres for day-time support). In: Brągiel, J. and Badora, S, (eds), *Formy opieki, wychowania i wsparcia w zreformowanym systemie pomocy społecznej* (*Forms of Care, Child-rearing and Support in the Reformed System of Social Assistance*), Opole: Uniwersytet Opolski: 551-561.

Sikorski W. (2002) *Psychoterapia grupowa różnych pokoleń* (*Group Psychotherapy of Different Generations*), Warszawa: Wydawnictwo Akademickie „Żak".

Weissbrot-Koziarska, A. (2005) 'Szkoła jako środowisko opiekuńczo-wychowawcze'. (School as a care and child-rearing environment). In: Brągiel, J. and Badora, S. (eds), *Formy opieki, wychowania i wsparcia w zreformowanym systemie pomocy społecznej* (*Forms of Care, Child rearing and Support in the Reformed System of Social Assistance*), Opole: Uniwersytet Opolski: 65-73.

Widelak, D. (2007) 'Miejsce wyższego szkolnictwa niepublicznego w polskim systemie edukacyjnym' (The place of the private school system in the Polish education system). In: Chepil, M. and Kuchta, R. (eds) *Europejska wspólna przestrzeń edukacyjna a przeobrażenia oświatowe w Polsce i na Ukrainie 1989-2005* (*The European Common Educational Space and the Educational Transformations in Poland and in Ukraine 1989-2005*), Drohobycz-Lublin: Wydawnictwo: Oddział Redakcyjno-Wydawniczy Państwowego Uniwersytetu Pedagogicznego w Drohobyczu: 189-199.

18 Work with families to prevent social problem behaviour

Miriam Niklová
University of Banská Bystrica, Slovak Republic

Introduction
Families are the most important contributors to people's socialization, having a decisive influence both on the physical and also on the mental development of human beings. This is so not only in childhood, but also in adolescence and maturity. When families fail to meet their responsibilities in this role, schools have to substitute for them, at least partially. Preventing and eliminating social problem behaviour and emotional and behavioural disorders among young people requires families to cooperate with schools and social agencies. Families make the most important contribution in prevention. The school's contribution to preventing emotional and behavioural disorders requires special attention to be paid by teachers at school to pupils coming from dysfunctional families, drugs users and children whose families exhibit similar problems.

Drug misuse
Drug misuse is a major area of social problems affecting families and schools. The need for prevention is highlighted by the national programme in Slovakia to combat drugs misuse, which was adopted by the Slovak government in August 1995. This sets the main programmre for a partnership to combat drug addiction, to decrease illegal sale of drugs. It establishes the main goals for medical and social care of people who have been snared by drug addiction (Pánisová, 1999: 149). The basic principles and key roles of a multidisciplinary approach to the problem of drugs are set out. A practical programme for gradual implementation of anti-drug policy shapes tasks for individual executive departments and central state authorities.

The updated national programe to combat drug misuse covers the period up to 2004 with a strategy extending to 2008. It states that the Slovak Republic will 'support early and effective prevention of the emergence and spread of drug addiction, securing holistic and sustained care of drug addicts and will decisively repress the production, transit and trading traditional and synthetic drugs so that the anti-drug policy of Slovak Republic prevails through complex, balanced and coordinated procedures, while supporting collective responsibility for the health and life of citizens (Národný program boja proti drogám na roky 2004 s výhľadom do roku 2008: 3).

The requirement at an international level to implement prevention comes from EU legislation and policy. The Council of the European Commission approved in June 2005 an EU anti-drug operational plan for years 2005-2008. This pperational plan maintains the structure and goals of the EU anti-drug strategy for 2005-2012 and pubished about a hundred specific regulations to be implemented by member states in the period up to the end of 2008. The EU anti-drug strategy for 2005-2012 focuses on a number of areas, areas, including coordination and the main crosscutting themes are information, research, and evaluation.

School-based prevention of social problem behaviour
It is inevitable that school preventive activities aiming at the prevention of social problem behaviour require carefuly coordination. This is organized by headteachers, education counsellors, school psychologists, and prevention coordinators. The leading role is undertaken by a prevention coordinator appointed by the school headmaster.

The powers of the coordinator of preventive work with pupilas affected by social problem behaviour are regulated by the education management rules published by the Ministry of Education for schools and similar organisations, including the education authorities adminstering local eductaion provision. The prevention coordinator fulfils the following tasks with families:

- school counselling on questions of drug and other addictions
- counseling and professional liaison with coluntary organisations involved in prevention
- coordinating and directing the approach taken in preventive anti-drug educational and informative strategies of teachers in schools
- systematically monitoring and evaluating the long-term development of pupils
- informing parents about preventive counseling and other professional approaches and their potential to prevent drug and other addictions.

While the issues that many schhols face require professional performance of the role of the prevention coordinator, it is often entrusted to teachers without knowledge of social issues and prevention, add this role to their existing workload. This often results in poor effectiveness. So, it is desirable for the prevention coordinator role to be performed by a social pedagogue as a skilled professional who theoretically, conceptually, and methodologically prepared for this work.

The professional position of 'social pedagogue' at elementary and secondary schools has not yet been established in law. Therefore, it has been valuable for the Teaching Methods Centre in Banska Bystrica to develop professional standards for specialist social pedagogues. The project prepared a proposal to systematize a role of a social pedagogue in schools. Emmerová (2007: 61) suggests that the main activities of a social pedagogue at elementary and secondary schools us should focus on the following issues:

- As part of their focus on primary prevention of emotional and behavioural disorders, they would coordinate prevention of drug addiction and of other behaviourla problems,
- Social counselling,
- Active work with pupils from disadvantaged family environments,
- Cooperation with parents.

Recent developments
New legislation in 2008 about the roles of professional staff in schools and similar agencies permits schools to employ social pedagogues. Another important role in preventing social problem behaviour is that of educational advisor, who, with parents' cooperation, helps pupils with in careers guidance and preparation for professional education.

An emphasis on mutual cooperation between school and family is crucial to increasing the effectivess of prevention processes, although increased attention also needs to be paid to pupils coming from dysfunctional and imperiled families. The basis for an effective prevention and education remains a focus on coordinated and systematic work the the factors that affect socialization: family, school and more specialised agencies, such agencies working on educational special needs or the police).

Family support
The appearance of social problem behaviour among young people require social intervention through measures such as family support centres designed to prevent later educational problems . Family support centres provide additional assistance to pupils coming from dysfunctional and at-risk families with the aim of improving family functioning. Social pedagogues in family support centres fulfil the following tasks:

- social and individual counselling for parents, teachers,
- active cooperation with families,

- organizating prevention programmes,
- courses for parents
- visiting families and others in the child's social network.

Youth offending
Another area of social pedagogy practice is casework with families is in the youth offending department. Youht offending practice focuses on preventiing crisis situation in families from arising. The social worker fulfils the following tasks, maintaining a family focus:
- participation in preparing for the dischange of offenders from pena,
- influences family setting of the deliquent,
- makes easier the come back of the deliquent to families and other.

Conclusion
Increasngly, young people disclose experience of alcohol drinking alongside a more tolerant attitude to it among the members of their own family. This is an example of the role of family is a fundamental unit of society and the dominant factor socialization, which influemces the positive development of an individual. Children to a great extent accept family values, including the way drug problems are discussed within the family circle. This forms their attitudes, because the family forms an environment for modeling human behavior. According to J. Hroncová (2007: 12) 'The best prevention is a good family'. However, teachers and parents offering a positive model of the legal drug consumption influences the creation of positive attitudes among children.

Bibloigraphy

Dôvodová správa k zákonu č. 305/2005 Z. z. *O sociálnoprávnej ochrane detí a o sociálnej kuratele.* In: www.rokovania.sk.

Emmerová, I. (2007) Social pedagogue at elementary and secondary schools in the Slovac Republic – present situation and perspective. *New Educational Review.* 2(12)

Hroncová, J. (2007) Prevencia sociálnopatologických javov v školskom prostredí. (w:) *Problematika sociálno-patologických javov v školskom prostredí – stav, prevencia, riešenie,* K. Tišťanová – T. Jablonský (red.), Ružomberok: PF KU.

Koncepcia prevencie sociálnopatologických javov u detí a mládeže na obdobie rokov 2007-2010

Ondrejkovič, P., Poliaková, E. (1999) *Protidrogová výchova.* Bratislava: VEDA.

Zákon č. 305/2005 Z. z. *O sociálnoprávnej ochrane detí a o sociálnej kuratele a o zmene a doplnení niektorých zákonov.*

19 University of the Third Age as the form of social work

Zenon Jasiński
Opole Universtiy

Introduction
The idea of the Universities of the Third Age goes back to people's and adult universities, which originated in Europe in the 19th century. However, their activity was aimed at young people and others who were still at a productive age. On the other hand, the Universities of the Third Age dealt with older people who stopped working; calling this period of life 'the third age' or 'the autumn of life' was widely accepted. The first University of the Third Age started in France, thanks to Professor Pierre Vellas, in Toulouse in 1973 at the Institute of Social Science (Sztajer 2006: 1) and the International Society of the Universities of the Third Age has been active as early as since 1975 (Association International des Universités du Troisieme Age, abbrev.: AIUTA).

The idea was quickly adopted in Poland. In 1975 in Warsaw, on the initiative of the Professor of Medicine Halina Szwarc, the first University of the Third Age (often called: U3A) (http://www.cmkp.edu.pl: accessed: 15th March 2009). in Poland came into existence at the Postgraduate Medical Training Centre in Warsaw. More U3As were created during the 1970s in places like: Wrocław, Opole, Szczecin, Poznań, Łódź; these were followed by others in the 80s. Anyway, the most such universities started in Poland at the turn of the 21st century.

Social conditions for the rise of Universities of the Third Age
There are some reasons for a strong interest in the U3As. Firstly, it is related to the economic transformation of retirement of a vast group of people, a group that used to be very active during their working life, with a strong need of affiliation and educational needs not fully satisfied in spite of the education that they had already received. It was an intellectually competent group, wishing to share their experience, skills and knowledge. Secondly, it is associated with increasing standards of living and appreciation for an individual in the society.

Last but not least, U3A forming in Poland was also influenced by development of such academic disciplines as: adult learning, gerontology, social pedagogy focusing on the life and quality of life of older people, connected with satisfying their needs.[16]

The need to create new U3As arises from various reasons. Firstly, due to social progress, retiring people are generally in good physical and psychological health. The number of these people is quite high as technological and social change makes them redundant and leads to earlier retirement than in the past. In many occupations, the retirement age has been lowered, especially for women (for some jobs and countries even to people aged 55). Projections of the number of people in a post-productive phase of life in Poland indicate that there will be a considerable increase in the near future; if there were 5,765 thousand in 2002, the number is estimated to reach 7,468 thousand in 2015. For example, if in Opole Voivodship (county council area) in this period, people in a post-productive phase constituted 15% of the Voivodship population; in 2015 the percentage will amount to 20, 2% and in 2030 will increase to as much as 28, 6% (Szukalski, 2008: 37). Therefore, Professor Rajkiewicz claims that: 'The problem of old people should be the problem of the strategic importance to our country (Rajkiewicz 2008: 24).

As a result of the transformation of the economic system in Poland, many factories and companies were closed down and their employees were retired early, considerably increasing the number of third age people. These people have often unsatisfied educational needs which could not be brought to fruition due to a difficult situation in Poland after the 1939-45 war, as the country concentrated rather on rebuilding and reestablishment of the new areas brought into the nation at the end of the war.

The pensioners have relatively a lot of free time and they are willing to use it for such activities as learning, and maintaining social relations. After retiring, people previously active feel emptiness, loneliness, a decline in prestige; they complain about being redundant or worsening financial situation (Zych 1999: 107-113). At the same time, they are aware of their

---

[16] For more on olderpeople needs, see for example R. Andrzejczyk, *Starzenie się społeczeństwa*. Warszawa 2007; K. Baczewski, *Starzy ludzie i starość w społeczeństwie i kulturze*, Lublin 1994; T. Buklewicz, *Ludzie – starość*, PWN Warszawa 2000; W. Diakonowicz, *Psychologia starości*, PWN Warszawa 2000; L. Dyczewski, T. Grabowski, *Starość –czas odpoczynku*, Branta Bydgoszcz 2006; B. Klonowicz, *Oblicza starości*, Warszawa 1979; P. Laszkowski, *Seniorzy*, Warszawa 2005 l. Romaniuk, L. Ligocka, *Problemy ludzi starszych. Wybrane zagadnienia*, PWN, Warszawa 2005; T. Sadowski, M. Zbolecki, *Krótkie Życie*, PWN Warszawa 1998; *Wybrane problemy procesu starzenia się człowieka*, ed. St. Rogala, WSZiA Opole 2007; M. Susłowska, *Psychologia starzenia się i starości*, PWN Warszawa 1989, A. Zych, *Człowiek wobec starości. Szkice z gerontologii społecznej*, Katowice 1999.

abilities and personal or professional experience acquired during their lifetime. They want to be part of their community, to be visible, and they want and should be active. We have to agree with Szarota's statement that contemporary retired people want to be active, don't want to be marginalized, want to be noticed in a society (Szarota 2007: 132-134). Not all of them are able to arrange their life after retirement. Psychologically, it is a very difficult period for a lot of people (Schulz 2008: 9-12). The U3As, by undertaking suitable activities, can help with adaptation to old age. Jankowski speaks about 'creating social stimulators and conditions for developing one's interests and exploratory activities' not only by organized forms of broadening awareness, including the U3As, but also a variety of community associations (Jankowski 2008: 200).

The roles of U3As can be considered from the point of view of adult education, psychology and social psychology and social work as well.

Existing U3As most frequently aim to:

- disseminate educational initiatives,
- building up the intellectual, psychological, social and physical functioning of older people,
- deepen and broaden retired people's knowledge and skills,
- facilitate relations with community organisations such as: health services, cultural centres and rehabilitation centres,
- engage the students in activities benefiting their community,
- maintain social bonds and interpersonal communication among retired people (http://www.utw.pl/: accessed: 16th March 2009).

Table 19.1 *The oldest Polish Universities of the Third Age*

Name	Place	Year of origin	Number of students in 2007
Uniwersytet III Wieku im. Haliny Szwarc	Warszawa	1975	1100
Uniwersytet III Wieku przy Uniwersytecie Wrocławskim	Wrocław	1976	651
Stowarzyszenie Uniwersytetu III	Opole	1977	721

Wieku Przy Miejskim Ośrodku Pomocy Rodzinie			
Stowarzyszenie Uniwersytet III Wieku w Szczecinie	Szczecin	1978	300
Uniwersytet III Wieku	Poznań	1979	1300
Łódzki Uniwersytet III Wieku im. Heleny Kretz	Łódź	1979	1000
Jagielloński Uniwersytet III Wieku	Kraków	1982	180
Uniwersytet III Wieku w Uniwersytecie Śląskim	Katowice	1982	500
Uniwersytet III Wieku przy Uniwersytecie Rzeszowskim	Rzeszów	1983	350
Lubelski Uniwersytet III Wieku	Lublin	1985	1000

Source: Extracted by the author from: *Repozytorium Uniwersytety III wieku*, parts I-V, „e-mentor" 2007 nr 18-22

Constituting universities led to a metamorphosis in predecessor organisation: the first were founded by educational societies, often by the Polish Association for Adult Education, partly by colleges which dealt either with adult education or with old age. Colleges had no finance for this purpose, they were usually academic patrons and formally U3As were run by the departments of culture or social welfare. Out of 126 U3A active in 2007, 26 were under the auspices of colleges, six under the management of permanent learning centres or even high schools, 10 managed by cultural centres, six under the auspices of community organisations and trade unions. In 48 cases it was impossible to find out who actually runs a U3A. At present, most U3As work under patronage of municipal social welfare centres and other municipalities. In practice, it is valuable that a local agency manages them. It is worth emphasizing that many state vocational colleges, which were founded in small local environments, took U3A over.

At present, although U3As in Poland do not operate independently and do not have legal status, they stay under care of:

- colleges or academies,
- adult education organisations, for example regional or educational societies, or centres of learning and training
- social welfare centres, cultural centres and retired people's day centres managed jointly by different agencies in the local community.

Table 19.2 *The location of U3As in Poland in 2007*

Voivodship	Number of universities	Number of students
Dolnośląskie	10	1932
Kujawsko-pomorskim	5	1478
Lubelskie	11	1974
Lubuskie	9	1643
Łódzkie	4	1980
Małopolskie	9	1864
Mazowieckie	22	1457
Opolskie	7	1261
Podkarpackie	4	899
Podlaskie	4	750
Pomorskie	9	2440
Śląskie	13	3450
Swiętokrzyskie	3	547
Warmińsko-Mazurskie	3	1268
Wielkopolskie	7	2366
Zachodniopomorskie	6	549
Total	126	25858

Source: Extracted by the author from:*: Repozytorium Uniwersytety III wieku w Polsce*, part I-V, „e-mentor" 2007 nr 18-22.

Zdzisław Sztajer, the chairman of the Halina Szwarc U3A board at the Postgraduate Medical Training Centre, points out the various functions of U3A as: a teaching-academic function, preventive function (in gerontology), educational function (how to live in new circumstances), medical function (supporting fitness and psychological and physical capacity) (Sztajer 2006: 9).

The functioning of Polish U3As varies, depending on the managing organsiation, tradition and opinion in the local community. The biggest, such as the one at Jagiellonian University or the Halina Szwarc U3A in Warsaw, have over 1000 students. In the last few years over 130 U3As have started in Poland. It shows a good demand for this form of activity and its popularity in our society. In years 2007-8 the press reported that not everyone wishing to start this activity was accepted due to the lack of places.

Table 19.3 *Forms of activity of the chosen U3A in Poland*

Name/Year of Origin/ Place	Forms of activity
The Halina Szwarc U3A at the Postgraduate Medical Training Centre in Warsaw 1975	- Lectures, seminars - Foreign language learning (English, French, German, Italian) - IT courses; literary group, memoirs group; painting group, drawing school, photographic courses, *bel canto* choir, traveller's club, bridge group, cultural events group, library; movement rehabilitation consulting; gymnastics group, tourist-sightseeing group; - Going to sanatoriums and rest trips; - students' record group, Cooperation with U3A group, administrative-organising group, friend-to-friend help group, 'information bulletin' planning for 2008-9;
U3A at Wrocław University. Wrocław 1976	- Lectures, seminars, foreign language learning, movement rehabilitation and rehabilitative gymnastics, swimming, tourism, the theatre of poetry, cabaret, painting and dancing workshops, meetings, inspiring the students' creativity, 'the U3A Daily'
Association of the U3A at the Municipal Family Service Centre. Opole 1977	- Lectures on: medicine, psychology, gerontology, physical education, history, culture and art; - classes on foreign languages (English, French, German, Esperanto); -circles and sections: art, literature, gymnastics, swimming, knitting, gardening, bridge, interactive help and a choir;
Association of the U3A in Szczecin. Szczecin 1978	- Lectures and section activities: bio-medical, gymnastics, art history and museum management, historical, linguistics, culture science, Japanese culture and language, puppet-show, literary, social science, art, swimming, psychological, stage, theatrical, tourist; - macramé and literary workshops; - courses on foreign languages (English, French, German, Esperanto, Spanish,

	Japanese, Russian, Italian);
The U3A. Poznań 1979	- Lectures and section activities: physical activities (walking tours, Hatha yoga, Qi gong, swimming, rehabilitation exercises in the swimming pool, gymnastic section, therapeutic dance), culture and art (history of art, history of architecture, 'Camerata di Musica' choir, art section), computer section, astronomy and others; - foreign languages (English, French, German, Spanish and Italian); - circles, for example: University Chaplaincy, globe-trotters, theatre lovers, skittles, history lovers, bridge, literary, cyclist, flowers lovers;
The Helena Kretz U3A in Łódź. Łódź 1979	Lectures on various subjects; activities within sections: bio-medical, gymnastic, art history and museum management, historical, linguistics, scientific culture, Japanese culture and language, puppet-show, literary, social science, art, swimming, psychological, stage, theatrical, tourist; moreover, there are macramé and literary workshops; students can also attend foreign languages courses (the U3A in Łódź offers courses on the following languages: English, French, German, Esperanto, Spanish, Japanese, Russian, Italian);
Sopot U3A at the permanent learning centre. Sopot 2003 - (1100 students)	Lectures on various fields of science and culture – open lectures covering other academic fields, meetings with representatives of the cultural industries; -workshops: computer, activities improving and maintaining dexterity (artistic workshops), physical activity classes (gymnastics, self-defence), tourist and dance therapy workshops; - presentation of famous film masterpieces; - cooking workshops; - language courses at a beginner and advanced level (English and German) and regular workshops dealing with interpersonal communication, psychology of advertising,

	psychology of love and relaxation workshops. The workshops on mind gymnastics attract great interest. There are also rehearsals of reciters' group and a dancing group *U3A Zorba*;

Source: Extraxcted by the author from: *Repozytorium Uniwersytety III wieku*, part I-V, „e-mentor" 2007 nr 18-22; comp.: www.utw.uni.wroc.pl; hwww.cmkp.edu.pl; www.utw.poznan.pl; sutwszczecin@op.pl; utw@sopot.pl; www.3wick.uni.lodz.pl.

Comparing activities in the oldest Polish U3As, with the U3A in Sopot which started as late as in 2003 allows some generalizations (see Table 3). The Sopot University belongs to this group of new universities which very quickly gathered many participants and already in 2007 it numbered 1000 students. This comparison indicates that activities in U3As are very similar and can be categorized as follows: intellectual activity (lectures, seminars, discussions), creative and hobby activity (artistic, art, dancing, recitation teams, choirs, cabarets), physical and healthy lifestyle activity (gymnastics, tourism, self-defence, trips, therapeutic and rehabilitation visits), communication activity (foreign language learning, interpersonal communication, use of the Internet), public activity (voluntary work, interpersonal help groups), social activity (bridge sections, various clubs), manual activity. It seems that these forms of U3A activity met the students expectations.

Two trends can be distinguished in the work of U3As. The French trend leans towards intensive work, with high academic standards; thus, the classes are run by the college lecturers, there is division into terms, students have credit records, a secondary education certificate is a condition to be acceptance. The English model is more extensive, aimed at meeting students' expectations, where classes resemble an English club and are run by people from the local community. In this model, maintaining relationships is more important than gaining new competences (Szarota 2008: 3).

> U3A enables people who have finished their employment to acquire knowledge, fulfilling their interests as well as performing active and creative work in their community (Broczek 2007: 2).

U3A can satisfy educational needs and support older people by adjusting the curricula (Rogala 2008: 222-225). Professor Halina Szwarc, the founder of the first Polish U3A, paid special attention help and support for older people (Szwarc 1990: 88).

Problems of U3A

In 2008, a futures committee 'Poland 2000 plus' of the Presidium of Polish Academy of Sciences, addressed a memorandum to important organisations in the Polish Republic about a programme fpr improving the situation of older people. In the memorandum, the issue of the education for the retired, IT education, supporting their cultural and social activity as well as the development of Universities of the Third Age were all highlighted, separately from the material, health and nursing matters (Memorial of Prognosis 2008: 27).

The development of U3As interested Polish-American Freedom Foundation which started in 2005, through the Jagiellonian University, the programme of support for U3A in Poland. The programme has resulted not only in the increase of the amount of U3A activity and the number of students (from 28 in 2005 to 180 U3As in 2009, with about 60 thousand students) but, also very important, in creating in December 2007 the National Federation of U3A Associations. The main goal of the Federation is representing U3A to state and non-governmental authorities and colleges when they are considering U3A activity and problems of older people. It strives not only to create a favourable climate, but also to establish a legal and financial basis for educational and development projects for retired people, creating common ground for cooperation between colleges or academies and U3A. Other results of this programme were academic conferences organized in the Polish Parliament[17] and local communities[18], as well as a competition for the small and big projects for U3A[19]. From this, universities that received grants could improve their work. Most U3As struggle with financial problems and insufficient space for their activities. Low membership fees don't cover the

---

[17] See letter of Wiesława Borczyk, the chair of the Board of the National Federation of Universities of the Third Age Associations, dated 22nd January 2009 to Senator Mieczyslaw Augustyn, chair of Parliamentary Group for Older People on the activities of the Federation, letter dated 8th November 2008 to Dr Michał Boni, the Chief of Prime Minister's Strategic Advisors' Team.

[18] 5th International U3A Conference: 'U3A as the supporter of social intergration in Europe' (9-10th November 2008); 4th International U3A Conference: 'Active Third Age' (Płock 11-12th November 2007); 3rd International U3A: 'U3A – for itself and for others' (Słupsk 15-17th November 2006); Universities of the Third Age. possibilities and practice, (Warszawa 25th May 2007, Polish Parliament, Warszawa.

[19] As a result of the competition 19 larger projects were granted with the sum of 419.2 thousand PLN and 27 small projects with the sum of 234.5 thousand PLN, http://www.utw.pl/.

maintenance costs. Therefore, the U3A Federation does its best to create legal opportunities for financing universities through the state budget.

Each U3A has their own self-governing body and acts through its membership groups. The internal structures of particular universities depends on the number of participants, their needs and local opportunities. For example, the H. Szwarc Warsaw U3A has its own legal identity and employs three people, manages its own finances, office and numerous groups. However, most U3A rely on voluntary work of their students.

Final remarks

Democratization processes in Poland, society appreciation for an individual, increased activity in local communities create a favourable climate for developing the highest quality permanent education for people in the post-productive phase of their lives; at the same time, it is extremely valuable kind of social work in a society where people's knowledge and skills create social capital. It iscrucial, though, according to the Board of the National Federation of Universities of the Third Age Associations, to adopt system solutions which can create an effective legal and financial base for U3A work.[20]

Translation: Marzanna Pogorzelska

---

[20] Letter of Wiesława Borczyk, chair of the Board of the National Federation of Universities of the Third Age Associations, dated 8th November 2008 to Dr Michał Boni, the Chief of Prime Minister's Strategic Advisors' Team, Warszawa on the declaration of participation in discussion about retired people in the context of the report 'Polish Intellectual Capital'. Website http://www.utw.pl.

Bibliography

Broczek K. (2007) *Starzenie się i starość w opinii słuchaczy Uniwersytetu Trzeciego i Wieku Szkoły Głównej Handlowej i studentów Akademii Medycznej w Warszawie E – mentor* 4.

http://www.cmkp.edu.pl *Uniwersytet Trzeciego Wieku im. Haliny Szwarc przy Centrum Medycznym Kształcenia Podyplomowego w Warszawie*. Directory for the academic year: 2008/2009.

http://www.utw.pl/ homepage of National Federation of Universities of the Third Age Associations.

Jankowski D. (2008) *Edukacja, aktywność kulturalna, rekreacja ludzi* [in:] *Polska w obliczu starzenia się społeczeństwa, Komitet Prognoz 'Polska 2000 plus' przy* Warszawa: *Prezydium* PAN, , for more information, see: D. Jankowski (2006), *Aktywność kulturalna dorosłych w sytuacji potężnienia rynku kultury i bezwładu edukacji ogólnej. Wyzwania dla animacji*. In: Akademickie kształcenie animatorów i menadżerów kultury w Polsce, (ed.) B. Jedlewska, Lublin: UMCS: 195-211.

Memorandum of the Futures Committee 'Poland 2000 plus' at the Presidium of Polish Academy of Sciences addressed to the leading organisations of the Polish Republic regarding improving the situation of older people. In: *Polska w obliczu starzenia się społeczeństwa, Komitet Prognoz 'Polska 2000 plus' przy Prezydium*. Warszawa: PAN: 2008.

Rajkiewicz A.(2008) Polska w obliczu starzenia się społeczeństwa. In: *Polska w obliczu starzenia się społeczeństwa, Komitet Prognoz 'Polska 2000 plus' przy Prezydium* Warszawa: PAN:4-26.

Rogala S. (2008) Psychologiczno-spoleczene uwarunkowania procesu starzenia się społeczeństwa. In: *Polska w obliczu starzenia się społeczeństwa, Komitet Prognoz „Polska 2000 plus" przy Prezydium*. Warszawa: PAN:220-245.

Schulz A. (2008) Znaczenie aktywizacji psychicznej ludzi starszych. In: *Uniwersytety Trzeciego Wieku - Aktywny trzeci wiek*. Kraków:1-14.

Szarota Z. (2008) Lęki i niepokoje pokolenia '60+' w kontekście ekskluzji społecznej. In: Rogala, St (ed)(2007) *Wybrane problemy procesu starzenia się człowieka*. Opole: WSZiA por. *E-mentor* 2008, 3:2-10.

Szarota Z. (2008) Przestrzeń edukacyjna Uniwersytetu Trzeciego Wieku, *E- mentor* 2008, nr 3:2-12.

Sztajer Z. (2006), Idea powstawania i działalność uniwersytetów trzeciego wieku, *Edukator zawodowy: The magazine for teachers, counsellors, methodology advisors, educators in vocational education* 12th April 2006:1-10.

Szukalski P.(2008) Polscy seniorzy w przyszłości. In: *Polska w obliczu starzenia się społeczeństwa, Komitet Prognoz 'Polska 2000 plus' przy Prezydium.* Warszawa: PAN:196-210.

Szwarc H. (1990) Działalność uniwersytetów trzeciego wieku i innych organizacji gerontologicznych na rzecz opieki i pomocy ludziom starym. *Praca Socjalna* 3-4: 89-112.

Zych A. (1999), *Człowiek wobec starości. Szkice z gerontologii społecznej.* Katowice: Wydawnictwo Śląsk.

20   Helping individual caregivers of people who are dying using a groupwork intervention

Margaret Reith[21]
Senior Social Worker, Princess Alice Hospice, Esher, UK (now senior social worker, Epson and St Helier University Hospitals NHS Trust, UK)

Context
The setting in which this group work took place was a hospice in England. The hospice has 28 beds and provides a specialist palliative care service to a catchment population of over one million people in the Surrey and South West London area. In addition to the in-patient unit, 750 dying people are supported in their own homes by the hospice community team of specialist palliative care nurses. People in the area with a diagnosis of a terminal illness are referred by their family doctors to the hospice for palliative care. Their family caregivers may also need support from the hospice to help them as they care for their relative.

Why do adults who are caring for dying relatives need support?
Traditionally health and social care services have tended to focus on the needs of the service user and may even have overlooked the equally important but different needs of the caregiver. Payne suggests in Chapter 2 of this volume that this has been an important recent development in UK adult social care policy. A diagnosis of terminal illness affects the whole family. 'In some cases, the carers are in more distress than the dying person. Not only will they be struggling with the emotional turmoil of seeing their loved one dying, but they may also find themselves exhausted by their caring duties' (Leason, 2004: 208). Caregivers often find themselves having to take on new roles that were previously carried out by the person who is ill.

The burden of caring should not be underestimated: 'Caring is hard work, becomes a full time job and forces life changes of great magnitude to the extent that one's former life is lost' (Brown, 2003: 73). These changes may be associated with financial, practical, physical and emotional demands being made of the caregiver. The caregiver's own health can suffer with the result that physical and mental health issues may arise for the carer. People caring for another family member may experience a range of emotions including anxiety, fear, anger, sadness, despair, resentment and guilt. For

---

[21] Margaret.reith@esth.nhs.uk

example, maintaining hope in the face of despair can lead to feelings of dishonesty. Similarly, a caregiver who experiences a sense of relief at the prospect of the caring role coming to an end can also feel guilt. Caregivers are likely to experience mixed emotions because the task of caring is so complex.

As a result of the many issues that arise when a family member takes on the task of caring caregivers often feel bewildered, isolated and alone facing new challenges and responsibilities with which they are not familiar. Research into the experiences of caregivers looking after someone with motor neurone disease highlighted that 'carers felt insufficiently cared for themselves, particularly in terms of emotional support' (Brown, 2003: 74). Against this background it can be seen that adult social care services should take into account the needs of the caregiver in addition to those of the service user. Rabow and his associates identify five 'burdens' of family care-giving as: time and logistics, physical tasks, financial costs, emotional burdens and mental health risks and lastly physical health risks (Rabow et al, 2004). Not only is it important for caregivers to be able to access support for themselves but this is likely to have secondary gains for the patient. 'Family care-giving is typically at the core of what sustains patients at the end of life' (Rabow et al, 2004). Caregivers may experience the task of caregiving as a 'burden' but they may also experience caring for the person they love at the end of life as immensely rewarding and enriching, particularly if they feel adequately supported along their journey.

Why offer a group intervention?
A group of people sharing similar problems can offer more than can be provided individually. While such help can be provided individually there is some research that shows that some of these 'important processes occur only, or occur best, in a group setting' (Sutton and Liechty, 2004: 19), and Firth points out that 'groups can be very effective in returning power and control to people who are particularly vulnerable (Firth, 2000: 34). UK government guidance recommends that all specialist palliative care providers should provide support for caregivers and families by setting up 'arrangements for families and carers to meet other families and carers who have experienced similar situations, if wished' (NICE Guidance 2004, 12.25). When 'caregivers find themselves in support groups with other "like" members, these barriers are removed, and members are able to share their feelings openly and honestly' (Sutton and Liechty, 2004: 521).

Having considered this evidence it was agreed that a group intervention would be offered to caregivers who are providing care to a family member who is already known to the palliative care service offered by the hospice.

However, this decision requires further thought about what sort of group intervention model to adopt.

Different models of groupwork intervention
Should the group be open or closed? Should there be a fixed number of sessions or should the group be open-ended with no fixed time-limit? How frequently should the group meet? How long should each session last? How are caregivers referred to the group? Who should facilitate the group? How many members make the group viable and helpful? We piloted three models of group intervention before arriving at the current model as our preferred choice.

First we tried an open group that was open-ended and met monthly. This proved unsatisfactory because the meetings were too infrequent to enable a sense of continuity to develop. Second, we tried several closed groups that met for six or eight sessions over twelve or sixteen weeks, each session lasting an hour and a half. Using this model it was difficult to know exactly when the next group would be starting so it was hard to maintain momentum. Also members felt it was unhelpful for their source of support to cease after just a few weeks. Following evaluation of each pilot we revised the model in the light of feedback from the group members and the experience gained by the facilitators.

Our model of group intervention
We now run an open, ongoing group that meets weekly for one and a half hours. The average weekly attendance is between four and nine caregivers. We always run the group with two leaders who co-facilitate the group. Initially, in the first few groups, we kept the facilitators the same for each closed group. But with an ongoing group we had to change this model to give group leaders a break from time to time. We prefer to have two facilitators who come from different disciplines. We have found it helpful to have a nurse and a social worker whose skills and knowledge complement each other. But both the occupational therapist and the chaplain have shared the facilitation role. The present group has been meeting weekly for nearly three years.

Referrals to the group come from the hospice community palliative care nurses, the day hospice and the hospice social workers.

Bereavement issues
It was important to ask the group members at an early stage before any of the caregivers' relatives had died what they would want to be shared within the group when a relative dies. They made it very clear they wanted openness

and honesty and for information about the death to be shared within the group. They also wanted to be able to still attend the group at least once or twice more afterwards to say goodbye to people they had shared so much with.

Recurring themes
The facilitators kept notes on the content and process of each session. From their recording it was possible to identify the concerns and issues most frequently raised within the group. These themes fall broadly into two categories: emotional and practical. Emotional themes predominate.

Emotional concerns
The emotional content included many discussions about depression and low mood. Group members talked about feeling trapped, 'a prisoner in their own homes'' this gave rise to loneliness and isolation. Sometimes it was sheer exhaustion that led to depression. Anxiety and worry tended to result in poor sleep patterns and exacerbated exhaustion and fatigue.

Communication issues were another topic to which group members frequently returned. These included relationship issues especially with the sick partner. One person discussed with the group how she could not talk to her husband about his dying, his sadness and his funeral wishes, and how this distressed and troubled her. The group offered a number of strategies for opening up difficult areas of communication and the following week the person concerned reported that as a result of the help she had received from the group she had the courage and confidence to broach these difficult subjects with her partner. As a result they were able to share their distress that they were both feeling but hiding from each other. She said she felt much better, no longer burdened by the barrier between them. Within the group, empathy and compassion were demonstrated in powerful ways as people supported each other following receiving bad news about lack of treatment options or deterioration in their partner's condition.

Caregiver fatigue, already mentioned, was a common problem but caregivers benefited from encouraging each other to find time during the week for themselves as well as identifying the need for regular respite breaks which were offered by the hospice. This enabled them to legitimize their need for breaks from the demands of caring and helped reduce the guilt experienced by many when they took time away from their partners for themselves.

Adjusting to the role of caring was another issue that affected everyone. Taking on new and unfamiliar roles, coming to terms with the loss of their previous lives, the loss of a future together, the loss of their partner's role and adjusting to the power imbalance in their changed relationship were all areas of difficulty highlighted by group members. However, they enabled each other through mutual support and encouragement to face these difficult changes in their lives.

Guilt was another emotion shared by many within the group. For example, someone might report feeling at the end of their tether and so not always as patient as they would wish when their partner was demanding, slow, incontinent etc. By offering alternative ways of reframing the problem and so helping people to recognize the difference between guilt and regret it enabled them to see the appropriateness of regret and the inappropriateness of guilt.

One of the strengths of the group was that people felt able to trust each other with uncomfortable emotions such as feelings of anger and resentment, which they were often unable to express elsewhere. For some caregivers, particularly younger ones, they articulated their sense of being cheated of a future, of their own lives being either on hold or even destroyed. They felt resentful of friends who were not living with similar burdens. Without a safe space to express the negative side to caregiving, such thoughts and feelings could become quite destructive.

All group members shared difficulties about coping with the wider family and other people's distress. For example, they were relieved to find they were not alone in crossing over the road to avoid acquaintances. Group members looked together at how to talk to their children and grandchildren about what is happening and how best to prepare them.

Practical issues
In addition to these emotional issues many practical concerns were also addressed. Information about equipment, services, helpful tips on the task of caregiving and so on were shared and offered to each other. Information about welfare benefits, care packages, care agencies, nursing homes, legal issues and obtaining travel insurance were some of the topics discussed.

Each person was on an individual and unfamiliar journey, but by pooling information they were able to signpost each other in the right direction, because they had been on at least part of the same road.

Food and nutrition were recurring topics, both in connection with the sick person and for the caregivers themselves. Caregivers shared experiences of struggling to find food to cook that their partner would enjoy, only to throw it away when not eaten. In relation to being in the caregiving role, they could see the importance of looking after themselves, but talked about not wanting to eat if their partner was unable to share in the meal. They also recognized that for some of them comfort eating was an issue. For many months, group members regularly made cakes to bring with them to share in the group session.

Challenges
One of the ongoing challenges has been recruitment and maintaining the level of referrals. As people die, the group changes and new caregivers join it. Maintaining awareness of the caregivers' group in the minds of all potential referrers remains an issue for us, but has been alleviated by having a dedicated volunteer whose role is to make contact with potential group members and welcome them on arrival. Interestingly the UK government guidance on providing palliative and supportive care identifies caregiver recruitment as a common problem with caregiver groups (NICE, 2004, 12:48). Leaving their sick partner at home so that they can attend the group is understandably a real barrier to attendance. However, our experience is that while it may be difficulty, if the caregiver can overcome their initial resistance their commitment to the group counteracts this. As a result, people go to great lengths to ensure that their partner can be left safely to enable them to attend. Harding and his colleagues, evaluating a closed, short-term group found similarly, that caregivers were highly ambivalent both to their own needs and to accessing supportive interventions (Harding et al, 2004). In our group, by being supportive of each other, caregivers were empowered through the group experience to recognize their own needs and feel able to address them.

Running an open-ended group required us to ensure continuity of leadership, while changing the facilitators from time to time so that they could take annual leave and have breaks from running the group. We hope we have achieved a balance between continuity and flexibility by handing over the facilitation to two more leaders after three or four months and having a small pool of social workers and nurse specialists and an occupational therapist who share the leadership role.

A third challenge is to ensure that new members are included and feel welcome when they come to an already established group. We have done this by asking existing members always to make a point of telling new members of their own experiences of how they felt when they came to their first session. Many found the initial meeting stressful, but after getting to know the others in the group they come to describe the group as being 'a life line' and enormously important to them.

Challenges for caregivers

As described above, many caregivers do not see themselves as people who join groups, and this is a hurdle to overcome with help from the others. A second hurdle is feeling that it is possible to leave their sick relative at home to attend. NICE guidance (2004: para 27.3) reports that caregivers are often reluctant to consider their own needs and 'tend to put the needs and interest of the patients above their own'. We have found this less of a difficulty once a routine has been established.**Evaluation**

To evaluate the group we asked for feedback from group members using a questionnaire. The fact that most people attend the group very regularly for as long as they are looking after their relative is in itself evidence of a service that is meeting the needs of its attendees. The commitment on the part of individuals to the group, to looking out for each other and to sharing very personal and painful experiences indicates its value to its members. The feedback highlighted the strength of feeling from caregivers describing the group as a 'lifeline', of not wanting to miss sessions and not wanting a time-limited group. Members emphasized the value and power of sharing common experiences with others in a similar situation to their own, the safety of the group being fundamental. They identified the importance of being able to laugh and to cry, of being able to explore distressing emotions and realize they are not alone. Perhaps two of the most important features of the group are the safe space it provides to express negative thoughts without being judged or criticized, and the fact that there is always a place for sharing humour within the group.

Conclusion

'Clearly a support group for carers cannot meet all the needs of palliative carers' (Hearn, 2004: 204), but we have found that the direct sharing of experiences between caregivers is a powerful means of empowering people to help each other. Recently one member told the group how she had been to see a psychotherapist. When the other members asked her how it had been for her, she replied that she much preferred the group because she felt safe, knew she could trust the others in the group and felt she could discuss and confide in a totally honest and open way with people who understood because they had shared the ups and downs of caregiving.

The experience of running a group for people who are caring for a family member with a terminal illness has strengthened our resolve as health and social care professionals to offer caregivers the opportunity to meet together to enable them to support each other.

Bibliography

Bowen, S. (1999) *Record and Evaluation of Carers' Group* unpublished report

Brown, J. (2003) User, carer and professional experiences of care in motor neurone disease *Primary Health Care Research and Development* **4**: 207-217

Firth, P. (2000) Picking up the Pieces: Groupwork in Palliative Care. In Manor O (ed) *Ripples: groupwork in different settings.* London: Whiting and Birch: 30-7

Harding, R., Higginson, I., Leam, C., Donaldson, N., Pearce, A., George, R., Robinson, V., and Taylor, L. (2004) Evaluation of a short-term group intervention for informal carers of patients attending a home palliative care service *Journal of Pain and Symptom Management* 27(5): 396-408

Harding, R. and Leam, C. (2005) Clinical notes for informal carers in palliative care: recommendations from a random patient file audit *Palliative Medicine* 19: 639-642

Hearn, F. (2004) Setting up a support group for carers in palliative care *European Journal of Palliative Care* 11(5): 204-206

Leason, K. (2004) Final Farewell *Community Care* 3-9 June: 28-29National Institute for Clinical Excellence NICE (2004) *Improving Supportive and Palliative Care for Adults with Cancer* London: NICE

Rabow, M., Hauser, J., and Adams, J. (2004) Supporting Family Caregivers at the End of Life *JAMA* 291(4): 483-491

Reith, M. (2004) *Carers' Group Evaluation Report submitted to Princess Alice Hospice Clinical Issues Committee*

Sutton, A., and Liechty, D (2004) Clinical Practice with Groups in End-of-Life Care. In Berzoff, Joan., and Silverman, Phyllis. (eds) *Living with Dying: A Handbook for End-of-Life Practitioners* New York: Columbia University Press   508-533.

www.ingramcontent.com/pod-product-compliance
Lightning Source LLC
Chambersburg PA
CBHW070908270326
41927CB00011B/2491